# 2001 AMERICAN GUIDE TO U.S. COINS

Charles F. French
Edited by Scott Mitchell

A FIRESIDE BOOK
Published by Simon & Schuster
NEW YORK   LONDON   TORONTO   SYDNEY   SINGAPORE

**FIRESIDE**
Rockefeller Center
1230 Avenue of the Americas
New York, NY 10020

Copyright © 1964, 1965, 1968, 1970, 1972, 1973, 1974, 1975, 1976, 1977, 1982, 1983, 1984, 1985, 1986, 1987, 1988, 1989, 1990, 1991, 1992, 1993, 1994, 1995, 1996, 1997, 1998, 1999, 2000 by Simon & Schuster, Inc.

All rights reserved,
including the right of reproduction
in whole or in part in any form.

FIRESIDE and colophon are registered trademarks
of Simon & Schuster, Inc.

Manufactured in the United States of America

10 9 8 7 6 5 4 3 2 1

ISBN 0-684-87185-8

# CONTENTS

## PART ONE: SOME HISTORY AND SOME ADVICE

| | |
|---|---:|
| Introduction: A Brief History of American Numismatics | 13 |
| 1. Early American Coins | 18 |
| 2. Pirate and Revolutionary Money | 21 |
| 3. Gold Dollars and Golden Eagles | 22 |
| 4. Private Gold Coins | 25 |
| 5. The Coins of the Mormons | 28 |
| 6. Civil War Money | 32 |
| 7. Hard Times Tokens | 36 |
| 8. Commemorative Coins | 38 |
| 9. Teddy Roosevelt's Twenty-Dollar Gold Piece | 41 |
| 10. America's First Colonial Coins | 44 |
| 11. Christian Gobrecht's Flying Eagle Dollar | 45 |
| 12. History of the "Dollar" | 46 |
| 13. Our First Gold Coins | 48 |
| 14. How to Determine Whether a Coin Is Uncirculated | 49 |
| 15. Proof Coins Must Be Perfect | 55 |
| 16. Beware of Counterfeits | 57 |
| 17. Mint Errors and the Rating Scale | 61 |
| 18. Shall I Clean My Coins? | 63 |
| 19. How to Sell a Coin Collection | 66 |
| 20. Coin Values Are Determined by Demand and Condition | 70 |

## PART TWO: THE COINS LISTED

| | |
|---|---:|
| Abbreviations Used in the Coin Value Lists | 74 |
| 21. Colonial Coins Before the Declaration of Independence | 75 |

| | | |
|---|---|---:|
| 22. | State Coinage | 78 |
| 23. | First Mint Issues | 83 |
| 24. | Half-Cent Pieces | 84 |
| 25. | One-Cent Pieces | 87 |
| 26. | Bronze Two-Cent Pieces | 97 |
| 27. | Nickel Three-Cent Pieces | 98 |
| 28. | Nickel Five-Cent Pieces | 99 |
| 29. | Silver Three-Cent Pieces | 105 |
| 30. | Half Dimes | 106 |
| 31. | Dimes | 109 |
| 32. | Twenty-Cent Pieces | 118 |
| 33. | Quarter-Dollars | 118 |
| 34. | Half Dollars | 127 |
| 35. | Silver Dollars | 137 |
| 36. | Trade Dollars | 144 |
| 37. | Silver Commemorative Coins | 145 |
| 38. | Gold Commemorative Coins | 148 |
| 39. | Proof Sets | 149 |
| 40. | Gold, Gold, That Magic Word | 150 |
| 41. | Gold Dollars | 152 |
| 42. | Quarter Eagles ($2.50 Gold Pieces) | 155 |
| 43. | Three-Dollar Gold Pieces | 160 |
| 44. | "Stella" or Four-Dollar Gold Pieces | 162 |
| 45. | Half Eagles ($5 Gold Pieces) | 163 |
| 46. | Eagles ($10 Gold Pieces) | 170 |
| 47. | Double Eagles ($20 Gold Pieces) | 176 |
| 48. | Private and Territorial Gold Coins | 181 |
| 49. | Hard Times Tokens | 188 |
| 50. | Civil War Tokens | 189 |
| 51. | Coins of Hawaii | 190 |
| 52. | Philippine Islands | 191 |

# AMERICAN GUIDE TO U. S. COINS

Part One:
# SOME HISTORY AND SOME ADVICE

# INTRODUCTION: A BRIEF HISTORY OF AMERICAN NUMISMATICS

The discovery in 1843 of the celebrated 1804 silver dollar is one of the earliest indications we have of interest in American numismatics. While there is a great deal of discussion regarding this coin's authenticity, it is generally agreed that the earliest were struck with the revision of Mint operations during the 1836–40 period. From 1858 on, the United States Mint struck proofs for collectors and, although not many of these were issued, this shows that there was numismatic interest at that time.

The middle of the nineteenth century saw great interest in revising our coinages. It was the policy of the Mint to strike "trial" or experimental coins, and there appeared such unusual denominations as two-cent, three-cent, and twenty-cent pieces, none of which met with much popularity in circulation. They therefore were ultimately discontinued. Trial pieces became very popular with collectors in the 1860s and 1870s and it is possible that a good many of these were struck purely for the delight of the collector. Usually only a dozen or so patterns were needed, but quantities up to five hundred of some were struck.

The latter part of the nineteenth century saw the start of the American Numismatic Association and the publishing of America's first monthly magazine devoted exclusively to numismatics. Students came into being who ardently studied their particular field, and many books of value were published towards the end of the century. The majority of these books were about cents and half cents; other topics covered were Colonial coins, half dimes, quarters, halves, and dollars. The continuing popularity of large cents explains why there were so many publications about these interesting coins.

The following authors were pioneers in their subjects and paved the way for the many publications that have since appeared: Ebenezer Gilbert, Ed Frossard, Sylvester Crosby, W.W. Hays, Thomas Elder, F.W. Doughty, George H. Clapp, H.R. Newcomb, H.P. Newlin, D.W. Valentine, A.W. Browning, J.W. Haseltine, M.L. Beistle, Dr. M.W. Dickeson, Dr. Edward Maris, Philip Nelson, Sydney P. Noe, Carl Wurzbach, and Miller-Ryder.

There is no accurate record of the number of collectors in those days, but I would estimate that they must have numbered between three and five hundred. There were no "coin boards" or plastic holders. Collectors had to improvise. The wealthier had wooden cabinets built, fitted with velvet-lined trays; others lined cigar boxes and velvet and placed their coins in these. Many a pleasant hour was spent going over coin collections, pointing out prized pieces to friends. Trading and exchanging coins with fellow numismatists became the thing to do.

Probably the first coin holders to become popular were the small round cardboard "pill" boxes manufactured by T. James Clarke of Jamestown, New York. Mr. Clarke, being a well-known collector of large cents, sold these boxes as containers for large cents, for they were just the right size. Collectors would put cotton in the bottom of the box, place the coin in it, and write its description on the cover.

At the beginning of the twentieth century, coin collecting was a hobby only for the few deeply interested in the subject. There were perhaps several thousand collectors at this time. They formed a national "clique" deeply interested in coin research, finding new rarities and new varieties. One of the first boons to the hobby was the issue of several million Columbian half dollars during the World's Fair in Chicago in 1892. This was the first coin struck in America commemorating an event and offered for sale to all. It opened the eyes of the public to the possibilities of coin collecting and showed how it could be interesting and even profitable. Collectors fondly kept those commemorative memoirs of the World's Fair. The success of this first commemorative encouraged the issue of many more from 1915 on and while these helped keep the hobby active, they did not materially increase the number of collectors.

In the middle of the 1920s, the largest coin dealer was B. Max Mehl, who used the radio and national newspaper advertising to foster the sale of his new and excellent coin book, the "Star Rare Coin Encyclopedia." This book gave collectors buying prices for all United States coins and also had many articles of interest on coins from all parts of the world, plus information about coin collecting. The book was a truly educational volume. It cost him thousands of dollars to advertise, but since he sold hundreds of thousands of books at a dollar each, we suspect he didn't lose any money. Mehl's coin book helped give the public a new awareness of numismatics, an awareness that was so far-reaching that even today we occasionally hear his great slogan, "I'll give fifty dollars for a 1913 Liberty-Head nickel." In fact, it was B. Max Mehl who made the 1913 nickel such a popular and desirable coin.

Up to the depression of 1929–33, coin values had gradually increased, as had new coin collectors. I would estimate that in 1930 there were probably ten thousand coin collectors in the USA—many of them hard-pressed for money due to the depression. During those years collectors' coins could be purchased very reasonably. With the return of prosperity, a new stimulus came to numismatics. The many new issues of commemorative coins in 1935 and 1936 caused coin speculation on a large scale for the first time. Easy profits brought the speculator into the field. Commemorative prices skyrocketed, and all United States coins were affected; values rose substantially. As might have been expected, when commemoratives crashed in 1937–38 many of the "fast-buck boys" lost interest in the hobby.

The first auction sales took place very early in the nineteenth century. There were only one or two well-known coin auctioneers at that time. Toward the latter part of the 1930s, many new auctioneers went into the business. I still have a letter from a well-known dealer and auctioneer, Thomas Elder, bemoaning the fact that with all the auctions being conducted and coins being offered, prices would surely crash and coins become valueless. If only he had lived to see what has occurred and how greatly the hobby has grown!

In the beginning of the 1940s, many coin minded people were confident of the future of numismatics. They reasoned that if the number of collectors continued to increase and there were no more coins to be had, prices would rise. They began accumulating uncirculated rolls of current coins against future demands. These investors would secure the rolls at their banks, or send away to dealers who specialized in this kind of business, and store them in safe deposit boxes. Uncirculated rolls were excellent investments, for how could one lose? At worst, the coins could be deposited in their bank at face value. Those who held these rolls long enough made small fortunes.

During the depression, the Whitman Publishing Company first nationally put on the market an attractive, reasonably priced series of coin boards designed to encourage new collectors. They showed the novice what and how to collect, mostly, from his pocket change, and were offered throughout the United States in many kinds of stores. They steadily increased the number of coin collectors and are still a major factor in encouraging new ones.

Another great boon to numismatics was the resumption of the manufacture of proof sets in 1936 by the United States Mint in Philadelphia. Not many proofs were sold from 1936 through 1942 and none were made during the war years of 1943–49. The record of the number of proof sets coined from 1950 on clearly indicates their increasing popularity. When one considers that there were 51,386 sets coined in 1950 and 3,950,762 in 1964, the answer is obvious as to the interest in coin collecting as a hobby.

Many people ask "Why do collectors like proof sets?" The first answer occurs when you consider the care and accuracy with which they are coined, and also their beautiful mirror-like finish. Second, there is a great appeal to collecting a series. Third, their value has constantly increased and they have been an excellent investment in the past.

Probably one of the greatest boons has been the introduction of coin newspapers, weekly and biweekly publications that reach all coin collectors, dealers and even people who are only slightly interested in coins. Shortly after the first issue of the coin newspapers, their circulation was nearly a hundred thousand; this was a great surprise to all "old time" numismatists, many of whom did not realize how wide the interest in coins had become.

Another useful innovation is the advertised "bid" and "ask" prices, by dealers, of uncirculated rolls, proof sets, and commemoratives. These give the collector and investor an idea of current value. Weekly published "trends" give an idea of how the market on all regularly issued coins is faring. For today's prices change very rapidly, sometimes up and sometimes down. Those interested are coin collectors of all classes, beginners, Whitman board collectors, speculators, investors, regular collectors, dealers, and students. The majority are new to the hobby and have a great deal to learn.

The law of supply and demand governs prices. When the supply is short and demand great, values are bound to increase. When certain pieces rise to very high prices, a great many small collectors are frozen out of the market for these particular coins. However, this only applies to coins that run well into the thousands of dollars per coin.

The American Numismatic Association conducts a national convention once a year in August held in various cities of the United States. Years ago, coin clubs began springing up throughout our country. Today there are very few cities of respectable size that do not have their own clubs. They meet, usually once a month, conduct their business meetings, have talks on numismatics, occasionally conduct a club auction, buy and sell coins, and even have displays. They are always interested in gaining new members. More recently, the Internet has become a hugely popular meeting place for coin collectors, whether they are discussing coins or conducting transactions.

The large number of collectors and clubs has encouraged the forming of regional associations and you will find that these associations cover practically the entire country. Joined by clubs and collectors in their regional territory, these associations hold either one or two conventions per year. Many have auction sales conducted during their convention and a bourse where dealers from all over the United States congregate to offer their coins for sale. Collectors are encouraged to display their collections and are awarded prizes for their efforts on a competitive basis.

Numismatics today is well organized. Since its start in 1891, the American Numismatic Association has grown slowly; today there are more than 500 local chapters. Under this parent organization come the regional associations and then the local coin clubs. In addition to the above, there is the American Numismatic Society in New York

City, which maintains an outstanding museum of rare coins. The society has a remarkable library and issues many new publications, devoting its efforts to research.

# 1.
# EARLY AMERICAN COINS

Were we to transport ourselves back three centuries to the early days of Colonial America, we would find that industry was very small and that business, for the most part, was conducted by barter and trade. While the need of coins was felt, the shortage was not as important as later, when Colonial America became more industrialized and succeeded in acquiring wealth. Even so, attempts to issue coins were made.

Massachusetts experimented with its NE (New England) shillings, sixpence, and threepence. These very crude and rare coins are credited with being the first coins struck in the territories then known as the American Colonies.

Following quickly came the Willow, Oak, and Pine Tree series. Some were to find use in circulation, for in those days a coin was a coin regardless of who issued it, and the amount of metal it contained determined its value. This first series was strongly disapproved of by Charles II of England, and the coinage was stopped.

There were other very early experiments in coinage in other Colonies. The Mark Newby halfpence, struck in Dublin in 1678, was originally coined for Ireland but found its way to New Jersey. There were also the Lord Baltimore pieces for Maryland, which were coined in England and brought over for circulation here.

After these early attempts, we find little activity numismatically until the first part of the eighteenth century, when a small flurry again occurred. We have the Gloucester tokens of 1714, and the Wood or Hibernia series and Rose Americana coins of 1722 and 1724. There were the early French Colony coppers of 1721–22; and a little earlier, the Elephant tokens of 1694. With the exception of the Gloucester tokens, of which little is known, the rest were struck in foreign lands and shipped here for use, due to the dire need. The Higley, or Granby, coppers of 1737–39 saw considerable circulation, even though they were unauthorized and coined on this continent.

As we enter the second period of inactivity, the 1767 French Colony pieces, with the exception of the 1760 Voce Populi coins, find little or no interest in "coins for America." The next and most important era commenced around the time of our embarking on the American Revolution. From this time until the opening of the first United States Mint, in 1792–93, we find innumerable varieties, experiments, in fact all types of coins. Some received recognition and actually circulated. Others should be classified as pattern or experimental pieces. Of these I shall first discuss the State cents.

New Hampshire, as early as 1776, struck coppers. As shown by their great amount of wear, they must have circulated considerably, even though very few are known. Vermont issued many varieties and quite a few cents from 1785 through 1788, and they were actively used in circulation. New York, too, issued cents from 1786 through 1787, some of which could be considered experimental pieces, others actually circulated. Connecticut probably had the most active coinage system from 1785 through 1788. All of her coins were circulated extensively. Massachusetts struck some early experimental pieces around 1776 and went into regular coinage during 1787 and 1788. New Jersey issued a wide variety of cents from 1786 through 1788. Virginia, in 1773, struck pennies and halfpennies with George III on them.

During this time, just prior to the Revolution, a wide variety of experimental coins or tokens appeared. The majority did not see circulation even though some are known to have been used. In this group we find the rare pewter pattern Continental dollars of 1776; the Nova Constellatio coppers of 1783–85–86; the

19

Immune Columbia pieces, the Confederatio cents; Brasher's experimental pieces, and Chalmers Annapolis (Maryland) shillings, sixpence, and threepence. Belonging here, too, are the U.S.A. Bar cents, Mott tokens, Talbot, Allum, and Lee tokens, Georgius Triumpho tokens, Auctori Plebis tokens, Kentucky tokens, Myddleton tokens, North American tokens, Pitt tokens, Rhode Island Ship tokens, and Franklin Press cents.

Now we come to what may be the forerunners of our first regular coinage, the Washington pieces. George Washington's great popularity at the end of the Revolution made it natural to want to copy the practice of foreign nations and place the head of the ruler on the obverse of the coin. There being no "ruler" of the United States, the president was the logical equivalent. If this practice had been accepted and carried out until today, we would have had a change in coin design with each president; the bust or head of each president would have appeared on our coins while he was in office. This would have been an interesting series for our coin collectors, but the many changes might very possibly have confused our coinage. (This frequent changing of coin designs did not occur in kingdoms, for the rulers were in for life.)

The practice of using Washington's head was therefore discarded and the Liberty-Head designs adopted. Many of the designs from Washington pieces, however, were adopted either partly or entirely.

The reverse of the Unity cents of 1783 is almost identical to the reverse design adopted on the wreath-type cents of 1793 and the following years. The eagle on the reverse of the various cents and half dollars is very similar to the eagle adopted for the reverse of our silver coins.

The designs of the half disme, disme, Birch cent, and silver-center cents are almost identical to the designs adopted on our coins of 1793. The Fugio cents of 1787 which actually saw circulation, while authorized by Congress, were coined privately.

You will notice that all of the above were coinages designed to fill the need of minor coins, mostly cent and half-cent sizes; this was the size that was needed most. Business requirements in larger transactions were carried on in gold Spanish-American doubloons and their fractions, English guineas, and even French louis d'or. Silver requirements were largely supplied by the masses of one-, two-, four-, and eight-real coins of Spanish America.

# 2.
# PIRATE AND REVOLUTIONARY MONEY

Our coasts were infested with pirates and privateers during the early days of our Colonial History. This made shipping hazardous and uncertainty was the order of the day. British, French, and particularly Spanish ships were liable to be boarded, stripped of their cargo and then sunk. With the exception of the Spaniards shipping gold and silver treasure back to Spain other cargoes usually consisted of articles sorely needed by settlers in the new world; guns, ammunitions and luxuries desired by the rich.

Gold and silver were not always in coin form for bullion was found to be more easily handled.

The Spaniards lost many ships of treasure, either through pirate raids or sunk by hurricanes. Gold coins, subjected to the action of salt water are not harmed at all, neither are rare jewels, but silver is badly affected by the corrosive action of the salt and these must be treated carefully to remove the corrosion and encrustations they acquire after centuries of lying under salt water.

During the American Revolution, the need for hard money was so great in the United States that it encouraged our authorizing private shipowners to turn "pirate." Known as privateers, these sleek fast ships roved our coast and captured any ship they could as a prize of war, placing their American crews on them and sending them to the Colonies. For the ship captains and owners this was a very lucrative business and many of the wealthy clipper ship owners of the next fifty years started out in this manner. The wealth of unobtainable material these privateers brought to the revolting Colonies was of terrific aid to the successful consummation of the war. Not only were goods brought to our shores, but a sorely needed quantity of hard money. Many English gold guineas were confiscated as they were being shipped over to the continent to pay English armies.

We must try to visualize the situation of that day in order to realize the need of this money. The early Americans had always considered hard coins the only money of real value; gold coins were used for business transactions of merit. It made no difference from what country the coins came as long as they were coins; this also applied to silver and copper. The dire needs of the war caused the individual colonies to issue paper currency, which was not looked upon with much favor.

When the Continental Congress began issuing paper currency to pay bills, their money was looked down upon and inflation swept the country to a degree that almost wrecked the war efforts. The expression "Not worth a Continental" comes to us from those days when everyone shied away from these bills. They never were redeemed and finally became of no value. For the most part, however, the earlier notes issued by the individual colonies were redeemed, but in varying percentages of their face value. To aggravate the situation further, the British resorted to counterfeiting our paper money and attempting to circulate it.

3.
GOLD DOLLARS
AND GOLDEN EAGLES

Prior to the establishment of our United States Mint, a proposal was made, in 1785, to coin five-dollar pieces, but the actual approval of our first gold pieces did not come until 1792 when Congress passed an act authorizing the coinage of eagles ($10.00), half eagles ($5.00), and quarter eagles ($2.50). The eagles were to be 247½ grains pure, 270 grains standard. Half eagles were to be 123¾ pure, 135 grains standard; quarter eagles were to be 61⅞ pure and 67½ grains standard. The standard weight included an alloy to make the coins wear better.

These gold coins were pegged to silver on a 15 to 1 ratio, namely fifteen ounces of silver to one ounce of gold, and while this ratio was all right at the time the bill was passed, by 1799 the ratio in Europe had reached 15¾ to 1 and the overvalued gold coins began to flow out of the country or were melted down to get the extra value they contained. Gold therefore disappeared from circulation, as did silver dollars.

It wasn't until June 28, 1834, that a new law reduced the weight of gold coins. From that time on, our gold pieces appeared in the new smaller size, returned to circulation, and created a new interest in and demand for gold. Gold mines profitably increased their production. Our mint first struck twenty-dollar double eagles, and experimented with fifty-dollar coins in 1849. We also find our first gold dollars appearing, closely followed by threes. The three-dollar gold piece, first coined in 1854, was never a popular coin. It was frequently linked with bad luck by the superstitious.

The quantities of gold and shortages of gold coins in the west prompted the coinage of pioneer pieces in many denominations. Privately issued and not under rigid regulations, many of these were not up to standard fineness; as late as the latter part of the 1920s these pioneer pieces were looked down upon as low-grade, undervalued coins and were redeemed by financial institutions at less than face value. Today, these low-grade coins are rare and worth high premiums, not for their gold value but for their numismatic value.

From the time shortly after the Civil War until the banking holiday in 1933, numismatic interest in collecting gold coins was not high, perhaps because of the coins' face value. Anyone who wanted to collect them could easily have secured the majority of all denominations for very little over face value, even back to 1834, when the new smaller size was adopted. A great many of the first gold pieces prior to 1804 could have been purchased for much less than their rarity should have dictated.

Proof gold coins were not popular with collectors. With the exception of the last few years, only twenty-five to forty proof gold dollars have been struck each year! Similar small quantities were coined in proofs for quarter eagles, threes, half eagles, eagles, and double eagles. The largest quantity of gold proof dollars of any year were struck in 1889, and this only amounted to 1,779 pieces! The majority of proofs struck in all denominations per year usually ran from twenty to forty specimens! Over ten times that amount or more were struck for coins in silver and copper. It is no wonder that perfect gold pieces bring very high prices today.

Due to the depression of 1929-33 and the uncertainty of the country's financial position, hoarding of gold coins by individuals became so common it seriously endangered our financial structure. This was one of the major reasons for the government order that all gold coins be turned in. The purpose of this order was to end hoarding and get gold back where it could do the country more good. The first announcement of the government order was widely publicized and stressed the penalties for failure to comply, which at the time were drastic, with stiff jail sentences. The order accomplished what it intended and millions of dollars in gold coin were deposited in banks and Federal Reserves.

It is regrettable that, because of the hysteria of the time, many really rare gold coins were turned in. The government was not interested in the coins themselves, but only in hoards. Within a few weeks the original order, which exempted gold coins in quantities of $100 was amended to exempt gold coins that were considered rare and held in coin collections. Over a period of years subsequent amendments gradually continued to ease the stringency of the original order. At first limits were lifted with the exception of two-and-one-half-dollar pieces. Restrictions on the two-and-one-half-dollar pieces limited ownership to not more than two of any date or mint mark. This restriction was lifted next and the offense was changed from a criminal to a civil one with a fine.

Since the Hoarding Act of 1933, interest in gold coin collecting has been growing by leaps and bounds. As soon as the government discontinued making gold coins, collectors began taking great interest in them.

There are no restrictions regarding the export or import, purchase, sale, or collecting of gold coins in the United States of any date.

# 4.
# PRIVATE GOLD COINS

Necessity has brought into reality many things, and so, through a necessity, we have our private territorial gold coins. These pieces were issued between 1830 and 1862 in different parts of our country to answer a demand for denominations lacking in regular issues. While there were laws that forbade the individual states striking gold coins, there were none forbidding private persons or private companies doing so.

In 1787, the year before Washington was elected to the presidency, a jeweler named Ephraim Brasher, whose place of business was on Cherry Street in New York City, appealed to the state legislature for permission to strike copper coins to circulate in that state. Permission was refused, but that did not stop him from using the dies he had made. He struck his coins in gold, their intrinsic value being $16, the same as the Spanish doubloons. They were known as the Ephraim Brasher doubloons. The one with EB on the right wing of the eagle is one of the highest priced coins in the world.

The years 1830–40 saw great industrial development and territorial expansion in our country. The first steam locomotive, streetcar, and omnibus were put to use; the Erie Canal was built and the telegraph invented.

In 1830, a treaty with Great Britain opened to American commerce the ports of the West Indies and South America; a treaty with Turkey opened the Black Sea. Around the same time, Templeton Reid, assayer, located near the gold mines in Lumpkin County, Georgia, issued the first of his private gold coins. It is not definitely known just how long his business existed or just when it started, but the first coins to bear his stamp were dated 1830. The coins issued from his Georgia establishment contained gold of a higher standard and fineness than any other ever issued by either private persons or the government. It is reasonable to assume that this is why so many were melted, resulting in their great scarcity.

Christopher Bechtler's establishment was located in Rutherford County, North Carolina. The first of his coins, although undated, are attributed to the early part of 1831. About 1842, he passed his business on to his son August, who continued until about 1852. The gold for these pieces came from North Carolina and Georgia.

When Texas was admitted to the Union as an independent state, arbitration over the boundary resulted in the war with Mexico and ended with the Treaty of Guadeloupe in 1848. For $18,000,00 Mexico sold all of her northern territory to the United States. This territory included the region known as California, Utah, Nevada, New Mexico, and part of Colorado and Arizona.

Civilization had already pushed its way westward when the cry of "gold" came from California and resounded from coast to coast. There was a great exodus from the east; people poured into the west in droves. The trials and hardships of the cross-country trek with inadequate means did not stop them. With the influx of prospectors, traders, merchants, and people from every walk of life, towns grew up overnight. It was the dawn of a Golden Age. The forty-niner was staking his claim.

The discovery of gold in California was a boon to a world suffering from a gold shortage. It changed the whole outlook of industry and commerce. Prices skyrocketed to unbelievable heights. For a while gold dust was used as a medium of exchange, but this was soon found to be cumbersome and impractical. The demand for gold coins was great but there were no mints in the west. To ship gold dust to the east to be minted into coins was out of the question. Besides not having adequate means for shipping, there were the hazards of holdups, Indians, and slow progress overland. An attempt was made by the provincial government in the Oregon Territory to establish a mint, but this failed. A private organization, the Oregon Exchange Company, started operations in Oregon City in 1849. They employed a blacksmith to make the apparatus and an engraver, who happened to be one of the company's members, to make the dies.

The Mormons, who for years had been migrating westward, having been expelled from New York, Illinois, and Nebraska, finally settled on the shores of the Great Salt Lake in Utah, while it was still Mexican territory. They started their mint in 1849, striking coins from the gold dust received from California. Their twenty-dollar gold piece was the first to be struck in this country, but the intrinsic value was found to be only between $16 and 18.

There were about fifteen private mints operating in California between 1849 and 1855, striking millions of dollars worth of gold coins. Norris, Greig & Norris coined the first, a five-dollar coin of 1849; Moffat & Company struck the first ten-dollar coin; Baldwin & Company, the first twenty; Moffat & Company, the first fifty. The fifty-dollar coin was octagonal, bearing the stamp of the United States Assayer Augustus Humbert F.D. Kohler & Company and Moffat & Company issued ingots stamped from gold bars. The last private issue coins from California came from the mints of Wass, Mollitar & Company and Kellogg & Company, dated 1855, just one year after the San Francisco Mint was opened.

In 1857 a panic overtook the country due to over-capitalization, over-building of railroads, rise of prices, speculation, bad crops, bad state banking, and diminishing gold output. While there was agitation between the states over the question of states' rights and the Dred Scott Decision, the first Atlantic cable was being laid. Silver was discovered in Nevada and a new gold district was discovered in the west. The forty-niner rush was repeated but not in the same proportions as the rush a decade before, the states' rebellion had become a serious issue.

There were three private minting firms in Colorado. The first coins to be struck were by Clark, Gruber & Company, in 1860. Coins of all United States gold denominations with the exception of ones and threes were issued. In 1862, the government purchased the Clark, Gruber establishment, which was thereafter conducted as a United States Assay Office. The original bill called for a government mint at Denver, but this did not materialize until 1906.

John Parsons & Company, Tarryall Mines, and J.J. Conway & Company, Georgia Gulch, operated their private mints at about the same time for a limited period. Parsons issued quarter eagles and half eagles; Conway, quarter eagles, half eagles, and eagles. None of the coins bore dates, but they are said to have been struck in 1861. All are quite rare, Conway's exceedingly so.

The designs on these privately issued gold coins are varied. Some are very plain with only the name of the mint or minter, date, and denomination or weight. Others have very attractive original designs, and still others are so very much like the regular government coinage that to the ordinary layman they are easily mistaken.

## 5. THE COINS OF THE MORMONS

"During the year 1846, the beginning of the great exodus from Nauvoo, Illinois, to Salt Lake Valley, Utah, there appeared a strange little brass token that has created and attracted the attention of church members and collectors from all over the country" (*Numismatist*, July, 1911, p. 241). The date and Brigham Young's favorite emblem—the beehive, meaning "Let everyone do his duty," and clasped hands, signifying friendship—indicate very strongly that the coin is associated with the Mormons. However, some believe that it is in no way connected with the Mormons, because the emblem of the beehive was first thought of after their arrival in the valley. We do not know whether this token was used as an exchange medium or as a commemorative issue, nor do we know what its value was. Its size was about that of a dime.

When the Mormons went west, they took very little money with them and droughts, insects, and other adverse conditions drained what money they had. Hard work ultimately conquered all their handicaps and eventually Indians were no longer a threat. Trade and barter were their mediums of exchange. A Mormon battalion in the Mexican War brought home with them, in 1847, a certain amount of money which circulated. It is recorded that Captain James Brown left the valley in 1847 to collect his men's back pay, returning with $5,000 in Spanish gold doubloons valued at $16 each. Many other instances of small quantities of coin coming into the hands of the Mormons are on record, but the discovery of gold in the ground was the start of a desire to issue coins.

A very interesting and integral part of the Mormons' history was contributed by Thomas Rhoads, more commonly referred to as Father Rhoads. Rhoads and his family left Missouri in the spring of 1846 for Sutter's Fort on the Sacramento River. Upon arriving at the fort, Rhoads and his five sons signed up for service in the Mexican War. After termination of their services they returned to Sutter's Fort just in time to help organize a party for the purpose of rescuing a snowbound Donner party trapped in the California mountains. The small rescue party was successful in its attempt to locate the lost Donner party, but unfortunately did not arrive in time to save the group from starvation. Only a few members of the Donner party survived.

On their way home, hunger once again reared its ugly head, for the bears had eaten the supplies that members of the rescue party had tied to the trees to aid them on their return trip. The party finally reached civilization once again, but not before scarcity of food compelled them to eat the rawhides from their snowshoes.

When gold was discovered in the channel of the mill race at Sutter's Sawmill, Rhoads and his sons joined the other adventurers in their quest for gold, which later proved very rewarding. After accumulating a small fortune, Rhoads and his family left California for Great Salt Lake in the latter part of 1848. News of the Rhoads fortune leaked out and while they were making their way through the California mountains they were attacked by bandits. Had it not been for the intervention of some passing travelers, the ambush might have been successful. With the help of the travelers, the Rhoads family was able to repel the attack.

According to Colonel Lock, Father Rhoads brought with him several sacks of gold, among which there was a 60-pound sack, the largest amount that had been brought into the valley. Father Rhoads turned all the gold over to Brigham Young, who in return had a home built for Rhoads and allowed him to withdraw from the tithing office all the food supplies that he deemed necessary. Rhoads also received a herd of cattle in consideration for the gold dust. It was customary for each individual to give one-tenth of his accomplishments to the church, whether cattle, produce, or money, in order to aid their common cause. But Father Rhoads contributed his entire amount in order to accelerate the progress of the Mormon people. The famous 60-pound sack of gold was the chief topic of the people in the valley at that time and for quite some time to come.

Concerning gold dust that was brought into the valley, William T. Fullett, a battalion member, was credited with having made the first deposit on December 10, 1848. He deposited fourteen and one-half ounces of gold dust which was then worth $232, equal to $16 per ounce. Within four months, close to $8,000 in dust and a little coin was deposited in the "bank." Entries of deposit show that battalion men deposited 77 percent, and 135 others, 35 percent of the total.

Since the city was fairly well supplied with gold dust, the council unanimously agreed that it was time to convert the dust into coins. In order to accomplish this, President Young solicited the aid of John Kay and John Taylor in planning the first mint ever to be established in the Great Salt Lake Valley.

John Kay, skilled in patternmaking, and John Taylor were persuaded to work on suitable designs for the coins. After some time and difficulty, the preparations were finally completed and Kay began to melt the gold and roll it into sheets. A punching press was then used in punching out the gold discs, while a coining press stamped the designs on the discs.

Kay turned out ten-dollar pieces which were paid out at a premium of fifty cents on the piece. Whether the coins were at a premium because of the novelty value or because of overweight is not known. Twenty of them were charged out to Brigham Young and five to John Kay. A week later twenty-one pieces were coined and charged out at par to Brigham Young. No more were coined until September, 1849, because the crucibles were broken in the preliminary runs and melting could not be continued until others were obtained.

Since the coining could not be continued, the punching press was dismantled and shipped by ox team to Parowan where it could be put to use while the crucibles were being made. During the short time the press was in Parowan, it was used for cutting nails. The sheet iron was cut into strips and then headed in a vise. On October, 1848, the press was returned to the valley where it was used in connection with the coinage of the 1849–50 gold coins and later, the 1860 gold coins.

Finally, the patternmaker Kay completed his work on refining the gold dust, and at last the mint was ready for operation. In order to test the crucibles, Kay struck a few pattern pieces bearing a design on only one side. This time the crucibles did not break. Apparently the workers were satisfied with the results, because the mint went into full production and remained so for the remainder of the year.

Joseph Fielding Smith, church historian, made the following statement concerning the men who participated in the coining of these gold coins:

> When the Desert Mint was built, Alfred B. Lambson forged all the dies and punches, in fact all that pertained to the mint with the exception of the drop hammer, which was forged by Martin H. Beck. John Kay cut the dies and coined the money, William Clayton and Thomas Bullock being associated with him as accountant and weigher. As an expedient, before this Dr. Willard Richards weighed the gold dust brought from California and placed it in small packages, representing from $1 to $20 which passed current for money.[1]

The designs on the pieces were not too elaborate, but one must admit originality and much praise should be forthcoming for the job they did with such limited facilities.

The following is a description of the gold coins minted in Salt Lake City: on the obverse in the center, there are clasped hands with the date 1849 below; the legend reads "G.S.L.C.P.G." (Great Salt Lake City Pure Gold), "Two and half Do." On the reverse is a crown over the all-seeing eye, around the edge of which are the words "HOLINESS TO THE LORD." The designs on the 1849 and 1859 coins were all the same with the exception of the 1850 five-dollar piece. This had nine stars around the edge and a slightly different crown.

It is generally believed that during the early coinage no effort

---

[1] By permission of the Church Historian, Church of Jesus Christ of Latter-Day Saints; reprinted from *Mormon Money* by Sheridan L. McGarry.

was made to assay or refine the gold because there was no one connected with the mint capable of determining such standards. This fact has been substantiated by Captain H. Stansbury in his report on his exploration and survey of the Great Salt Lake. The coinage was done in good faith, however, because of the then prevailing theory of "relative fineness"; in other words, the Mormons based the worth of all gold upon the purity of California gold. Little did they realize that the coins minted from native gold were very low in assay due to the fineness of the gold, although it was full weight. According to Colonel Lock, the 1849 five-dollar gold piece was actually worth $4.51. This mistake was later brought to light but not before losses had been sustained by many who had purchased gold on the relative-fineness theory.

# 6.
# CIVIL WAR MONEY

Southern guns roared on Fort Sumter and the Civil War had begun. Our nation had started the bloodiest war in its history.

Patriotism ran high in the newly formed Confederacy, and the cry went out for all to help in the war effort by turning in their gold, silver, and other precious metals in exchange for both state and Confederate notes. Southern bonds were issued to finance the war—all with promises to pay a certain number of years after the ratification of peace between the North and South. There was no question about who would win—the South of course! And this temporary paper money was just as good as having the gold coins it represented—or so they thought.

Financing the war was no easy task. The South, not having much heavy industry of its own, had to rely on foreign aid for its sorely needed supplies—which it had to pay for with hard cash.

Coins soon went out of circulation. There was an attempt to continue operation of the New Orleans mint, but due to lack of metal, this failed, and the only coins that were struck there for the Confederacy were the cent and half-dollar—both experimental pieces, and very rare. The Dahlonaga and Charlotte mints were closed for good.

As the war progressed and things began looking blacker, public confidence waned. There was a scramble for gold, and some state bank notes (formerly considered "as good as gold") were redeemed for gold at "20 cents on the dollar."

As more and more money was needed, more and more Confederate paper was printed. Great quantities were printed in 1864—the last year this paper money was issued. Printing presses were turning out denominations anywhere from fifty-cent notes up to five-hundred-dollar bills.

The collapse of the Southern effort put an end to this, and rendered all Confederate money valueless; the land was left destitute as a result. While much of the money was destroyed, some found its way into attics, in cartons and trunks, where it lay for decades—a useless reminder of the great war effort. Many stories have been told since of old Southern families with trunks full of Confederate money stored in their attics.

The vastly increased interest in numismatics over the past two decades has brought much of this currency out of its storage places. There are a few rarities in existence, such as the Montgomery, Alabama $1,000 and $500 notes, plus a few others, which are worth more today than their original face value. The majority, however, are worth less.

The start of the war in the North was quite different, however. Heavily industrialized, the North was far better equipped to cope with the problems presented by the war.

There too, small change soon went out of circulation. The loss of the New Orleans mint cut coin output in half, throwing the burden of coin manufacture on the shoulders of the Philadelphia and San Francisco mints. Although these mints were also hampered by the shortage of metal, they were not nearly as hard hit as the South.

Contributing to the great shortage of hard cash was the desire of many to hoard and the greatly increased need for small change in day-to-day business transactions. Housewives going to market were constantly plagued by a lack of change; merchants, therefore, were compelled to improvise methods of providing change, with the result that postage stamps were frequently used for this purpose. While a necessity, the use of stamps for this purpose was a nuisance since the stamps often stuck together, lost their gum (one reason why so many of our early issues are found in mint condition without gum), and were very fragile.

A year after the war began, a Mr. J. Gault patented the first encased postage stamps. This consisted of a round brassy metal frame in which stamps of various denominations were inserted and covered with a transparent mica cover. It protected the stamp, served the purpose of a coin and could be used much longer because of its cover. Denominations issued were for one, two, three, five, ten, twelve, twenty-four, thirty, and ninety cents.

The enterprising Mr. Gault arranged to have advertising placed on the back cover, and while many have his name on them, dozens of Northern firms paid to use this convenient method of providing change. Outstanding among these are such concerns as Ayers Pills, Drakes Plantation Bitters, Burnetts Cooking Extracts, Lord and Taylor, North American Insurance Co., etc. All of these encased postage stamps are quite rare—the highest-valued ones being those stamps in the higher denominations.

Another answer to the coin shortage was the series known as Civil War Tokens. They first appeared the latter part of 1861, and were coined in great quantities until 1864, when laws—still in effect today—abolished all *private* money coining. It is estimated that about fifty million of these tokens were coined during this period, in two main varieties: patriotic ones, with novel political legends—"our flag, should anyone tear it down, shoot him on the spot"; "millions for contractors, not one cent for widows", etc., and merchants' tokens, which appeared with legends advertising wares. Although these were not legitimate money, they were used as cents.

The war had caused the suspension of specie payments, and

all coins had gone out of circulation; hoarding was universal. Copper-nickel cents of 1859-64 were worth a premium.

The situation was serious, something had to be done. In 1862, Congress passed a bill authorizing postage currency. Notes in denominations of 5c., 10c., 25c., and 50c., had facsimiles of the current 5c. and 10c. postage stamps printed on them. This was brought about by the wide use of postage stamps as small change. While not favored, the system was used.

In 1863, a new act was passed authorizing the first issue of Fractional Currency. This currency circulated until as late as 1876, when an act authorized its redemption in silver coin.

During 1866 and 1867, the Treasury Department made up special Fractional Currency shields. These were an ornate arrangement of specimen notes, printed on one side and framed. They included notes of all issues, both obverse and reverse, for the first three series. The 15c. Grant and Sherman notes were included, even though these never appeared in circulation. Shields were distributed to banks to assist them in detecting counterfeits. These shields are quite rare and difficult to find in good condition. Many were taken apart in the hope that the notes could be sold or spent.

Before the Civil War, State Bank charters were easy to obtain. The rapid expansion of our economy had created the need for more money and State Banks were authorized to issue paper money against their deposits. This system was satisfactory as long as there was prosperity; in recession, however, deposits were withdrawn, banks closed their doors, and money became valueless.

While paper money was looked upon with suspicion, the government was compelled to issue its first currency: the demand notes of 1861 and the legal tender notes of 1862 and 1863. Issued in denominations of from one dollar to one thousand dollars, they were called "greenbacks" from the color on the reverse side.

The one-dollar and two-dollar denominations were often sent to the "boys in blue" at the front. It became the practice to pin these notes to a heavy piece of paper so they could not be detected in the mails, and stolen. Many of the notes of this series we find today have these pin holes in them.

With the termination of hostilities, changes in minting procedures came about. In the South, the mint in New Orleans was not permitted to resume operations until 1879, and for over a decade it only issued silver dollars. In the West, a new mint was opened in 1870 at Carson City. The San Francisco mint continued to operate, turning out gold coins. The Philadelphia mint bore the brunt of our nation's small-change needs. As the economy gradually got back on a normal footing, change was again available in our pockets.

# 7.
# HARD TIMES TOKENS

During the stirring period from 1832 to 1844, politics and the economy of the country produced the Hard Times Tokens.

President Andrew Jackson disapproved of a fiscal system under which public funds were deposited in a single, privately controlled institution—the Bank of the United States. In 1832 Jackson vetoed the bill to continue the Bank's existence after the expiration of its charter in 1836. This was in opposition to Clay and the financial interests of the country. This caused an upheaval in both political parties.

Jackson's party split into two opposed groups. And Clay's supporters fought to restore the bank. Jackson and his successor,

Martin Van Buren, succeeded in warding off the attacks and put in reforms.

They discontinued depositing funds in the Bank of the United States and established a Sub-Treasury system. Metallic currency was the only medium of payment for public lands.

At the time the country was undergoing a severe depression. That, plus the uncertainty of the banking system, led to hoarding hard money. Paper money was so unreliable, nobody wanted to accept it. The demand on the large cent, and the disappearance of small change, led to the manufacture of the Hard Times Tokens. Those with political slogans were the first campaign tokens.

Some of the legends on the Political Tokens are as follows:

"Andrew Jackson President Elected 1828 re-elected 1832— We commemorate the glorious victories of our hero in war and in peace."

"Gulian C. Verplanck Our Next Govnr A Faithful friend of our Country."

Small bust of Jackson with "My Substitute for the U.S. Bank. My Experiment, My Currency, My Glory." A running boar: "My Victory, My third Heat, Down with the Bank, Perish Credit, Perish Commerce."

Running Jackass: "I follow in the steps of my illustrious predecessor." Turtle with strongbox on its back marked "Sub Treasury." "Executive Experiment."

Balking horse: "Constitution as I understand it," "Roman Firmness," "A Plain System Void of Pomp."

Jackson sitting in a strongbox with a sword and a bag of money: "I take the responsibility." Sailing vessel named "Constitution" wrecked: "Van Buren Metallic Currency."

Phoenix: "Substitute for shin-plasters," "Specie payments suspended May 10, 1837" in wreath.

Ship "Constitution" under full sail: "Webster credit Currency." Ship named "Experiment" wrecked on the rocks: "Van Buren Metallic Currency."

Slave tokens: "Am I Not a Man and Brother." Another: "Am I not a Woman and Sister."

There are many varieties of "Liberty Heads" similar to large United States cents. Some are very ugly. In addition to some of the reverses already mentioned they are also found with "Millions for Defense, Not One Cent for Tribute"; "Mint Drop Bentonian Currency"; "Mint Drop Benton Experiment"; Ugly Head obverse with "Loco Foco" instead of "Liberty" on headband.

Many enterprising merchants of the day issued tokens advertising their wares to be used as small change. Some of these tokens have the same obverses as the Political Tokens.

Others have the type of business on them—a clock-màker has a clock; a boot-maker, a boot; a barber, a comb and scissors. A gold-beater has an arm and sledge, an anvil represents hardware and cutlery. A circus rider on two horses stands for the Hippodrome, and a railroad coach for the New York and Harlem Railroad.

Edwin Parmele's liquor store has an inebriate with a glass. An agriculturist has a bull. An umbrella-maker has an open umbrella, and a chair-maker, an upright chair. Public baths are indicated by a nude.

Lyman H. Low listed 183 Hard Times and Merchants' Tokens from 1832 to 1844. While many are easily available, there are others which are rare.

They were made in bronze, brass, and white metal, the bronze being the commonest. The majority were made the size of large cents but there are a few of smaller.

# 8.
# COMMEMORATIVE COINS

The opening of the Chicago World's Fair in 1892 was the occasion for the issue of our first commemorative coins, the Columbian half dollars. Designed to help defray expenses, they did not at first meet with great enthusiasm. A good many were coined in 1892 and still more in 1893. It was hoped that nearly 2,500,000 of both dates could be sold at one dollar each.

Many were sold, brought home by visitors, and kept for years as souvenirs of the exposition. A great many, however, did not sell and ultimately were placed in circulation at face value. For many years it was not unusual to receive one of these Columbian half dollars, particularly one dated 1893, in one's pocket change. The Isabella quarters, struck in 1893, were issued in much smaller quantities and therefore were not a drug on the market as the Columbian halves were.

Even though these commemoratives did not meet with great enthusiasm, the series was started, as if by accident, and the idea of selling special coins at premiums to raise money for special events took hold.

In 1900 we had our first commemorative dollar, the Washington Lafayette. Until this time no special denomination had been adopted for commemorative coins and they began to appear in all kinds. With the advent of the 1903 Louisiana Purchase commemorative gold dollars, we have the first of a series of gold dollars and quarter eagles. The Panama-Pacific fifty-dollar slugs, which appeared in 1915, became very rare. Coined in very limited numbers they were issued more as historical souvenirs than as coins. Even so, at the time of issue, trouble was encountered disposing of them at over face value.

People resented having to pay a premium for a coin, no matter how interesting it was or how small an issue. Little did those buyers know how greatly they would increase in value. Even in the late 1920s, dealers were more than pleased to get their capital investment out of the Panama-Pacific fifty-dollar piece plus a small premium for their efforts. I can remember the pair, both octagonal and round, being offered, uncirculated, for as little as $125 for the pair! Twenty-five dollars over face value!

While approximately a thousand of these Panama-Pacific fifty-dollar pieces were struck of each type, nearly half of them were turned in to the mint to be melted up. This leaves a little over a thousand of both in existence today.

The Panama-Pacific set—the two fifty-dollar gold pieces, a gold quarter eagle, a gold dollar, and a fifty-cent piece—created the first urge to encourage more of this interesting series. This commemorative, having adopted so many different denominations, helped decide what future denomination was to be used— the half dollar. Since both the price and the size of the half dollar were the most popular, future commemorative coins were struck in this denomination. In 1918 the Lincoln Centennial half dollar was issued, and from 1920 on, one or more different commemoratives came out every year.

Difficulty was found selling all the commemoratives that were authorized, for while the series had enlisted many ardent followers, there were not as many as there were coins. Many were available and kept the values down for a long while. Collectors were told these commemoratives were limited issues and would become valuable, but did not respond.

In 1921, the idea of making varieties that would be rarer than the regular series was first put into effect. We find the Missouri Centennial with and without star and the Grant Memorial with and without star and the two Alabamas. This was the first step toward trying to sell more coins to a limited number of buyers. As time went by, many commemorative halves were issued, some by associations which only wanted to dispose of enough coins to fill their need for funds. More enterprising concerns had the halves made for many years, from many mints, and with all kinds of minor varieties to create rarities.

The quantity of commemorative coins issued hit a peak around 1935–36. Interest at that time also hit a peak. Speculators and collectors were getting on the band wagon, buying commemoratives in quantities, making up sets, and carrying around graphs showing the fluctuations of price trends. It was not unusual for "the boys" to deal in hundreds and thousands of one issue. It was similar to stock market speculation. Some rare issues skyrocketed from $5 to $75 within a week! Such rapid profits were unheard of in the numismatic world.

As might have been expected, it couldn't last. The crash came. Overnight no one wanted to buy any commemoratives and everyone was loaded with hundreds of one kind. It took many years to get over this debacle and for holders of commemoratives to dispose of their hoards. When this finally occurred, most issues were widely distributed, and a gradual and more secure rise in values began.

The sale of new issues after 1936 was very difficult, and the government approved few. For many years the only new commemoratives struck were those under authorization from previous years, such as the Boone, Oregon Trail, Texas, and Arkansas. Very few coins were struck each year because of the sharply reduced demand and the repetition of designs. Collectors were disgusted with the "rackets" as they called them. Some hope was raised with the issue of the 1946 Iowa Centennial, for this was a new, single, and interesting coin. However, it was quickly followed by the mass of varieties of the Booker T. Washington and Washington-Carver series, the last of which, with thirty different varieties, ended in 1954.

There followed a thirty-year lapse of commemorative production. The administration, on the advice of the Mint, frowned upon commemorative issues. The exploitation of many issues of the series has caused a good deal of discontent. The feeling was that the Mint was too busy to issue these special coins and that commemoratives tend to confuse the coinage of the country, creating too many designs. It was also felt that commemoratives should be issued in the form of medals. Medals, however, have never reached the popularity among collectors that coins have; the collector likes to feel his collection is of basic intrinsic value, no matter how small. The number of medals versus proof sets issued by the Mint is evidence of this.

In 1982, the administration resumed producing commemoratives with the issue of a 250th-anniversary George Washington coin. Within a few years, the popularity of commemoratives had again soared, and there followed a number of issues, including a Statue of Liberty coin and Olympic coins in gold and silver. Today, commemoratives are thriving.

# 9.
# TEDDY ROOSEVELT'S TWENTY-DOLLAR GOLD PIECE

The Smithsonian Institution received the donation by Cornelius Roosevelt, of Washington, D.C., of an experimental high-relief double eagle or twenty-dollar gold piece, dated 1907, designed by Augustus St. Gaudens at the request of President Theodore Roosevelt. This is one of the great rarities of the United States coin series and has, in addition, an unusual historical connotation since it was owned originally by Theodore Roosevelt, who devoted considerable efforts toward its design and production.

In fact, in the winter of 1905, Theodore Roosevelt met at a dinner in Washington with Augustus St. Gaudens, whose sculptures the president admired greatly. The conversation drifted to the beauty of ancient Grek coins, described by St. Gaudens as almost the only coins of real artistic merit. Why couldn't the United States have coins as beautiful as the Greek ones, the president wished to know. If St. Gaudens would model them, the president said, he would have them minted.

Thus started a unique venture in modern monetary history. Manifesting his versatility and extraordinary energy, Theodore Roosevelt found the time personally to conduct the campaign for a more artistic series of United States coinage designs. On November 6, 1905, in a letter to St. Gaudens regarding these designs, the president said:

> I want to make a suggestion. It seems to me worthwhile to try for a really good coinage; though I suppose there will be a revolt about it! I was looking at some gold coins of Alexander the Great today, and I was struck by their high relief. Would it not be well to have our coins in high relief, and also to have the rims raised? The point of having the rims raised would be, of course, to protect the figure on the coin; and if we have the figures in high relief, like the figures on the old Greek coins, they will surely last longer. What do you think of this?

For two years president and sculptor gave much time and energy to the task of producing the new coin designs. The models finally adopted for the double eagle were of unusual artistic merit. The obverse showed a standing figure of "Liberty," holding aloft in her right hand the torch of enlightenment and in her left, the olive branch of peace. On the reverse side was a rendering of a flying eagle above a rising sun.

A few experimental pieces having an extremely high relief were struck at the president's order. These exceedingly rare pieces can be easily distinguished from the ones issued later for general circulation, which also have a very high relief. The field of the rare experimental pieces is excessively concave and connects directly with the edge without any border, giving it a sharp knifelike appearance. Liberty's skirt shows two folds on the side of the right leg; the Capitol building in the background at the left is very small; and the date, 1907, is in Roman numerals. The sun, on the reverse side, has fourteen rays.

In addition to these experimental pieces, 11,250 high-relief twenty-dollar gold pieces were struck on a medal press for general distribution and may be found today in many collections. Their relief is somewhat lower than that of the experimental pieces. They have a border around the edge; Liberty's skirt has three folds on the side of the right leg; the Capitol is considerably larger; and the date, 1907, is indicated in Roman numerals. On the reverse, there are only thirteen rays extending from the sun.

For practical reasons and especially since these high-relief coins could not be struck on a regular coin press and would not stack, it was decided soon to revert to the customary flat relief. A large number of similar flat-relief double eagles were issued in 1907 (these pieces show the date in Arabic numerals) and in later years up to 1933, when the issuance of gold coins was discontinued.

Theodore Roosevelt's twenty-dollar gold piece, donated by Cornelius Roosevelt, is placed on permanent display in the Smithsonian Institution's hall of monetary history. It should remind us of Roosevelt's words about this piece: "Certain things were done, of which the economic bearing was more remote but which bore directly upon our welfare, because they add to the beauty of living and therefore to the joy of life."

# 10.
# AMERICA'S FIRST COLONIAL COINS

The first New England coins, crude silver pieces with a simple design "NE" on the obverse, "XII" on the reverse, were the first coins struck in the Colonies. Shortage of change and the inability to get relief from the mother country prompted the Massachusetts Colony to embark upon this coining adventure to alleviate this shortage in New England. The famous Pine Tree Shilling shown below was part of this series to be struck by John Hull, who was appointed Mint Master.

After several years, when the coining operations were brought to the attention of King Charles of England, action was taken to prohibit any further issues.

While the majority were dated 1652, it is thought that they were coined for thirty years despite the King's disapproval. These crude and early pieces are actively sought by collectors and bring good prices today. They were coined in shillings, sixpence, three-pence and two-penny pieces.

# 11.
# CHRISTIAN GOBRECHT'S FLYING EAGLE DOLLAR

In the year 1836 interest was revived in the coining of silver dollars, as none had been coined since 1803. With the proposed passage of a law reducing their weight, permission was granted to resume minting this denomination.

Christian Gobrecht, famed engraver, executed the dies for this beautiful coin shown here. The Liberty Seated design was submitted by Thomas Sully, famed Philadelphia artist, and the Flying Eagle on the reverse was designed by Titian Peale, son of Charles Willson Peale, famous painter.

In 1836, 1838 and 1839 limited quantities of these dollars were struck with minor varieties on a more or less experimental basis. All are very rare.

It was not until 1840 that the dollar came into its own. Robert Ball Hughes, an Anglo-American sculptor, was the designer. He closely copied the Liberty Seated design on the obverse, but changed the Eagle to a standing position on the reverse. This famous Liberty Seated design was used on dollars and smaller denominations from then until 1891.

# 12.
# HISTORY OF THE "DOLLAR"

From the time of the Roman Empire, and through the Dark Ages the predominant size of silver coins was copied after the Ancient Roman Denarius, about the size of our present day dime. Times were pretty lean and silver pieces were consequently few and far between.

In the year 1516 a rich silver mine was discovered in Joachim's dale, a mining district in Bohemia. The count of Schlitz, by whom it was appropriated, struck a great number of large silver coins. The first had the date 1518 and the effigy of St. Joachim upon it. These were to be of the same value in silver as the many gold *gulden* then in use in trade. This Joachimsthaler has the distinction of being known as the first "Thaler" or silver coin of approximately one ounce in weight and around the size of our silver dollars.

From that time on the "thaler" became one of the most popular coins in Europe. Most countries and German states issued hundreds of varieties of these. The French issued coins of similar size "Ecus," the English their "Crowns," the Spanish their "Pieces of 8" (8 Reals). The name of such coins in other countries were changed to "Daler," "Dalar," "Daalder," "Tallero."

In the Western Hemisphere the Spanish "Pieces of 8" circulated widely during Colonial days. The British kept as much English Specie as possible from the American Colonies, creating serious shortages here. They also prohibited the coinage of coins. It is therefore not surprising the Spanish 8 Real coins soon became the principal medium to circulate and soon became known as the "Spanish Milled Dollar."

It is said that the Dollar George Washington threw across the Rapahannock River was one of these and indeed it must have been for our country did not coin any silver dollars until 1794.

We sometimes wonder why we did not adopt the English Denominations when we first started coining. Pounds, shillings and pence were used in all transactions with England, the parent country, during the Colonial days. We find that early Colonial paper money was issued in English denominations but during and after the Revolution one finds the gradual change to dollars and cents, some of the earlier notes even being redeemable in "Spanish Milled Dollars." No doubt antagonism over the war with England and the use of the Spanish coins influenced our country to adopt the dollar and cents denominations.

Our silver dollar has had a stormy path. From 1794 through 1803 they were coined in varying quantities. From 1803 through 1840 we have a gap of thirty-seven years when none were coined for circulation. It seems the amount of silver contained in the early dollars was too great. In 1837 Congress passed a law providing that $3\frac{1}{2}$ grains of the alloy be extracted from the authorized weight of the dollar, which at that time weighed 416 grains. This made the new dollar weight $412\frac{1}{2}$ grains. The only dollars struck between 1803 and 1840 were the 1804s of questionable authenticity, and the rare pattern or experimental pieces of 1836, 1838 and 1839, forerunners of the regular issued Liberty Seated dollars of 1840.

Standard silver dollars were again suspended with the issue of Trade dollars in 1873, designed to capture trade in the Orient. As these were not successful they were terminated in 1878 and standard silver dollars were again coined from then on until 1904. The few Trade dollars that were issued between 1879 and 1885 were struck for collectors only. In 1904 all dollars were discontinued due to the lack of bullion.

The Peace dollar first made its appearance in 1921, seventeen years later, and was coined continuously from then until 1935, the last year silver dollars were struck.

In 1971 the Eisenhower dollar appeared. It had a seven-year run and was then supplanted by the Susan B. Anthony dollar, which was wildly unpopular. It was discontinued after only a few years. As of this writing, we are anticipating a new dollar coin to be issued in the fall of 1999.

# 13.
# OUR
# FIRST GOLD COINS

The half eagle, or five dollar gold piece, was the first gold coin struck by our mint in accordance with the Coining Act of April 1792. Dated 1795, it had liberty's head facing right with a turban-like address. The reverse shows an eagle with spread wings, holding a wreath of laurel in its beak and standing on a palm branch. The original of this design was thought to be copied from a Roman first century B.C. onyx cameo, of similar design.

In addition to half eagles, limited quantities of quarter eagles and eagles were coined, but only on demand. Half eagles were our mint's major output. Even so, these were issued in very limited quantities.

The revaluation of our gold coins in 1834 is felt responsible for the extreme rarity of our early pieces. It is thought many were returned to the mint to be melted in order to get the benefit of the new values. For each $100 worth of old type coins, one could get at least $106.

Reverse designs were changed in 1797 to a spread eagle shown above. It was not until 1807 with the second design change that denominations were placed upon our gold.

# 14.
# HOW TO DETERMINE WHETHER A COIN IS UNCIRCULATED

I cannot stress enough the importance of accurate classification on condition in coins. If one becomes a coin collector, this exacting work should be the first to be mastered. A good amount of money can be lost by paying high prices for coins or coin collections that have been grossly overrated. If, when buying coins, there is any doubt in your mind as to whether a certain piece is in the condition represented, take it to an expert or another experienced collector. He will gladly give you an opinion free of charge. When purchasing a large collection, don't hesitate to have a dealer appraise it for you and give you his written expert opinion. It may cost you a fee for an expert appraisal, but this sum may save you many hundreds in the long run. Dealers KNOW what to look for. Another option is to purchase "slabbed" coins, which have been professionally graded and encapsulated in plastic. Slabbed coins can provide a high degree of buyer confidence, but the price usually reflects the added value of professional grading.

With the steadily increasing values of uncirculated coins it is essential that the serious collector know how to determine whether or not a coin is really uncirculated. Because of some of the cleaning processes used today, very careful scrutiny is necessary. I do not mean a cleaned coin cannot be considered uncirculated; what I mean is that many cleaned coins look like uncirculated pieces when closer scrutiny shows they have some wear.

It must be remembered that truly uncirculated pieces, if properly cleaned, are not decreased in value, even though under some circumstances it is preferable to have uncirculated pieces in their natural state. Too frequently, we look at a coin and, because it appears bright and new, consider it uncirculated, when the actual wear upon such a piece should be the determining factor.

I shall try to describe what I have found to be the first spots to wear on a coin, the first places to look for wear on what appears to be an uncirculated coin. I shall also mention other telltale defects to watch for.

Lincoln cents show their first wear on the cheekbone of Lincoln's bust. In the twenties, for a few years, Lincoln cents were struck very poorly so the coinage appears blurred, and these would be exceptions to the rule. Such blurred coins, even though uncirculated, would not be considered choice uncirculated coins.

Indian Heads first show wear on the obverse at the lock of hair at the lower right-hand bottom part of the bust. The ribbon hanging down is next to show wear. On the reverse, the highlights of the bow at the bottom of the wreath first wear.

The tip of the headdress above the word "Liberty" first shows wear on a large cent back to 1840. Prior to that date, the hairlock below the headdress, the eyebrow, and the cheek give telltale evidence. On the reverse, the highlighted leaves in the wreaths must be watched for wear. These coins are rather well struck. They should also be watched for minute scratches on the field of the obverse and reverse, on the head, and most important of all, on the edges of the coin. I have seen large cents that appear to have no wear at all, but close examination shows they contain many tiny scratches and nicks which immediately remove them from the uncirculated category.

Color plays a vitally important part in the valuation of large cents. Rich browns and steel color are the most desirable. Partially red, red, and brilliant are less desirable because they are apt to corrode under certain conditions.

The earlier large cents are a study for an expert. Being crudely struck and with so many varieties, it is difficult to name any specific places of where to look for wear. Each coin must be examined with the greatest care. Look for minute tiny scratches. Examine the color of the coin and its glossy surface. Should one of these "seem" to be worn slightly, it might well be the manner in which it was struck.

The most desirable condition for an early large cent is one with a rich dark brown, glossy surface, well centered, evenly struck, with no apparent signs of wear, corrosion, tiny nicks, scratches , and the like. Large cents in this condition are very valuable and should be carefully handled to maintain their status.

The description of wear for large cents covers that of the half-cent series.

The Eagle cents of 1856 through 1858 first show signs of wear upon the eagle's breast directly below the wing. The wing tip and eyebrow should also be examined. Some Eagle cents exist with very smooth tail feathers. This does not indicate wear, however, for many were lightly struck there.

Two-cent pieces are easy to detect for the "we" of the motto is the first item to go. Blurred horizontal lines in the shield are frequent, but these are not necessarily signs of wear, for many were coined in this manner.

The lock of hair above the ear first shows signs of wear on the three-cent nickel piece. These should also be closely examined for color, for soiled or discolored pieces are not desirable. Mint bloom should be evident upon these.

The Jefferson nickel wears first on Jefferson's cheekbone. On the reverse, just below the dome of Monticello, first signs of wear can be detected by a slight dulling or discoloration from the original glossy uncirculated look of the rest of the coin. These may be cleaned, but it is very difficult to erase this dulling effect.

Buffalo nickels are about the most difficult to identify in uncirculated condition. First, examine them for their original glossy mint bloom or color. If this is satisfactory, then examine the sharp edges of the coins for slight telltale hairlike scratches that will indicate circulation.

After this, closely examine the shoulder of the buffalo which will appear worn, for Buffalo nickels were coined in this manner, but examine the smooth shoulder for more telltale hairlike scratches. His hip, tail tip, and horn should be sharp. Next examine the cheek and just above the braid on the Indian's head for the same hairlike scratches. If the coin has no wear, no hairlike scratches on the above spots, and has its original mint bloom, you can assume it is a truly uncirculated coin.

The Liberty nickel first shows wear on the lock of hair over the temple and on the reverse highlights of the leaves in the wreath. The majority of Liberty nickels were struck very sharp, but blurred coinage is known in the years of 1911 and 1912. Slight dulling of the original mint bloom on the highlights is the first sign of wear, as was the case with the Jefferson nickel.

The tiny crosslike emblem atop the shield of the Shield nickel shows evidence of wear first. On the reverse, examine the "5" for minute, hairlike scratches and signs of wear.

A great many of the three-cent silver pieces were not struck very sharply. Of the first design, these should have mint bloom and lack light hairlike scratches. The type II three-cent piece, from 1854 on, has sharply defined lines around the star. These are the first spots to wear although these tiny coins usually wear fairly evenly all over.

The first signs of wear on Liberty-Seated coins, whether they are half dimes, dimes, quarters, halves, or silver dollars, appear on the ear of the head (some are known to have been struck blurred, however), then on the thigh of Liberty Seated. The ribbon below the wreath, on the reverse of the dime and half dime, wears first. Quarters and halves first show wear on the eyebrow and upper beak of the eagle, then on the upper wing tips.

Bust-type quarters and halves wear first on the lock of hair near the ear, next on the clasp on the ribbon at the lower part of the bust. On the reverse, the eagle's upper bill and the top edges of the wings wear first. Some of these coins are known to have been lightly struck so the general appearance of the rest of the coin must be taken into consideration.

Telltale signs of wear first show up on the eagle's wing, right in the center of the coin, on a Peace dollar. On a Morgan dollar wear appears first on the eagle's breast and head. With both of these coins, the reverse seems to show wear a good deal faster than the obverse.

Barber quarters, halves, and dimes wear first on the obverse on the lock of hair over the forehead and temple directly below the word "Liberty." The cheek next shows discoloration and dulling. The reverse of the quarters and halves wears first directly above the eye of the eagle and the claws in his left talon.

The Liberty-Walking half-dollar coins first show wear on the breast of the eagle on the reverse. The head, breasts, and left leg of Miss Liberty are the next telltale signs. Franklin half dollars show their first sign of wear right in the center of the bell and on the cheek of Franklin. A slight dullness is the very first sign of wear.

Liberty-Standing quarters first show signs of wear on the knee of Miss Liberty. A slight flattening appears as the first telltale sign of wear. A number of these quarters were coined with flat heads, which appear worn, but this does not necessarily mean the coin is not uncirculated. Watch that knee for the first real signs of wear. On the reverse, the eagle's breast wears first, but not nearly as soon as the knee on the obverse. I have seen many beautiful (cleaned) Liberty-Standing quarters with full head, but with that telltale sign of wear on the knee. Don't be fooled by this one! Washington quarters first wear on the eagle's breast.

Now consider our early types of silver dollars. The type with flowing hair wears first on the eagle's breast and on the lock of hair directly behind the ear. The bust type, small eagle, on the reverse shows wear on the eagle's breast, on the obverse on the draped bust, directly above the first two digits of the date and to the extreme right bottom. The cheek wears next.

On Liberty Seated silver dollars, the first wear shows on the right thigh, closely followed by the forehead and the word "Liberty" on the shield; on the reverse, the eagle's beak and upper tips of wings wear first. On trade dollars, the knee, left breast, and head on the obverse show the first signs of wear; on the reverse the eagle's left leg, then upper tips of wings.

Commemorative coins should be examined carefully as many show wear, particularly in the early series. The first spots to wear are listed below:

*Columbian Half Dollars*
   *Obverse:* cheek and center lock of hair
   *Reverse:* center sail of ship; next, center of globes
*New Rochelle, New York, 300th Anniversary*
   *Obverse;* the calf's hip
   *Reverse:* highlights of the fleur-de-lis
*Iowa Centennial*
   *Obverse:* the eagle's breast
   *Reverse:* center columns, building, and the tower
*Booker T. Washington Memorial*
   *Obverse:* cheek and nose
   *Reverse:* highlights of center letters
*Washington-Carver*
   *Obverse:* the prominent cheek
   *Reverse:* the whole map of the United States
*Isabella Quarter*
   *Obverse:* cheek
   *Reverse:* head and left forearm
*Lafayette Dollar*
   *Obverse:* cheek of Washington
   *Reverse:* leg of equestrian; next, head
*Panama-Pacific Exposition (1915)*
   *Obverse:* head and left arm
   *Reverse:* eagle's breast

*Lincoln, Illinois, Centennial*
   *Obverse:* cheekbone
   *Reverse:* eagle's breast directly below forward part of left wing
*Maine Centennial*
   *Obverse:* fingers of left figure on scythe
   *Reverse:* ribbon holding wreath at bottom
*Pilgrim Tercentenary*
   *Obverse:* cheek, hatbrim, and book tip
   *Reverse:* high side of ship
*Missouri Centennial*
   *Obverse:* cheek and side of hat
   *Reverse:* pioneer's arm, both heads
*Alabama Centennial*
   *Obverse:* Kilby's cheek and forehead
   *Reverse:* eagle's breast directly above left leg
*Grant Memorial*
   *Obverse:* hair at temple
   *Reverse:* leaves of trees
*Monroe Centennial*
   *Obverse:* cheek and hair over temple
   *Reverse:* the faint figures in the maps of North and South America; examine coin for light hairlike scratches (This is a lightly struck coin hard to tell when slightly used.)
*Huguenot-Walloon Tercentenary*
   *Obverse:* outstanding rim and top of hat, also cape
   *Reverse:* hull of ship and shrouds
*Lexington-Concord Sesquicentennial*
   *Obverse:* fingers holding the gun
   *Reverse:* point of block house at center

# 15.
# PROOF COINS
# MUST BE PERFECT

Proof coins are described by most publications as "Coins specially struck with mirror-like surface, for collectors, at Philadelphia only. Also sandblast and mat proof." But there is a lot more to them than that.

Today, they are very carefully struck to insure perfect specimens. Proofs are currently struck at San Francisco, and bear the "S" mint mark on the obverse. Until recently, they were struck by hand to insure perfection. At all times, the dies used were polished, as were the planchets. This gave the coins their mirrorlike finish.

A genuine proof must be perfect. Its field, including the tiny spaces between letters and designs, must have this mirror-like finish. The highlights of the coin are sharp and have a "frosted" or "uncirculated" look, causing the designs to "stand out" from their mirror-like background. The edges are usually sharp and the coin is perfectly centered.

Proof coins are truly beautiful coins, whether they are of gold, silver, or copper. Sandblast or mat proofs have all the above qualifications, with the exception of the mirror-like finish; they have a dull velvety-type surface instead.

While the first regularly recognized issue of proofs for collectors commenced in 1858, proofs were coined before that time. The first early proofs were trial or experimental pieces to test designs and dies. Very few were struck and consequently they are very rare. These were usually not offered for sale to collectors but were more "presentation" pieces, samples of coinage, and so forth.

In 1858, when proofs were first offered for sale to collectors, the number struck was very small. Records of how many proofs were coined prior to 1877 are spotty, but from what information we have we can tell that the quantities were very small. By examining the records one can see how the interest in proof coins steadily increased as the years went by, popularity centering on the lower denominations.

During the nineteenth century, proof sets were offered as minor sets, complete sets, and those with gold. The minor sets were by far the most popular, the complete sets following second in popularity. Gold coins were not very popular in proof even though their premium cost was very little over the face value. Probably, this was due to the initial face-value investment involved. The coinage of proof double eagles ranged from only 20 to 158 proofs per year from 1865 to 1907.

Proofs were discontinued in 1915 and were not resumed again until 1936. The maximum number of proofs struck in 1915 for any denomination was around 1,000. The number struck in 1936 that can make up proof sets was around 3,300. This was quite an increase, but nothing like what occurred from 1936 to 1957 when 1,000,000 or so proof sets were coined.

From 1936 through 1942, proofs were not sold as "sets" only, as they are today. One could purchase any quantity of any denomination; you had to make up your own sets. From 1950 on, proofs have been sold as sets only.

Many "early strikes" of regular issue coins appear to be proofs, for the new dies frequently give the coins a mirror-like surface. This is often true with branch mint coins, but it must be remembered that no proofs were ever struck at any of the branch mints. While it is very difficult to detect these, it will be found that they never have the sharp, well struck edges of a genuine proof. The highlights are usually not sharp and the coin is not perfectly centered.

One frequently comes across attempts to fake proofs. Buffing will give an uncirculated coin a mirror-like finish, but this usually can be detected because the mirror-like finish is on the designs as well as the field. Even coins done more carefully, so that the designs are not buffed, can be detected by examining the tiny surfaces between the letters and designs where a buffer cannot get to. Of course the sharp edges of a genuine proof on such coins are lacking also.

Uncirculated coins that most frequently look like proof coins when they are not are: silver dollars, 1878 up, from all mints; Liberty-Seated halves, prior to 1890; quarters, prior to 1890; a few dimes in the 1870s; the 1866 nickel; the 1865 three-cent piece; gold dollars, particularly in the 1880s; and some of the later three-dollar gold pieces. With regard to the gold two-and-one-half-, five-, ten-, and twenty-dollar pieces, these sometimes are found with proof-like luster but are usually somewhat scratched, indicating contact with other coins.

Several of the scarcer, shorter issues, such as the four-dollar Stellas; the three-dollar coins of 1873, 1875, and 1876; the twenty-cent pieces of 1877 and 1878; the nickel three-cent pieces of 1877 and 1878; and the two-cent pieces of 1873, were only struck in proof, even though used specimens or "debased" proofs are occasionally found of these coins.

The three-dollar series, the nickel three-cent pieces, and the two-cent pieces were coins purely for collectors, to maintain a consecutive run of dates. The 1873 two-cent pieces and the 1877 and 1878 twenty-cent pieces struck for this reason turned out to be the last of the series.

The four-dollar Stellas were really trial or experimental pieces and were never coined for actual use.

Some denominations during the 1880s became unpopular for regular use but were coined for a decade or so in small quantities, probably to satisfy the collectors' demand for a complete "run of dates."

# 16.
# BEWARE
# OF COUNTERFEITS

The rapid price rise of nearly all United States coins has created a flood of counterfeits, altered dates, and other kinds of forgeries, many of which are so clever that the best experts are sometimes fooled. Below are those to watch out for:

*Twenty-dollar gold pieces.* All twenties are being coined, of the proper amount of gold, in foreign countries, designed to be sold to American collectors. They can be detected by examining the feathers in the center of the eagle on the reverse. These feathers are too sharply tooled. They also have a very proof-like, mirror-type surface. Beware of Liberty-Head types of rare dates, Philadelphia Mint, for the common branch mint coins are having the mint marks cleverly removed. Foreign made counterfeit Liberty Heads have very sharp milling—appear too new.

*Ten-dollar gold pieces.* Watch the 1858*P*; these are known to exist with their mint marks removed (branch mint). All tens are being coined in Europe at present.

*Five-dollar gold pieces.* Watch the 1909*O* as the *O* mint mark is known to have been added. All fives are being counterfeited.

*Three-dollar gold pieces.* There is a possibility that the later dates are being struck in Europe. They have a mirror-like appearance.

*Four-dollar Stellas.* Beware of gold-plated patterns struck in inferior metals and being sold as gold Stellas. The 1880 series coins are being struck presently in Europe.

*Quarter eagles* ($2.50). Both types, Indian Head and Liberty Head, are being struck in large quantities in Europe. They have the correct weight in gold and are very nearly perfect.

On fake Liberty Heads the head is too sharp, the edge of the coin is a trifle flat, and the milling is too sharp. These have a granular surface and they come in many dates. As to the Indian Heads, it is difficult to tell, but there again the milling is too fine and sharp.

*Gold dollars.* Coins of pretty nearly every date and mint have been copied. These, for the most part, have a granular surface, the beading on the edge tends to be too flat, the milling much too sharp, the deep-cut word "Liberty" on the headdress is usually sharp in the center and weak toward the end of each word. These are the new counterfeits struck in Europe and are very dangerous, being of the correct weight and fineness of gold. Old counterfeits are very easy to detect, for the gold content is inferior. The very rare 1854C has been faked by adding a sweated letter C to it; I have seen two of these in the last six months. Mint marks also are known to have been sweated to nearly all of the rarer branch mint gold dollars. In all denominations, these new European gold counterfeits are made by the centrifugal molding process and are very cleverly done.

*Silver dollars.* Removing the mint mark from an 1895*O* or *S* is done to make it the rare 1895*P* dollar. This coin was only struck in proof and, to be genuine, should be a perfect proof.

*Half dollars.* There are no outstanding new forgeries of halves recently other than the well-known addition of a star to the Grant Memorial half dollar. This is easily detected because the Grant stars were coined first. When the star was removed from the dies, a few minor defects were also corrected, namely slight bulges at the neck and below the nose. These always appear on the genuine Grant stars and never on the Grant without star. Counterfeit Grant stars also, at times, have a flattened spot on the reverse.

*Quarter dollars.* The 1923*S*, being rare, is being made by changing the 8 on a 1928*S* to a 3. Also, the mint mark on a 1913*D* is being retooled to look like an *S*. 1932 with a *"D"* cleverly added.

*Dimes.* Beware of the 1916*D*! I have seen these altered in all conditions; recently I saw a "good" one altered from a 1919*D*. Many have been faked by sweating a *D* cleverly on to a 1916P. These can be detected under a 20-power glass; close examination of the *D* will show some slight discoloration around the initial. Very frequently, the initial is out of its correct position. If sweated on, close examination will show indications of the base of the *D* tending to "round in" where it is attached to the coin, rather than being part of the planchet. A dealer recently had a roll of 1916*D* Unc. dimes offered to him. He picked the false *"D*s" off of the coins and sent all back to the seller!

Another clever fraud is to take two dimes, a 1916*P* and a 1917*D* and mount them, with the 1916*P* obverse showing and the 1917*D* reverse showing, in an expensive plastic holder. In still another dangerous fraud, they punch the metal on the obverse out a little and fill it in so it is hardly noticeable; then with the bulge on the reverse they create a *D*. Very cleverly done! The celebrated 1894*S* has had *S* sweated on to the Philadelphia coin. I have not seen one of these, however, in thirty years.

*Nickels.* Watch 1950*D*. They are now cutting the tail off of 1959*D* to make it look like 1950*D*. Watch your 1937*D* three-legged nickels; they are now grinding off the one leg. To detect a genuine three-legged nickel, the point under the belly of the buffalo is long and very sharp; this does not appear on any other Buffalo nickel.

Watch this new angle. Dates are being put on dateless nickels by applying acids. The 1913 Liberty Head has for years been altered, either from a 1903 or a 1910. The 1895 nickels are being altered to 1885.

From 1866 through 1873 we had both the silver five-cent pieces of half dimes and the nickel five-cent pieces, two different types of this denomination. To top that off, the first Liberty nickels of 1883 did not have the word *cents* on them. After being gold-plated, they were frequently passed as five-dollar gold pieces, being the same size.

The twenty-cent coins were so similar to quarters that these two were frequently mistaken for each other. Last, but not least, a two-and-one-half-dollar gold piece is the same size as a cent. Many have been passed as cents, in error, due to this similarity.

I guess the five definitely different denominations we have today are the best.

*Cents.* This is the most popular series. The $D$ is cleverly being ground off of the 1960 cents to make them $P$, small date only. 1937$S$ cents are being retooled to look like 1931$S$. The 1922$D$ cents are being changed to 1922 plain cents.

The 1914$D$ is being made from an altered 1944$D$, with the first 4 being changed to a 1. The $D$ is being sweated on the 1914$P$ and the field is being ground down so that only the metal for the $D$ is left. These are the hardest to identify, because one must examine the field around the letter to detect the concave depression. On 1909$S$-$VDB$, the letter $S$ is being sweated to a common 1909$VDB$. (Initials of Victor D. Brenner, the coin's designer.) Indian cents apparently have not been tampered with. But watch the 1856 Eagle cent. These are commonly altered from an 1858.

Watch your coins; any coins valued at from a few dollars up are liable to be forged.

Be very careful of early rarities, particularly in Colonials, large cents and half cents; some of the electrotypes are so realistic they fool many an expert. An electrotype is a copperplated lead piece made as an exact copy of the original rare coin. Electrotypes are considered by the government to be counterfeits if they are made in imitation of regular United States coinages. I know of an antique dealer who payed $110 for an electrotype of the rare 1792 Washington Large-Eagle half dollar, not knowing that it was a fake. A customer of ours recently purchased a collection of half cents from another collector for a high price, only to find that the 1796, 1831, 1852 cents—all very rare dates—were electrotypes. Those three coins, if genuine, would have been worth the major cost of the collection.

How can you detect electrotypes? Sometimes it is easy, other times not. First, an electrotype never has any lettering or milling on the edges; at least, I have never seen one that did. Second, sometimes one can detect a fine crack in the middle of the edge running around the coin where the two copper coatings have been pressed together; sometimes this has been eliminated by careful smoothing off of the edges. In any event, one can usually see one or the other: a slight crack or evidence of light smoothing on the edges of the coin. Third, usually an electrotype does not ring true. Its ring is sometimes remarkably near that of an original coin, however, in that the old copper coins do not ring very much anyway. Fourth, unless an electrotype has been very heavily plated, it usually can be bent with the fingers because the lead inside is soft. The antiquated system of biting a coin to test its genuineness may work if the plating is not too thick. Fifth, scraping the edge with a sharp knife usually will expose the lead under the thin copper plating; however, some electrotypes are so heavily plated that to scrape through seriously damages the coin if it turns out to be genuine. This is all I can suggest concerning electrotype detection, and I repeat, electrotypes are found mostly of early American Colonials, large cents.

# 17.
# MINT ERRORS
# AND THE RATING SCALE

Coins that are off-center or that have something wrong with them, formerly known as freaks, have now been given the name of *mint errors*. In the manufacture of coins, the mint carefully checks the new coins as they are coined, but occasionally a misstamped coin, or bill for that matter, manages to escape the eyes of the checkers and get into circulation. A good many of these mint errors are unique, others are quite common due to the ease with which certain errors occur and are overlooked. There is an association for mint-error collectors.

The difficulty of describing mint errors prompted the rating scale, which makes it easier to understand what the error is. For instance, on off-center coins, the clock is used as a guide. If you place the coin in front of you, the top would be numeral 12, and the circle of the coin would be divided into twelve equal spaces like the face of a clock. Thus, if you have an off-center Lincoln cent and the design is off to the right at about the number 3 of the clock, it is known as a "3 o'clock" off-center coin. If the coin is off at the bottom of the planchet, it is "6 o'clock" and so on around the face of the clock.

Degrees of off-center are figured in fractions of an inch. If the design is halfway off, showing half the planchet blank, and to the right, as described above in the first example, it is "3, ½ off." If the degree off is one quarter, showing three quarters of the coin design and one-fourth blank, it is known as "3, ¼ off." Therefore, the professional description of the last coin is: Lincoln cent 1911*P* ¼ O.C. in 3 o'clock.

Coins slightly off-center, or eclipsed (a circular piece out of the edge of the planchet at some spot), are the most common mint errors. This does not mean that all are, however. I recently had a large cent with the rare date 1811 in almost uncirculated condition which was off-center about ⅛ at 2 on the obverse. The unusual thing about this cent was that, while it was the same amount off on the reverse, the design was *incused,* or cut in, rather than raised up and very sharp. This most likely was the result of two planchets being struck at once and the design of one cent being impressed in reverse on the other. The combination of errors, plus the rarity of the coin and its condition, make it very rare.

A popular type of mint error is the cent that is struck on a silver planchet. This can happen when a dime planchet gets mixed up with the cent ones; consequently the cent design is struck on the silver dime planchet. Many persons think these are very rare, but there are more of them than one realizes. A count made recently indicated that there were approximately forty-five known silver cents. They are frequently quoted as being worth thousands of dollars, but auction records indicate a bonafide sale of one of these at substantially less. Most dealers shy from this coin.

One of the most sought after and popular mint errors is the copper cent of 1943, the year they made steel cents only. Many people claim to have these copper cents, but close inspection shows that nearly all are fakes. It is very easy to copper-plate a steel cent, but this can be detected by giving it a magnet test. If the cent adheres to the magnet, you may be certain there is a steel cent under the plating.

Errors in paper money are also ardently sought. The commonest errors are bills that are slightly off-center. Also common are bills that had the paper folded slightly so that there is a "white spot" across some part of the note. Probably the most desirable are notes that have one denomination on one side, and another on the other. I recently saw one of these on exhibition, a one dollar reverse and a five dollar obverse.

Other very unusual mint errors are bills with composite folds that give a white, unprinted, accordion effect; notes printed heavily on one side of the reverse or obverse with ink fading to nothing on the other side; and notes with signatures and numbers upside down. All these are very rare. And one must remember that mint errors, as well as all coins, must be in perfect condition to demand the best prices. Even though the error is an unusual one, if the note has been used a lot, its value is one-tenth what it would have been had it been crisp-new.

# 18.
# SHALL I CLEAN
# MY COINS?

This age-old question has been bothering collectors and dealers for a long time. Originally, the cleaning of coins was taboo and those that first attempted cleaning did their best to have the coins they cleaned look as much as possible as if they had not been cleaned. Today, well-cleaned coins are accepted as readily as (and sometimes more readily than) those that have been kept in their original state, with exceptions. The coins cleaned and the cleaner used determine the desirability of the coin in question.

Never clean a badly worn coin of any kind. In the first place, it is a waste of time and, cleaning a coin that is in a condition inferior to very fine will never enhance it.

## PROOFS

Proofs in gold seldom if ever will need cleaning. In silver they frequently become tarnished and are preferred so by collectors. If the tarnish is not too dark, Silver Dip purchased in your local supermarket will brighten them without scratching. Don't leave the coin in the dip more than five seconds or so, and rinse immediately with water. Dry with a soft cleansing tissue. Proof nickels will react favorably to the foregoing treatment.

For bronze and copper coins, leave proofs alone. A nicely toned proof cent is more desirable than one that is brilliantly cleaned. If there are specks or corrosion spots on the coin, it will then have to be cleaned, but it is questionable whether the spots will come off and, if they do, whether the cleaning will not harm the proof surface. Silver proofs that have been cleaned seem to be more desirable to the collector than uncleaned ones because detection is difficult and they like their proofs bright in silver. In copper, however, toned ones are more desirable, for the brightness of a cleaned copper coin is easily detected.

## UNCIRCULATED COINS

Gold uncirculated coins rarely need cleaning. At times it might be advisable to wash them gently with Ivory soap and warm water. Silver coins, if lightly tarnished, can be brightened nicely by using Silver Dip as suggested for the proofs (a five-second dip and then a quick rinse). If heavily tarnished, silver coins should be cleaned as follows: make a paste of bicarbonate of soda and water. Do not use the ordinary inexpensive brand of soda available in grocery stores, but use the better grade found in drugstores; the texture of the cheaper brand is coarse and may scratch, whereas the better brand is smoother and does not tend to scratch as much. Be certain your fingers are soft and smooth with no nicks or scratches on the skin. It is a good idea to soak them a minute or so in warm water to soften. Then rub the coin gently with the paste until tarnish is gone. Don't forget the edges.

## COPPER COINS

Large cents or half cents in copper should never be cleaned. Indian Heads and Lincolns should not be cleaned if they are naturally brilliant or red. If they are toned down so that only a slight amount of red or no red shows, it probably is better to clean them today than leave them as they are, for a dark uncirculated cent of the small size does not seem to be as desirable as a cleaned brilliant one. A product called Care can be used on copper and bronze coins. This does not change their color but removes grease and dirt and gives them a glossy protective coating. Brilliantize does a good job even removing spots, provided one follows instructions. The cent will be very bright when finished and really nice looking, far superior to what it formerly looked like. Specks and spots can also be removed if they are on the coin. There is a tendency for copper coins to tone down more rapidly after cleaning than they would naturally, and this should be kept in mind.

## VERY FINE AND EXTREMELY FINE COINS

Gold rarely needs cleaning. Ivory soap and warm water should do, if it is absolutely necessary. Silver pieces can be cleaned with bicarbonate of soda following the instructions given for uncirculated silver pieces. This usually improves the looks of the coin. Copper or bronze coins in this condition should never be cleaned. They look better in their natural state.

Silver will tarnish very quickly, particularly if exposed to air and other chemicals that affect it. It is difficult to believe that brilliant uncirculated or proof coins as old as a hundred or more years could possibly have lasted all that while without ever having been tarnished. It is my opinion that nearly all choice silver coins have been cleaned at some time or other and perhaps many times. It hasn't hurt them; in fact, had tarnish been allowed to increase, the coin would finally have become black and the tarnish would have had a permanently bad effect on the condition of the coin. The surface of very badly tarnished silver coins begins to be eaten away and can never be brought back, the corrosive quality of the tarnish having deteriorated the value of the coin.

Many collectors of large cents prefer their uncirculated specimens in a rich brown or steel color that is acquired naturally through the years. The film that gives these cents this fine glossy surface is a protection preventing the annoying corrosion spots that so frequently appear on cents that are red or brilliant. This is not the case with collectors of small cents; with this series they want them brilliant or red even though these, too, are subject to the same annoying spots: I wonder when small-cent collectors will follow the large-cent collectors and will appreciate the value of rich, colored small cents, rather than the brilliant ones that are subject to deterioration.

# 19.
# HOW TO SELL A COIN COLLECTION

For some time I have wanted to write about the sale of coins, how to go about it and how to get what they are worth. A reader of mine wanted to know what a widow should do to sell a coin collection. This is a very difficult problem for an inexperienced person.

How to go about selling a collection depends upon the value of the collection. If it is a matter of a few hundred dollars, an outright sale is the best. If it is a collection running in excess of several thousand dollars, the story is entirely different.

In the first place, every collector should make arrangements for the sale of his collection while he is still collecting. Since he has dealt (and is dealing) with many large dealers he is in a good position to form an opinion as to whom he would trust his collection with and whom he would not. This information should be passed on to his heirs. The sale of a collection of size has to depend upon the absolute trust in the dealer purchasing it or handling its sale. There are many honest dealers in this country, but there are a few others who will use all kinds of slick tricks to get the most for the least amount of money.

When death occurs, the first step is that the collection will have to be appraised for both state and federal inheritance taxes. Appraisals can be done on both a low wholesale or a high retail valuation. Expert appraisers should give both the wholesale and retail valuation. For inheritance tax purposes, a figure between the two should be used.

It is advisable not to keep the appraisal valuations too low for this purpose, because when the collection is sold there would then be a much higher capital gains tax which would cost more than paying a higher inheritance tax.

The choice of an appraiser is very important. Get the best and to your knowledge the most honest. Pay his fee rather than accept a free appraisal. This keeps you from being obligated to any one person in the event of sale and should get you a better appraisal. There is a great temptation for appraisers to keep values down low on a free appraisal with an eye to purchasing the collection. An appraiser should be a disinterested party, not the prospective purchaser of the collection or his agent.

Computer owners will definitely want to purchase a program called Hobbysoft Coin Keeper. In addition to supplying a database with coin prices regularly updated, this excellent program provides a way to inventory your collection for tax and insurance purposes. It also supplies a "want list" feature to track prices on future purchases. Hobbysoft Coin Keeper is available for MS-DOS, Windows, and Macintosh. It is available from Ninga Software Corporation, 882 Pepin Crescent, Victoria B.C. Canada V8Z 6V6. Phone: (800) 656-4642 or Fax: (250) 881-8355. Free demos are available on their Web site: www.ninga.com.

Next we come to the manner of selling, whether it is outright for cash or at auction. If sold outright, one should expect to receive between 50 and 70 percent of the retail sales value. This does not mean the guide book or catalog value, but the amount the coins would actually sell for. This will vary considerably from guide book prices depending upon what the collection contains.

Proofs and key rarities usually retail for as much as full guide book prices, and in many instances for considerably above these valuations. Extreme rarities in great demand can go at two, three, and even ten times catalog value. Circulated coins of the more common variety, even ordinary uncirculated coins, rarely sell up to guide book valuations; usually they sell at from 20 to 40 percent under them.

The discount paid from retail values of 50 to 70 percent depends upon the type of material the collection contains and the amount of work involved in selling the material. One must always remember that a dealer is in business to earn his living and is entitled to his profits for his efforts.

Now we come to selling at auction. This is the manner in which all of the leading collections are sold. It has advantages and disadvantages. While cash advances on a consignment can usually be gotten, the final settlement is usually slower than a cash sale because of the length of time it takes to handle the sale. The advantages are first that the auctioneer is very anxious to realize as much as possible for the collection. The more he can realize, the more his commission will be. He will catalog the coins to their best advantage, and hidden or unknown rarities that otherwise might not be mentioned in an outright sale will be featured in order to get the most for the collection.

Surprises also occur which even conscientious dealers might not expect when purchasing outright. A coin which a dealer would normally purchase for full guide book price, suspecting it would sell for considerably more, sold recently at auction for three times guide book price!

Other advantages of the auction method include a complete published and printed record in the catalog of the collection. Also a complete printed and priced list is made of what the collection brought for every lot. And lastly, when desired, the name of the collector is published in conjunction with the sale of the collection, crediting him for his efforts in compiling it.

The auction method does take time. It will take the cataloger about a month to prepare the catalog. A month should be allowed to let the printer print it and get it into the mail. Then four to six weeks should be allowed for the collectors and dealers to send in their bids. At the termination of the sale, another month should be allowed for payments to come on the lots sold. So one can expect to have settlement in full thirty days after the termination of the auction sale. Insofar as one must wait six months for appraisal for inheritance tax purposes in order to have the profit from the sale come under capital gains rather than income tax, the length of time the auction method takes is no disadvantage.

The fee an auctioneer gets for his service ranges between 10 and 25 percent of the prices realized and should include all costs, insurance, advertising, printing, etc.

Inexperienced people sometimes fear the auction method, being afraid the coins will go for a price way below value. This is not the case. Auctioneers who run large, nationwide sales cover the market so completely, both as to dealers and collectors, there is little opportunity for any lot to go for a ridiculous price. Sometimes an unpopular item sells at a price that appears to be quite cheap, but that is really what it is worth.

The best auctions are those run by dealers who have specialized in this selling method for many years, for in so doing they have built up a clientele and a reputation that encourages good bidding. The best sales are a combination of mail bids and then a public sale commenced with the high mail bid. This system brings the best prices, encourages competition, and the prices realized are publicly announced.

## WATCH OUT FOR THE FOLLOWING WHEN SELLING FOR CASH:

*Downgrading.* Downgrading is listing or grading a coin as inferior to what it actually is. I know of a collection of beautiful proofs that was purchased several years ago as "uncirculated" by an unscrupulous dealer.

*Disinterest.* A common practice among "slickys" is to push the choice pieces aside, concentrate on a few common ones, pay a good price for these, and get the real rare coins for a song.

*Use of fear.* Many a gold coin has been purchased, under threat of penalty to own (a law which is nonexistent), at as low as half face value.

*Omission.* Lots of rare coins have been sold for a song simply by the purchaser forgetting to mention that they are rare and buying a group as a "lot."

## WATCH OUT FOR THE FOLLOWING WHEN SELLING AT AUCTION:

*High cash advances, too-low commission charges.* High cash advances and too-low commission charges are inducements that are likely to work to your disadvantage. They are come-ons to get your coins.

*Local club auctions.* These are honest sales but they do not have the number of bidders necessary to bring good prices. They are usually started with a minimum bid which causes a good percentage of the items to be returned unsold, as no one will take up the bidding. On the other hand, a majority of those that are sold go for the minimum, which may be very low.

*Part-time auctioneers.* They do not have the clientele or experience to do a good job on your collection. It takes many years of experience to catalog correctly, build a reputation, and get lots of active bidding from both dealers and collectors.

*Choice of a dealer to buy outright or sell at auction.* Every dealer will tell you how great and honest he is. Some will knock their competitors (beware of these!). The best test if you don't know any is to check his references, his bank, and his Dun & Bradstreet ratings. Also, get the names of half a dozen other collectors who have actually done business with him and find out whether they were satisfied.

It's not very nice to consign a collection to a dealer for outright sale or auction and have to wait and wait to get paid. If it's a cash sale, don't take it in installments; that can go on for years, the cream may then be gone, and you may have to take back what's left that the dealer couldn't sell.

Check the promptness with which your auctioneer will pay. We know a collector who sold an $80,000 collection at auction and had to travel 700 miles each month to get $10,000 each trip, when he should have been paid outright in thirty days.

## 20.
## COIN VALUES ARE DETERMINED BY DEMAND AND CONDITION

New collectors take up the hobby of coin collecting every day. Older coins disappear from circulation very quickly and the supply coming into the market from the break-up of collections cannot keep pace with the demand that comes from ever greater numbers of collectors of American coins. Thus, the demand for these coins grows while the supply diminishes. The result has been a steadily rising level in the value of American coins.

Besides rarity, however, there is another factor that affects a coin's value, namely, its state of preservation or condition. Collectors will often pay many times as much for a coin in superior condition than for a specimen that is just average.

The prices listed in this book are, for the most part, for "fine" coins. A "fine" coin is one that shows a reasonable amount of wear but is still a desirable coin. The basic outline is still clear but much of the fine detail is worn away. All lettering should be legible. The next grade below this is "very good," a much worn but not altogether unattractive coin. A coin in this condition should be free of serious gouges or other mutilations but it may be somewhat scratched from use. A coin that is rated only "good" is really a minimum condition coin. The date and mint mark would be legible and the major portions of the design distinguishable. "Fair" indicates a badly worn coin that is usually not acceptable to a collector. "Fair" coins are generally used as "space fillers," only until such time as a better coin can be acquired.

The grade above "fine" is "very fine," a coin on which the design is still quite clean, and which over all shows the very slightest amount of wear. An "extremely fine" coin shows the slightest signs of wear or rubbing only on the very highest points of the design. "Uncirculated" indicates a coin absolutely without wear. Above "uncirculated" is "proof," a coin which is a special coin with a mirror-like surface especially minted for collectors. The "proof" coin must be absolutely perfect.

*There is no iron-bound rule as to values* but the following pages should give you an *approximate* idea of what your coins are worth. The values shown are the prices the dealers charge when they sell coins. If a "fine" coin as listed in this book is listed at $10, you can expect dealers to pay you between 50 and 70 percent of the price shown. This will, of course, depend upon how badly the dealer needs the coin or coins. Dealers usually carry a large stock of coins and cannot be expected to pay high prices for those items that they have a lot of. On the other hand, if he needs your coin badly, he often will pay record prices.

# Part Two:
# THE COINS LISTED

# ABBREVIATIONS USED IN THE COIN VALUE LISTS

*Unc.*—Uncirculated
*Ex. Fine*—Extremely Fine
*V. Fine*—Very Fine
*V. Good*—Very Good

More detailed information about minor varieties can be found in the following books:

*A Guide Book of U.S. Coins*, Whitman Publishing Co. General information.
Miller-Ryder. *The State Coinages of New England*. Colonial Coins.
Dr. Edward Maris, *New Jersey Cents*. Colonial Coins.
Sydney P. Noe, *The New England and Willow Tree Coinages of Massachusetts*. Colonial Coins.
S. S. Crosby, *Cents and Half Cents of 1793*.
Gilbert Elder, *U.S. Half Cents*.
Wm. H. Sheldon, *Penny Whimsey*. Large cents.
D. W. Valentine, *U.S. Half Dimes*.
J. W. Haseltine, *Type Table of U.S. Dollars, Halves and Quarters*.
M. H. Bolender, *Silver Dollars 1794–1804*.

# 21.
# COLONIAL COINS BEFORE THE DECLARATION OF INDEPENDENCE: 1652–1776

## MASSACHUSETTS
### NEW ENGLAND PIECES
*SHILLING*

|  | Good | Fine |
|---|---|---|
| NE Shilling | 13,500.00 | 37,500.00 |
| NE Sixpence (6 known, very rare) | — | — |
| NE Threepence (2 known, very rare) | — | — |

### WILLOW TREE PIECES (1652)

| | | |
|---|---|---|
| Willow Tree Shilling | 12,500.00 | 35,000.00 |
| Willow Tree Sixpence | — | 37,500.00 |
| Willow Tree Threepence (3 known, very rare) | — | — |

### OAK TREE PIECES (1652)

| | | |
|---|---|---|
| Oak Tree Shilling | 1,150.00 | 2,500.00 |
| Oak Tree Sixpence | 875.00 | 2,500.00 |
| Oak Three Threepence | 875.00 | 2,500.00 |
| Oak Tree Twopence (1662) | 750.00 | 1,650.00 |

### PINE TREE PIECES (1652)

| | | |
|---|---|---|
| Pine Tree Shilling, Large Planchet | 1,100.00 | 2,350.00 |
| Pine Tree Shilling, Small Planchet | 1,000.00 | 2,150.00 |
| Pine Tree Sixpence | 700.00 | 1,850.00 |
| Pine Tree Threepence | 650.00 | 1,650.00 |

## MARYLAND (1658)
### LORD BALTIMORE COINAGE

| | | |
|---|---|---|
| Shilling | 1,300.00 | 5,000.00 |
| Sixpence | 1,200.00 | 3,800.00 |
| Fourpence | 1,300.00 | 4,750.00 |

## NEW JERSEY
### MARK NEWBY COINAGE

| | | |
|---|---|---|
| St. Patrick Halfpence | 185.00 | 550.00 |
| St. Patrick Farthing with Brass Plug on Obverse | 150.00 | 325.00 |
| St. Patrick Farthing without Brass Plug | 150.00 | 325.00 |
| St. Patrick Farthing, Silver | 1,100.00 | 2,000.00 |

## FLORIDA TOKEN

|  | Good | Fine | Unc. |
|---|---|---|---|
| (1688) Florida, James II Plantation Token, 1/24 part real—Tin | 200.00 | 500.00 | 1,750.00 |

## LONDON ELEPHANT TOKENS

|  | Good | Fine | Ex. Fine |
|---|---|---|---|
| (1664) Halfpenny GOD PRESERVE LONDON (Thick Planchet) | 200.00 | 450.00 | 1,000.00 |
| (1664) Halfpenny GOD PRESERVE LONDON (Thin Planchet) | 250.00 | 550.00 | 1,750.00 |
| (1664) Halfpenny GOD PRESERVE LONDON (Diagonals in center of shield) | 275.00 | 600.00 | 2,000.00 |
| (1664) Halfpenny, similar. Variety with sword in second quarter of shield instead of first (Rare) | — | — | — |
| (1664) Halfpenny LON DON | 500.00 | 2,250.00 | 6,750.00 |

## CAROLINA ELEPHANT TOKENS

| 1694 PROPRIETERS | — | 7,500.00 | — |
|---|---|---|---|
| 1694 PROPRIETORS | 2,750.00 | 5,750.00 | 12,500.00 |

## NEW ENGLAND ELEPHANT TOKENS

| 1694 NEW ENGLAND (Very rare) | 15,000.00 | 25,000.00 | — |
|---|---|---|---|

## FRENCH COLONIES

|  | V. Good | V. Fine | Ex. Fine |
|---|---|---|---|
| 1721 Mint Mark B, Sou | 175.00 | 500.00 | 675.00 |
| 1721 Mint Mark H, Sou | 100.00 | 300.00 | — |
| 1722 Sou | 100.00 | 300.00 | — |
| 1722 Sou, 2 over 1 | 175.00 | 300.00 | — |
| 1767 Sou | 75.00 | 200.00 | 500.00 |
| 1767 Sou Counterstamp "R.F." | 65.00 | 140.00 | 350.00 |

## WILLIAM WOOD'S COINAGE

### ROSA AMERICANA

|  | Good | Fine | V. Fine |
|---|---|---|---|
| Twopence (no date) | 100.00 | 250.00 | 500.00 |
| 1722 Twopence, Period after REX | 150.00 | 300.00 | 550.00 |
| 1722 Twopence, No Period after REX | 150.00 | 300.00 | 550.00 |
| 1722 Penny UTILE DULCI | 85.00 | 150.00 | 250.00 |
| 1722 Penny VTILE DVLCI | 85.00 | 150.00 | 300.00 |
| 1722 Halfpenny D.G. REX ROSA AMERI. UTILE DULCI | 80.00 | 200.00 | 375.00 |
| 1722 Halfpenny DEL GRATIA REX UTILE DULCI | 80.00 | 200.00 | 350.00 |
| 1722 Halfpenny VTILE DVLCI | 500.00 | 1,350.00 | — |
| 1723 Twopence | 100.00 | 200.00 | 375.00 |
| 1723 Penny | 75.00 | 125.00 | 250.00 |
| 1723 Halfpenny | 85.00 | 150.00 | 300.00 |
| 1723 Halfpenny Uncrowned Rose (Rare) | 725.00 | 1,300.00 | — |
| 1724 Penny (Rare) | — | — | 6,000.00 |
| 1724 Penny (Undated) ROSA:SPINE:SPINA (3 known) | — | — | 7,500.00 |

## HIBERNIA

|  | V. Good | V. Fine | Ex. Fine |
|---|---|---|---|
| 1722 Halfpenny, First Type, Harp at Left | 75.00 | 225.00 | 500.00 |
| 1722 Halfpenny, Second Type, Harp at Right | 50.00 | 125.00 | 250.00 |
| 1722 Farthing | 135.00 | 325.00 | 650.00 |
| 1723 Halfpenny | 50.00 | 100.00 | 200.00 |
| 1723 Over 22 Halfpenny | 75.00 | 275.00 | 500.00 |
| 1723 Farthing | 60.00 | 125.00 | 225.00 |

|  | Good | Fine | Ex. Fine |
|---|---|---|---|
| 1724 Halfpenny | 50.00 | 100.00 | 350.00 |
| 1724 Farthing | 75.00 | 175.00 | 550.00 |

## HIGLEY COPPERS

|  | Fair | Good | Fine |
|---|---|---|---|
| 1737 THE•VALVE•OF•THREE•PENCE—3 Hammers CONNECTICVT | — | 6,000.00 | 13,000.00 |
| 1737 THE•VALVE•OF•THREE•PENCE—3 Hammers—I•AM•GOOD•COPPER | — | 6,500.00 | 14,000.00 |
| 1737 VALUE•ME•AS•YOU•PLEASE—3 Hammers—I•AM•GOOD•COPPER | — | 5,500.00 | 12,000.00 |
| 1737 VALVE•ME•AS•YOU•PLEASE—3 Hammers—I•AM•GOOD•COPPER (rare) | — | — | — |
| (1737) VALUE•ME•AS•YOU•PLEASE—Broad Axe—J•CUT•MY•WAY•THROUGH | — | 6,000.00 | 13,000.00 |
| (1737) Similar. Wheel Design (Unique) | — | — | — |
| 1739 VALUE•ME•AS•YOU•PLEASE—Broad Axe—J•CUT•MY•WAY•THROUGH | — | 7,500.00 | 17,000.00 |

## VOCE POPULI

|  | V. Good | V. Fine | Ex. Fine |
|---|---|---|---|
| 1760 Halfpenny | 65.00 | 125.00 | 450.00 |
| 1760 Halfpenny VOOE POPULI | 70.00 | 150.00 | 500.00 |
| 1760 Farthing, Large Letters | 175.00 | 650.00 | 1,500.00 |
| 1760 Farthing, Small Letters (Rare) | 600.00 | 3,750.00 | 7,000.00 |

## PITT TOKEN

| 1766 Halfpenny | 200.00 | 750.00 | 1,350.00 |
|---|---|---|---|
| 1766 Farthing (Rare) | — | 4,000.00 | 7,500.00 |

## VIRGINIA

|  | V. Good | Fine | Unc. |
|---|---|---|---|
| 1773 Halfpenny, Period after GEORGIUS | 65.00 | 100.00 | 675.00 |
| 1773 Halfpenny, No period after GEORGIUS | 75.00 | 125.00 | 800.00 |

# 22.
# STATE COINAGE

## CONNECTICUT CENTS

|  | Good | Fine | V. Fine |
|---|---|---|---|
| 1785 Bust Right | 75.00 | 250.00 | 550.00 |
| 1785 Bust Left | 175.00 | 400.00 | 750.00 |
| 1786 Bust Right | 85.00 | 425.00 | 950.00 |
| 1786 Bust Left | 65.00 | 225.00 | 450.00 |
| 1786 Draped Bust | 85.00 | 300.00 | 650.00 |
| 1787 Mailed Bust Right | 100.00 | 425.00 | 1,500.00 |
| 1787 Mailed Bust Left | 60.00 | 175.00 | 400.00 |
| 1787 Draped Bust Left | 50.00 | 125.00 | 325.00 |
| 1788 Mailed Bust Right | 50.00 | 175.00 | 450.00 |
| 1788 Mailed Bust Left | 50.00 | 150.00 | 400.00 |
| 1788 Draped Bust Left | 50.00 | 200.00 | 400.00 |

(Note: There are many minor varieties of Connecticut Cents.)

## MASSACHUSETTS

|  | Good | Fine | Ex. Fine |
|---|---|---|---|
| 1787 Cent. Arrows in Right Talon (Ex. rare) | 3,500.00 | 9,000.00 | — |
| 1787 Cent. Arrows in Left Talon | 75.00 | 200.00 | 700.00 |
| 1787 Cent. Horn (Die Break) from Eagle's Head | 75.00 | 200.00 | 750.00 |
| 1787 Half Cent | 75.00 | 200.00 | 800.00 |
| 1788 Cent | 75.00 | 200.00 | 875.00 |
| 1788 Half Cent | 100.00 | 250.00 | 775.00 |

## NEW HAMPSHIRE

| | | | |
|---|---|---|---|
| 1776 New Hampshire Penny (Very rare) | 20,000.00 | — | — |

## NEW JERSEY CENTS

|  | Good | Fine | V. Fine |
|---|---|---|---|
| 1786 IMMUNIS COLUMBIA (Very rare) | — | — | 30,000.00 |
| 1786 Date under Plow Handle (Very rare) | — | 25,000.00 | 45,000.00 |
| 1786 No Coulter | 750.00 | 2,750.00 | 7,500.00 |
| 1786 Narrow or Wide Shield | 75.00 | 275.00 | 500.00 |
| 1787 Small or Large Planchet | 60.00 | 200.00 | 375.00 |
| 1787 Outlined Shield | 75.00 | 225.00 | 450.00 |
| 1787 Pluribs instead of Pluribus | 100.00 | 350.00 | 900.00 |
| 1788 Horse head Right | 75.00 | 225.00 | 450.00 |
| 1788 Horse head Left | 300.00 | 900.00 | 1,600.00 |
| 1788 Running Fox before Legend | 150.00 | 500.00 | 1,200.00 |

(Note: There are many minor varieties of New Jersey Cents.)

## NEW YORK CENTS

|  | Good | Fine | V. Fine |
|---|---:|---:|---:|
| 1786 NON VI VIRTUTE VICI | 4,000.00 | 7,750.00 | 15,000.00 |
| 1786 IMMUNIS COLUMBIA | — | — | 25,000.00 |
| 1787 Excelsior Cent. Eagle Right | 1,500.00 | 4,000.00 | 7,750.00 |
| 1787 Excelsior Cent. Eagle Left | 1,450.00 | 3,750.00 | 7,500.00 |
| 1787 Excelsior Cent. Large Eagle (Very rare) | — | — | 40,000.00 |
| 1787 Excelsior. Indian | 4,500.00 | 9,000.00 | 15,000.00 |
| 1787 Excelsior. George Clinton | 6,750.00 | 15,000.00 | 23,000.00 |
| 1787 Indian. Eagle on Globe | 8,000.00 | 16,500.00 | 27,500.00 |
| 1787 NOVA-EBORAC, Figure Right | 90.00 | 315.00 | 600.00 |
| 1787 NOVA-EBORAC, Figure Left | 100.00 | 325.00 | 650.00 |
| 1787 NOVA-EBORAC, Small Head | 2,000.00 | — | — |
| 1787 NOVA-EBORAC, Large Head | 400.00 | 1,000.00 | 3,000.00 |
| 1787 IMMUNIS COLUMBIA | 450.00 | 1,200.00 | 2,400.00 |

## VERMONT CENTS

|  | Good | Fine | V. Fine |
|---|---:|---:|---:|
| 1785 IMMUNE COLUMBIA | 2,500.00 | 5,000.00 | — |
| 1785 Mountain Scene, VERMONTS | 200.00 | 850.00 | 1,850.00 |
| 1785 Mountain Scene, VERMONTIS | 200.00 | 850.00 | 1,850.00 |
| 1786 Mountain Scene, VERMONTENSIUM | 175.00 | 750.00 | 1,750.00 |
| 1786 Baby Head. Bust Right | 300.00 | 800.00 | 2,500.00 |
| 1786 Bust Left | 150.00 | 700.00 | 1,500.00 |
| 1787 Bust Left (Rare) | 3,000.00 | 9,000.00 | — |
| 1787 Bust Right | 100.00 | 375.00 | 650.00 |
| 1787 BRITANNIA on Reverse | 100.00 | 250.00 | 450.00 |
| 1788 | 100.00 | 300.00 | 750.00 |
| 1788 GEORGIUS III REX | 275.00 | 900.00 | 2,000.00 |

## EXPERIMENTAL COINS
### CONTINENTAL DOLLAR

|  | Good | Fine | Ex. Fine |
|---|---:|---:|---:|
| 1776 CURENCY, Pewter | 2,000.00 | 4,250.00 | 8,500.00 |
| 1776 CURENCY, Brass (Very rare) | 12,000.00 | 22,500.00 | 40,000.00 |
| 1776 CURENCY, Silver (Very rare) | — | — | — |
| 1776 CURRENCY, Pewter | 2,250.00 | 5,500.00 | 11,500.00 |
| 1776 CURRENCY, Pewter, E.G. Fecit | 2,000.00 | 5,000.00 | 10,000.00 |
| 1776 CURRENCY, Silver. E.G. Fecit (Very rare) | — | — | — |
| 1776 CURRENCEY, Pewter (Very rare) | — | — | — |

## NOVA CONSTELLATIO (SILVER)

|  | V. Good | Fine | Ex. Fine |
|---|---|---|---|
| 1783 MARK (1000), Silver (Unique) | — | — | — |
| 1783 QUINT (500), Silver—Type 1 (Unique) | — | — | — |
| 1783 QUINT (500), Silver—Type 2 (Unique) | — | — | — |
| 1783 Bit (100), Silver (2 known) | — | — | — |

## NOVA CONSTELLATIO CENTS

| 1783 CONSTELLATIO, Small U.S. | 80.00 | 175.00 | 700.00 |
|---|---|---|---|
| 1783 CONSTELLATIO, Large U.S. | 85.00 | 200.00 | 850.00 |
| 1783 CONSTELATIO, Blunt Rays | 85.00 | 175.00 | 800.00 |
| 1785 CONSTELATIO, Blunt Rays | 85.00 | 200.00 | 850.00 |
| 1785 CONSTELLATIO, Pointed Rays | 80.00 | 175.00 | 800.00 |
| 1786 CONSTELLATIO (Very rare) | — | — | — |

## IMMUNE COLUMBIA CENTS

|  | Good | Fine | V. Fine |
|---|---|---|---|
| 1785 CONSTELLATIO (Very rare) | — | — | 12,500.00 |
| 1785 CONSTELATIO (Very rare) Known in Copper and Gold | — | 35,000.00 | — |
| 1785 George III Obverse | 3,000.00 | 5,500.00 | — |
| 1785 VERMON AUCTORI Obverse | 3,250.00 | 6,000.00 | — |

## CONFEDERATIO CENTS

| 1785 Stars in Large or Small Circle (All very rare) | — | — | 15,000.00 |
|---|---|---|---|

## THE FUGIO CENTS

|  | V. Good | Fine | Ex. Fine |
|---|---|---|---|
| 1787 Club Rays | 325.00 | 575.00 | 1,750.00 |

## POINTED RAYS

| 1787 UNITED above STATES below (Rare) | — | — | — |
|---|---|---|---|
| 1787 UNITED STATES at sides of circle | 200.00 | 325.00 | 850.00 |
| 1787 STATES UNITED at sides of circle | 200.00 | 300.00 | 800.00 |

(Note: There are several minor varieties of the Fugio Cents.)

# MISCELLANEOUS TOKENS
## RHODE ISLAND SHIP TOKEN

| | Good | Fine | Ex. Fine |
|---|---|---|---|
| 1778 Wreath below Ship | 225.00 | 600.00 | 1,200.00 |
| 1778 No wreath | 200.00 | 550.00 | 1,000.00 |

## NORTH AMERICAN TOKEN

| | Good | Fine | V. Fine |
|---|---|---|---|
| 1781 | 40.00 | 100.00 | 200.00 |

## GEORGIUS TRIUMPHO TOKEN

| | | | |
|---|---|---|---|
| 1783 GEORGIUS TRIUMPHO | 75.00 | 225.00 | 550.00 |

## J. CHALMERS
## ANNAPOLIS, MARYLAND

| | | | |
|---|---|---|---|
| 1783 Shilling—Birds, Long or Short Worm | 750.00 | 2,000.00 | 3,250.00 |
| 1783 Shilling—Rings (Ex. rare) | — | — | — |
| 1783 Sixpence, Small Date | 1,250.00 | 3,000.00 | 4,500.00 |
| 1783 Sixpence, Large Date | 1,100.00 | 2,750.00 | 4,250.00 |
| 1783 Threepence | 1,000.00 | 2,400.00 | 3,500.00 |

## THE BAR CENT

| | Good | Fine | Ex. Fine |
|---|---|---|---|
| Undated (1785) Bar Cent | 600.00 | 1,400.00 | 3,250.00 |

## AUCTORI PLEBIS TOKEN

| | Good | Fine | V. Fine |
|---|---|---|---|
| 1787 | 100.00 | 275.00 | 575.00 |

## BRASHER'S DOUBLOONS

| | | | |
|---|---|---|---|
| 1787 "E.B." on Breast or Wing (All very rare) | — | — | — |

## THE MOTT TOKEN

| | Good | Fine | Ex. Fine |
|---|---|---|---|
| 1789 Mott Token, Thick Planchet | 150.00 | 300.00 | 1,000.00 |
| 1789 Mott Token, Thin Planchet | 200.00 | 375.00 | 1,650.00 |

## STANDISH BARRY BALTIMORE, MARYLAND

| | | | |
|---|---|---|---|
| 1790 Threepence (Very rare) | 6,500.00 | 12,500.00 | — |

## ALBANY CHURCH PENNY

| | | | |
|---|---|---|---|
| (1790) | — | 8,000.00 | — |

## KENTUCKY TOKEN

| | V. Good | V. Fine | Unc. |
|---|---|---|---|
| Cent (1792–94), Plain Edge | 100.00 | 200.00 | 825.00 |
| Cent, Engrailed Edge | — | 525.00 | 2,500.00 |
| Cent, Lettered Edge | 80.00 | 225.00 | 1,000.00 |

## FRANKLIN PRESS CENT

| | V. Good | V. Fine | Unc. |
|---|---|---|---|
| 1794 | 125.00 | 275.00 | 750.00 |

## TALBOT ALLUM & LEE CENTS

| | | | |
|---|---|---|---|
| 1794 With NEW YORK | 75.00 | 225.00 | 1,175.00 |
| 1794 Without NEW YORK | 300.00 | 1,000.00 | 3,750.00 |
| 1795 | 75.00 | 200.00 | 1,000.00 |

## MYDDLETON TOKENS

| | Good | Fine | Unc. |
|---|---|---|---|
| 1796 Copper, Proof only | — | — | 7,500.00 |
| 1796 Silver, Proof only | — | — | 6,750.00 |

## WASHINGTON PIECES

| | Good | V. Fine | Ex. Fine |
|---|---|---|---|
| 1783 WASHINGTON & INDEPENDENCE Small Military Bust | 50.00 | 150.00 | 325.00 |
| 1783 Same, Engrailed Edge | 65.00 | 225.00 | 375.00 |
| 1783 Large Military bust | 45.00 | 135.00 | 300.00 |
| 1783 Draped Bust | 40.00 | 175.00 | 425.00 |
| 1783 Draped Bust with button | 75.00 | 250.00 | 525.00 |
| 1783 Restrike in Copper, Proof only, Plain Edge | — | Proof | 575.00 |
| 1783 Restrike in Copper, Proof only, Engrailed Edge | — | Proof | 500.00 |
| 1783 Restrike in Silver, Proof only, Engrailed Edge | — | Proof | 1,000.00 |
| 1783 UNITY STATES | 60.00 | 200.00 | 400.00 |
| (1783) Double Head Cent | 60.00 | 160.00 | 400.00 |
| 1784 Ugly Head (Very rare) | — | 35,000 | — |
| 1791 Cent, Small Eagle | 125.00 | 400.00 | 700.00 |
| 1791 Large Eagle | 125.00 | 400.00 | 725.00 |
| 1792 WASHINGTON PRESIDENT | 1,650.00 | 6,500.00 | — |
| (1792) WASHINGTON BORN VIRGINIA | 1,500.00 | 4,850.00 | — |

| | Good | Fine | Unc. |
|---|---|---|---|
| 1792 Roman Head (Rare) | — | Proof | 22,500.00 |
| 1795 Grate Cent, Lettered Edge | 100.00 | 200.00 | 1,400.00 |
| 1795 Grate Cent, Reeded Edge | 75.00 | 150.00 | 800.00 |

## WASHINGTON PENNIES AND HALFPENNIES

| | | | |
|---|---|---|---|
| (1795) Penny, Lettered Edge "LIBERTY & SECURITY" | 150.00 | 300.00 | 2,500.00 |
| 1791 LIVERPOOL HALFPENNY | 400.00 | 750.00 | 5,000.00 |

| | Fine | V. Fine | Ex. Fine |
|---|---|---|---|
| 1793 Ship Halfpenny | 175.00 | 325.00 | 650.00 |
| 1795 Liberty & Security Halfpenny, Plain Edge | 125.00 | 225.00 | 500.00 |
| 1795 Halfpenny, Lettered Edge | 120.00 | 200.00 | 450.00 |
| 1795 Halfpenny, Edge "AN ASYLUM FOR THE OPPRESSED OF ALL NATIONS" | 225.00 | 475.00 | 1,050.00 |
| 1795 NORTH WALES Halfpenny | 225.00 | 450.00 | 725.00 |
| SUCCESS Token Large, Plain & Reeded Edge | 175.00 | 425.00 | 750.00 |
| SUCCESS Token Small, Plain & Reeded Edge | 225.00 | 475.00 | 850.00 |

## WASHINGTON HALF DOLLARS

| | | | |
|---|---|---|---|
| 1792 Silver Half Dollar (Very rare) | — | — | — |
| 1792 Silver, Ornamental Eagle (Very rare) | — | — | — |
| 1792 Copper | 4,000.00 | 6,750.00 | 9,250.00 |
| 1792 Copper, Ornamental Edge | — | — | — |

# 23.
# FIRST MINT ISSUES

|  | Good | Fine | Unc. |
|---|---|---|---|
| 1792 DISME known in Silver and Copper (Very rare)... | — | 30,000.00 | 100,000.00 |

|  | Good | Fine | Ex. Fine |
|---|---|---|---|
| 1792 HALF DISME, Silver.......................... | 7,500.00 | 17,500.00 | 32,500.00 |
| 1792 HALF DISME, Copper (Very rare).............. | — | — | — |
| 1792 Silver Center Cent (Very rare).................. | — | — | 125,000.00 |
| 1792 BIRCH CENT (Very rare)..................... | — | — | 200,000.00 |

## 24.
## HALF-CENT PIECES—
## 1793–1857

*Note:* All half cents in *fair* to *about good* condition (i.e. unmutilated but worn) are valued at about one-third of the good column.

### LIBERTY CAP TYPE

              1793                                    1794–1797

|  | Mintage in Thousands | Good | Fine | V. Fine |
|---|---|---|---|---|
| 1793 | 35 | 1,500.00 | 3,450.00 | 5,500.00 |
| 1794 | 82 | 285.00 | 650.00 | 1,500.00 |
| 1795 Lettered Edge, Pole to Cap | 26 | 250.00 | 650.00 | 1,450.00 |
| 1795 Lettered Edge, No Pole to Cap | 109 | 240.00 | 625.00 | 1,350.00 |
| 1796 Plain Edge, Pole | 5 | 7,500.00 | 14,000.00 | 19,000.00 |
| 1796 Plain Edge, No Pole (Very rare) | 1 | 15,000.00 | 35,000.00 | 50,000.00 |
| 1797 Plain Edge, All Kinds | 119 | 265.00 | 875.00 | 1,700.00 |
| 1797 Lettered Edge | — | 675.00 | 2,500.00 | 4,850.00 |

### DRAPED BUST TYPE

| | | | | |
|---|---|---|---|---|
| 1800 | 203 | 45.00 | 85.00 | 185.00 |
| 1802 2 over 0, Rev. of 1800 | 20 | 15,000.00 | 30,000.00 | 45,000.00 |
| 1802 2 over 0, New Rev. | — | 600.00 | 3,500.00 | 8,500.00 |
| 1803 | 92 | 40.00 | 110.00 | 275.00 |
| 1804 Stemless Wreath | 1,055 | 35.00 | 65.00 | 135.00 |
| 1804 Stems to Wreath, Crosslet 4 | — | 35.00 | 55.00 | 120.00 |
| 1804 Stems to Wreath, Plain 4 | — | 50.00 | 165.00 | 275.00 |
| 1805 Stemless Wreath | 814 | 45.00 | 75.00 | 140.00 |
| 1805 Small 5, Stems | — | 700.00 | 2,250.00 | 4,250.00 |
| 1805 Stems to Wreath, Large 5 | — | 40.00 | 65.00 | 135.00 |
| 1806 Stemless | 356 | 40.00 | 60.00 | 110.00 |

|  | Mintage in Thousands | Good | Fine | V. Fine |
|---|---|---|---|---|
| 1806 Stems, Small 6 | — | 225.00 | 625.00 | 1,350.00 |
| 1806 Stems, Large 6 | — | 38.00 | 60.00 | 110.00 |
| 1807 | 476 | 38.00 | 70.00 | 165.00 |
| 1808 over 7, All Kinds | 400 | 135.00 | 575.00 | 1,350.00 |
| 1808 | — | 38.00 | 70.00 | 140.00 |

## TURBAN HEAD TYPE

| | | | | |
|---|---|---|---|---|
| 1809 over 6, All Kinds | 1,155 | 40.00 | 65.00 | 95.00 |
| 1809 | — | 35.00 | 55.00 | 75.00 |
| 1810 | 215 | 35.00 | 95.00 | 200.00 |
| 1811 | 63 | 135.00 | 575.00 | 1,675.00 |

|  | Mintage in Thousands | Good | Fine | V. Fine | Unc. |
|---|---|---|---|---|---|
| 1825 | 63 | 35.00 | 52.00 | 80.00 | 950.00 |
| 1826 | 234 | 35.00 | 52.00 | 70.00 | 625.00 |
| 1828 13 Stars, All Kinds | 606 | 35.00 | 50.00 | 65.00 | 350.00 |
| 1828 12 Stars | — | 35.00 | 55.00 | 95.00 | 1,250.00 |
| 1829 | 487 | 35.00 | 50.00 | 70.00 | 400.00 |

|  | Mintage in Thousands | Good | Fine | V. Fine | Unc. | Proof |
|---|---|---|---|---|---|---|
| 1831 | 2 | — | — | — | 11,000.00 | 8,500.00 |
| 1832 | 154 | 35.00 | 50.00 | 55.00 | 375.00 | 6,600.00 |
| 1833 | 120 | 35.00 | 50.00 | 55.00 | 350.00 | 6,250.00 |
| 1834 | 141 | 35.00 | 50.00 | 55.00 | 350.00 | 4,500.00 |
| 1835 | 398 | 35.00 | 50.00 | 55.00 | 350.00 | 5,500.00 |
| 1836 Original | — | — | — | — | — | 4,750.00 |
| 1836 Restrike | — | — | — | — | — | 4,750.00 |

## BRAIDED HAIR TYPE

|  | Mintage in Thousands | Good | Fine | Ext. Fine | Unc. | Proof |
|---|---|---|---|---|---|---|
| 1840–1849 Small Date, Proof only, each | | 3,800.00 | | | | |
| 1849 Large Date .... | 40 | 40.00 | 50.00 | 95.00 | 700.00 | — |
| 1850 .............. | 40 | 33.00 | 50.00 | 110.00 | 750.00 | — |
| 1851 .............. | 148 | 30.00 | 45.00 | 75.00 | 325.00 | — |
| 1852 Proof only ..... | — | — | — | — | — | 6,000.00 |
| 1853 .............. | 130 | 30.00 | 45.00 | 75.00 | 325.00 | — |
| 1854 .............. | 55 | 30.00 | 45.00 | 75.00 | 325.00 | — |
| 1855 .............. | 57 | 30.00 | 45.00 | 75.00 | 325.00 | — |
| 1856 .............. | 40 | 30.00 | 50.00 | 85.00 | 335.00 | — |
| 1857 .............. | 35 | 45.00 | 70.00 | 120.00 | 400.00 | — |

Note: In this book the value for Unc. is for M.S.-60 (i.e. "Mint State-60") to M.S.-63 condition. This grade range shows absolutely no wear, but may be toned, have bag or keg marks, or have an uneven strike.

# 25.
# ONE-CENT PIECES—
# 1793–1857

*Note:* All large cents in *fair* to *about good* condition (i.e. unmutilated but worn) are valued at about one-third of the good column.

## CHAIN TYPE

|  | Mintage in Thousands | Good | Fine | V. Fine |
|---|---|---|---|---|
| 1793 Chain type, AMERI. | 36 | 3,500.00 | 7,000.00 | 13,500.00 |
| 1793 Chain type, AMERICA | — | 2,650.00 | 5,250.00 | 10,000.00 |

## WREATH TYPE

| | | | | |
|---|---|---|---|---|
| 1793 Wreath type, Vine and Bars on Edge, All Kinds. | 63 | 975.00 | 2,650.00 | 4,250.00 |
| 1793 Wreath type, Lettered Edge | — | 1,000.00 | 2,850.00 | 4,500.00 |

## LIBERTY CAP TYPE

|  | Mintage in Thousands | Good | Fine | V. Fine |
|---|---|---|---|---|
| 1793 Liberty Cap type | 11 | 2,850.00 | 7,250.00 | 22,500.00 |
| 1794, All Kinds | 919 | 185.00 | 475.00 | 1,250.00 |
| 1794 Starred Rev | — | 9,000.00 | 24,500.00 | 37,500.00 |
| 1795 Lettered Edge | 37 | 225.00 | 575.00 | 1,150.00 |
| 1795 Plain Edge | 502 | 185.00 | 375.00 | 800.00 |
| 1796 Liberty Cap type | 110 | 200.00 | 775.00 | 1,500.00 |

## DRAPED BUST TYPE

| | | | | |
|---|---|---|---|---|
| 1796 Draped Bust type | 363 | 100.00 | 550.00 | 1,275.00 |
| 1797 Stems on Wreath, All Kinds | 898 | 70.00 | 250.00 | 500.00 |
| 1797 Stemless Wreath | — | 110.00 | 425.00 | 1,450.00 |
| 1798 over 97, All Kinds | — | 125.00 | 375.00 | 1,650.00 |
| 1798 | 1,841 | 45.00 | 150.00 | 375.00 |
| 1799 over 98, All Kinds | — | 1,450.00 | 7,250.00 | 16,500.00 |
| 1799 | 42 | 1,250.00 | 7,000.00 | 16,500.00 |
| 1800 over 1798, All Kinds | 2,822 | 45.00 | 250.00 | 675.00 |
| 1800 over 1799 | — | 45.00 | 150.00 | 500.00 |
| 1800 | — | 45.00 | 150.00 | 450.00 |
| 1801, All Kinds | 1,363 | 45.00 | 165.00 | 385.00 |
| 1801 3 errors—1/000, one stem and IINITED | — | 100.00 | 650.00 | 1,500.00 |
| 1801 Fraction 1/000 | — | 55.00 | 185.00 | 500.00 |
| 1801 Fraction 1/100 over 1/000 | — | 55.00 | 250.00 | 650.00 |
| 1802, All Kinds | 3,435 | 45.00 | 135.00 | 300.00 |
| 1802 Stemless Wreath | — | 45.00 | 160.00 | 300.00 |
| 1802 Fraction 1/000 | — | 55.00 | 250.00 | 575.00 |
| 1803, All Kinds | 3,131 | 42.00 | 145.00 | 300.00 |
| 1803 Large Date | — | 55.00 | 300.00 | 600.00 |
| 1803 Stemless Wreath | — | 42.00 | 165.00 | 375.00 |
| 1803 1/100 over 1/000 | — | 50.00 | 225.00 | 450.00 |

|  | Mintage in Thousands | Good | Fine | V. Fine |
|---|---|---|---|---|
| 1804 | 757 | 700.00 | 2,000.00 | 3,250.00 |
| 1805 | 941 | 45.00 | 165.00 | 375.00 |
| 1806 | 348 | 45.00 | 185.00 | 425.00 |
| 1807 over 6, Large Date, All Kinds | 727 | 45.00 | 135.00 | 300.00 |
| 1807 over 6, Small Date | — | 2,250.00 | 7,500.00 | 13,500.00 |
| 1807 All Kinds | — | 45.00 | 135.00 | 300.00 |

## TURBAN HEAD TYPE

|  | Mintage in Thousands | Good | Fine | V. Fine |
|---|---|---|---|---|
| 1808 | 1,109 | 60.00 | 275.00 | 600.00 |
| 1809 | 223 | 110.00 | 425.00 | 1,250.00 |
| 1810 over 9, All Kinds | 1,459 | 45.00 | 325.00 | 675.00 |
| 1810 | — | 55.00 | 325.00 | 625.00 |
| 1811 over 10, All Kinds | 218 | 70.00 | 525.00 | 1,450.00 |
| 1811 | — | 65.00 | 425.00 | 900.00 |
| 1812 | 1,076 | 45.00 | 275.00 | 575.00 |
| 1813 | 418 | 45.00 | 285.00 | 625.00 |
| 1814 Plain 4 | 358 | 55.00 | 275.00 | 575.00 |
| 1814 Crosslet 4 | — | 45.00 | 285.00 | 575.00 |

## CORONET TYPE

|  | Mintage in Thousands | V. Good | Fine | V. Fine | Unc. |
|---|---|---|---|---|---|
| 1816 | 2,821 | 13.00 | 35.00 | 100.00 | 475.00 |
| 1817, All Kinds | 3,948 | 13.00 | 27.00 | 70.00 | 400.00 |
| 1817 15 Stars | — | 14.00 | 30.00 | 100.00 | 3,250.00 |
| 1818 | 3,167 | 13.00 | 32.00 | 70.00 | 350.00 |
| 1819 over 18, All Kinds | 2,671 | 13.00 | 37.00 | 125.00 | 750.00 |
| 1819 | — | 13.00 | 30.00 | 70.00 | 400.00 |
| 1820 over 19, All Kinds | 4,408 | 14.00 | 30.00 | 125.00 | 825.00 |
| 1820 | — | 13.00 | 30.00 | 75.00 | 350.00 |
| 1821 | 389 | 27.00 | 140.00 | 450.00 | 10,000.00 |
| 1822 | 2,072 | 13.00 | 45.00 | 100.00 | 1,000.00 |
| 1823 over 22, All Kinds | 856 | 65.00 | 275.00 | 575.00 | 12,500.00 |
| 1823 | — | 70.00 | 325.00 | 700.00 | 12,750.00 |
| 1824 over 22, All Kinds | 1,262 | 18.00 | 75.00 | 325.00 | 5,000.00 |

|  | Mintage in Thousands | Good | Fine | V. Fine | Unc. |
|---|---|---|---|---|---|
| 1824............................ | — | 17.00 | 40.00 | 175.00 | 975.00 |
| 1825............................ | 1,461 | 14.00 | 40.00 | 135.00 | 1,400.00 |
| 1826............................ | 1,517 | 13.00 | 30.00 | 95.00 | 900.00 |
| 1827............................ | 2,358 | 13.00 | 30.00 | 80.00 | 725.00 |
| 1828............................ | 2,261 | 13.00 | 30.00 | 95.00 | 650.00 |
| 1829............................ | 1,415 | 13.00 | 30.00 | 100.00 | 750.00 |
| 1830............................ | 1,712 | 13.00 | 25.00 | 75.00 | 650.00 |
| 1831............................ | 3,359 | 13.00 | 25.00 | 65.00 | 375.00 |
| 1832............................ | 2,362 | 13.00 | 25.00 | 70.00 | 400.00 |
| 1833............................ | 2,739 | 13.00 | 25.00 | 65.00 | 450.00 |
| 1834............................ | 1,855 | 15.00 | 30.00 | 75.00 | 375.00 |
| 1835 Type of '34, All Kinds..... | 3,878 | 13.00 | 25.00 | 65.00 | 300.00 |
| 1835 Type of '36................ | — | 13.00 | 25.00 | 60.00 | 300.00 |
| 1836............................ | 2,111 | 13.00 | 25.00 | 60.00 | 375.00 |
| 1837 Plain Hair Cord, All Kinds . | 5,558 | 13.00 | 25.00 | 55.00 | 350.00 |
| 1837 Beaded Hair Cord.......... | — | 13.00 | 25.00 | 55.00 | 300.00 |
| 1838............................ | 6,370 | 13.00 | 25.00 | 55.00 | 300.00 |
| 1839, 9 over 6 .................. | 3,129 | 225.00 | 875.00 | 1,850.00 | — |
| 1839 Type of '38................ | — | 13.00 | 25.00 | 60.00 | 350.00 |
| 1839 Silly Head................. | — | 13.00 | 25.00 | 65.00 | 1,300.00 |
| 1839 Booby Head................ | — | 13.00 | 25.00 | 70.00 | 1,000.00 |
| 1839 Type of '40................ | — | 11.00 | 16.00 | 30.00 | 350.00 |

## BRAIDED HAIR TYPE

| | | | | | |
|---|---|---|---|---|---|
| 1840............................ | 2,463 | 11.00 | 17.00 | 30.00 | 300.00 |
| 1841............................ | 1,597 | 11.00 | 17.00 | 30.00 | 325.00 |
| 1842............................ | 2,383 | 11.00 | 17.00 | 30.00 | 250.00 |
| 1843 Obverse and Reverse of 1842, All Kinds ............ | 2,428 | 11.00 | 17.00 | 30.00 | 250.00 |
| 1843 Obverse of 1842, Reverse of '44........................ | — | 14.00 | 40.00 | 100.00 | 1,000.00 |
| 1843 Obverse and Reverse of 1844 ...................... | — | 12.00 | 21.00 | 30.00 | 250.00 |
| 1844, All Kinds................. | 2,399 | 11.00 | 17.00 | 30.00 | 275.00 |
| 1844/81 ....................... | — | 14.00 | 40.00 | 65.00 | 950.00 |
| 1845............................ | 3,895 | 11.00 | 14.00 | 27.00 | 175.00 |

|      | Mintage in Thousands | Good  | Fine  | V. Fine | Unc.   |
|------|---------------------:|------:|------:|--------:|-------:|
| 1846 | 4,121                | 11.00 | 14.00 | 25.00   | 175.00 |
| 1847 | 6,184                | 11.00 | 14.00 | 25.00   | 175.00 |
| 1848 | 6,416                | 11.00 | 18.00 | 25.00   | 200.00 |
| 1849 | 4,179                | 11.00 | 18.00 | 28.00   | 275.00 |
| 1850 | 4,427                | 11.00 | 18.00 | 25.00   | 175.00 |
| 1851 | 9,890                | 11.00 | 18.00 | 25.00   | 175.00 |
| 1851/81 | —                 | 13.00 | 25.00 | 60.00   | 650.00 |
| 1852 | 5,063                | 11.00 | 18.00 | 25.00   | 175.00 |
| 1853 | 6,641                | 11.00 | 18.00 | 25.00   | 175.00 |
| 1854 | 4,236                | 11.00 | 18.00 | 25.00   | 175.00 |
| 1855 | 1,575                | 11.00 | 15.00 | 25.00   | 175.00 |
| 1856 | 2,690                | 11.00 | 15.00 | 25.00   | 175.00 |
| 1857 | 333                  | 27.00 | 45.00 | 65.00   | 300.00 |

## FLYING EAGLE CENTS—1856–1858
### COPPER-NICKEL ("WHITE" CENTS)

|      | Mintage in Thousands | Good     | Fine     | V. Fine  | Unc.     | Proof     |
|------|---------------------:|---------:|---------:|---------:|---------:|----------:|
| 1856 | 1                    | 3,900.00 | 4,500.00 | 5,100.00 | 8,500.00 | 12,500.00 |
| 1857 | 17,450               | 15.00    | 25.00    | 36.00    | 325.00   | 11,000.00 |
| 1858 Large Letters, All Kinds | 24,600 | 15.00 | 25.00 | 38.00 | 350.00 | 10,000.00 |
| 1858 Small Letters | —           | 15.00    | 25.00    | 38.00    | 350.00   | 11,000.00 |

## INDIAN HEAD CENTS—1859–1909
### COPPER-NICKEL OR "WHITE"

    1859                        1860–1864

|      | Mintage | Good  | Fine  | V. Fine | Unc.   | Proof    |
|------|--------:|------:|------:|--------:|-------:|---------:|
| 1859 | 36,400  | 10.00 | 16.00 | 36.00   | 250.00 | 2,400.00 |
| 1860 | 20,566  | 7.00  | 13.00 | 15.00   | 140.00 | 1,500.00 |
| 1861 | 10,100  | 16.00 | 30.00 | 36.00   | 175.00 | 2,750.00 |
| 1862 | 28,075  | 6.00  | 10.00 | 14.00   | 110.00 | 875.00   |
| 1863 | 49,840  | 6.00  | 9.00  | 10.00   | 90.00  | 1,000.00 |
| 1864 | 13,740  | 13.00 | 25.00 | 32.00   | 140.00 | 1,000.00 |

## 1864-1909 BRONZE

|  | Mintage in Thousands | Good | Fine | V. Fine | Unc. | Proof |
|---|---|---|---|---|---|---|
| 1864 No L Bronze, All Kinds | 39,234 | 6.00 | 14.00 | 26.00 | 85.00 | 2,500.00 |
| 1864 L on ribbon | — | 42.00 | 80.00 | 115.00 | 350.00 | 40,000.00 |
| 1865 | 35,429 | 6.00 | 14.00 | 17.00 | 95.00 | 550.00 |
| 1866 | 9,827 | 35.00 | 52.00 | 80.00 | 250.00 | 375.00 |
| 1867 | 9,821 | 33.00 | 55.00 | 90.00 | 250.00 | 375.00 |
| 1868 | 10,267 | 31.00 | 47.00 | 75.00 | 225.00 | 375.00 |
| 1869 over 8, All Kinds | 6,420 | 100.00 | 200.00 | 270.00 | 500.00 | — |
| 1869 | — | 46.00 | 160.00 | 200.00 | 425.00 | 475.00 |
| 1870 | 5,275 | 36.00 | 140.00 | 190.00 | 375.00 | 375.00 |
| 1871 | 3,930 | 50.00 | 190.00 | 225.00 | 500.00 | 450.00 |
| 1872 | 4,042 | 55.00 | 230.00 | 250.00 | 500.00 | 475.00 |
| 1873 | 11,677 | 18.00 | 37.00 | 45.00 | 175.00 | 325.00 |
| 1874 | 14,188 | 12.00 | 25.00 | 41.00 | 170.00 | 325.00 |
| 1875 | 13,528 | 12.00 | 35.00 | 55.00 | 180.00 | 375.00 |
| 1876 | 7,944 | 22.00 | 37.00 | 65.00 | 200.00 | 350.00 |
| 1877 | 853 | 420.00 | 650.00 | 850.00 | 2,650.00 | 3,000.00 |
| 1878 | 5,800 | 22.00 | 45.00 | 70.00 | 250.00 | 250.00 |
| 1879 | 16,231 | 5.00 | 12.00 | 26.00 | 90.00 | 225.00 |
| 1880 | 38,965 | 3.00 | 6.00 | 9.00 | 85.00 | 225.00 |
| 1881 | 39,212 | 3.00 | 6.00 | 8.00 | 55.00 | 225.00 |
| 1882 | 38,581 | 3.00 | 5.00 | 8.00 | 70.00 | 225.00 |
| 1883 | 45,598 | 3.00 | 4.00 | 6.00 | 55.00 | 225.00 |
| 1884 | 23,262 | 3.00 | 6.00 | 11.00 | 95.00 | 225.00 |
| 1885 | 11,265 | 5.00 | 11.00 | 21.00 | 135.00 | 225.00 |
| 1886 | 17,654 | 3.00 | 15.00 | 36.00 | 170.00 | 250.00 |
| 1887 | 45,226 | 2.00 | 3.00 | 5.00 | 45.00 | 225.00 |
| 1888 | 37,494 | 2.00 | 4.00 | 7.00 | 90.00 | 225.00 |
| 1889 | 48,869 | 2.00 | 3.00 | 5.00 | 50.00 | 225.00 |
| 1890 | 57,183 | 2.00 | 3.00 | 4.00 | 50.00 | 225.00 |
| 1891 | 47,072 | 2.00 | 3.00 | 5.00 | 50.00 | 225.00 |
| 1892 | 37,650 | 2.00 | 3.00 | 5.00 | 50.00 | 225.00 |
| 1893 | 46,642 | 2.00 | 3.00 | 5.00 | 50.00 | 225.00 |
| 1894 | 16,572 | 3.00 | 8.00 | 12.00 | 60.00 | 225.00 |
| 1895 | 38,344 | 2.00 | 3.00 | 4.00 | 40.00 | 225.00 |
| 1896 | 39,057 | 2.00 | 3.00 | 4.00 | 40.00 | 225.00 |
| 1897 | 50,466 | 2.00 | 3.00 | 4.00 | 40.00 | 200.00 |
| 1898 | 49,823 | 2.00 | 3.00 | 4.00 | 40.00 | 200.00 |
| 1899 | 53,600 | 2.00 | 2.00 | 4.00 | 40.00 | 200.00 |
| 1900 | 66,834 | 1.00 | 2.00 | 3.00 | 25.00 | 200.00 |
| 1901 | 79,611 | 1.00 | 2.00 | 3.00 | 25.00 | 200.00 |
| 1902 | 87,377 | 1.00 | 2.00 | 3.00 | 25.00 | 200.00 |
| 1903 | 85,094 | 1.00 | 2.00 | 3.00 | 25.00 | 200.00 |
| 1904 | 61,328 | 1.00 | 2.00 | 3.00 | 25.00 | 200.00 |
| 1905 | 80,719 | 1.00 | 2.00 | 3.00 | 25.00 | 200.00 |
| 1906 | 96,022 | 1.00 | 2.00 | 3.00 | 25.00 | 200.00 |
| 1907 | 108,139 | 1.00 | 2.00 | 3.00 | 25.00 | 225.00 |
| 1908 | 32,328 | 1.00 | 2.00 | 3.00 | 25.00 | 225.00 |

|  | Mintage in Thousands | Good | Fine | V. Fine | Unc. | Proof |
|---|---|---|---|---|---|---|
| 1908S | 1,115 | 40.00 | 45.00 | 50.00 | 240.00 | — |
| 1909 | 14,371 | 3.00 | 4.00 | 4.00 | 35.00 | 225.00 |
| 1909S | 309 | 235.00 | 300.00 | 345.00 | 475.00 | — |

## LINCOLN HEAD CENTS—1909—Date

### 1909-1958           1959-1964

|  | Mintage | Good | Fine | V. Fine | Unc. | Proof |
|---|---|---|---|---|---|---|
| 1909 V D B | 27,995 | 3.00 | 4.00 | 5.00 | 10.00 | 3,000.00 |
| 1909 S. V D B | 484 | 360.00 | 450.00 | 510.00 | 750.00 | — |
| 1909 | 72,703 | 1.00 | 2.00 | 3.00 | 15.00 | 300.00 |
| 1909S | 1,825 | 37.00 | 57.00 | 105.00 | 135.00 | — |
| 1910 | 146,801 | — | — | 3.00 | 20.00 | 275.00 |
| 1910S | 6,045 | 6.00 | 8.00 | 21.00 | 60.00 | — |
| 1911 | 101,178 | — | 1.00 | 5.00 | 27.00 | 275.00 |
| 1911D | 12,672 | 4.00 | 7.00 | 35.00 | 80.00 | — |
| 1911S | 4,026 | 15.00 | 18.00 | 45.00 | 145.00 | — |
| 1912 | 68,153 | 1.00 | 2.00 | 11.00 | 35.00 | 275.00 |
| 1912D | 10,411 | 5.00 | 7.00 | 40.00 | 135.00 | — |
| 1912S | 4,431 | 10.00 | 15.00 | 40.00 | 100.00 | — |
| 1913 | 76,532 | — | 2.00 | 13.00 | 30.00 | 300.00 |
| 1913D | 15,804 | 2.00 | 4.00 | 26.00 | 90.00 | — |
| 1913S | 6,101 | 6.00 | 8.00 | 32.00 | 130.00 | — |
| 1914 | 75,238 | — | 2.00 | 10.00 | 40.00 | 275.00 |
| 1914D | 1,193 | 85.00 | 155.00 | 465.00 | 1,375.00 | — |
| 1914S | 4,137 | 9.00 | 12.00 | 45.00 | 300.00 | — |
| 1915 | 29,092 | 1.00 | 4.00 | 36.00 | 75.00 | 275.00 |
| 1915D | 22,050 | 1.00 | 2.00 | 11.00 | 65.00 | — |
| 1915S | 4,833 | 6.00 | 8.00 | 32.00 | 160.00 | — |
| 1916 | 131,834 | — | — | 4.00 | 20.00 | 450.00 |
| 1916D | 35,956 | — | 1.00 | 9.00 | 65.00 | — |
| 1916S | 22,510 | 1.00 | 2.00 | 10.00 | 85.00 | — |
| 1917 | 196,430 | — | — | 4.00 | 20.00 | — |
| 1917D | 55,120 | — | 1.00 | 8.00 | 75.00 | — |
| 1917S | 32,620 | — | 1.00 | 7.00 | 85.00 | — |
| 1918 | 288,103 | — | — | 4.00 | 20.00 | — |
| 1918D | 47,830 | — | 1.00 | 8.00 | 75.00 | — |
| 1918S | 34,680 | — | 1.00 | 8.00 | 85.00 | — |
| 1919 | 392,021 | — | — | 2.00 | 15.00 | — |
| 1919D | 57,154 | — | 1.00 | 6.00 | 55.00 | — |
| 1919S | 139,760 | — | 1.00 | 3.00 | 45.00 | — |
| 1920 | 310,165 | — | — | 3.00 | 15.00 | — |
| 1920D | 49,280 | — | 1.00 | 8.00 | 65.00 | — |
| 1920S | 46,220 | — | 1.00 | 7.00 | 110.00 | — |
| 1921 | 39,157 | — | 1.00 | 5.00 | 45.00 | — |
| 1921S | 15,274 | 1.00 | 2.00 | 16.00 | 100.00 | — |
| 1922D, All Kinds | 7,160 | 7.00 | 10.00 | 23.00 | 75.00 | — |
| 1922 No "D" | — | 290.00 | 425.00 | 1,475.00 | 9,500.00 | — |
| 1923 | 74,723 | — | — | 4.00 | 15.00 | — |
| 1923S | 8,700 | 2.00 | 3.00 | 21.00 | 225.00 | — |

|  | Mintage in Thousands | Good | Fine | Ex. Fine | Unc. | Proof |
|---|---|---|---|---|---|---|
| 1924 | 75,178 | — | — | 3.00 | 30.00 | — |
| 1924D | 2,520 | 9.00 | 12.00 | 65.00 | 250.00 | — |
| 1924S | 11,698 | 1.00 | 2.00 | 12.00 | 125.00 | — |
| 1925 | 139,949 | — | — | 2.00 | 15.00 | — |
| 1925D | 22,580 | — | 1.00 | 8.00 | 55.00 | — |
| 1925S | 26,380 | — | 1.00 | 6.00 | 80.00 | — |
| 1926 | 157,088 | — | — | 2.00 | 10.00 | — |
| 1926D | 28,020 | — | 1.00 | 6.00 | 65.00 | — |
| 1926S | 4,550 | 3.00 | 5.00 | 13.00 | 115.00 | — |
| 1927 | 144,440 | — | — | 2.00 | 10.00 | — |
| 1927D | 27,170 | — | 1.00 | 4.00 | 55.00 | — |
| 1927S | 14,276 | 1.00 | 2.00 | 9.00 | 75.00 | — |
| 1928 | 134,116 | — | — | 1.00 | 10.00 | — |
| 1928D | 31,170 | — | — | 3.00 | 40.00 | — |
| 1928S | 17,266 | — | 1.00 | 4.00 | 65.00 | — |
| 1929 | 185,262 | — | — | 1.00 | 10.00 | — |
| 1929D | 41,730 | — | — | 3.00 | 25.00 | — |
| 1929S | 50,148 | — | — | 2.00 | 15.00 | — |
| 1930 | 157,415 | — | — | 1.00 | 5.00 | — |
| 1930D | 40,100 | — | — | 2.00 | 15.00 | — |
| 1930S | 24,286 | — | — | 1.00 | 10.00 | — |
| 1931 | 19,396 | — | 1.00 | 2.00 | 22.00 | — |
| 1931D | 4,480 | 3.00 | 3.00 | 8.00 | 60.00 | — |
| 1931S | 866 | 37.00 | 43.00 | 48.00 | 75.00 | — |
| 1932 | 9,062 | 1.00 | 2.00 | 3.00 | 20.00 | — |
| 1932D | 10,500 | 1.00 | 2.00 | 2.00 | 20.00 | — |
| 1933 | 14,360 | 1.00 | 2.00 | 3.00 | 18.00 | — |
| 1933D | 6,200 | 2.00 | 3.00 | 6.00 | 17.00 | — |
| 1934 | 219,080 | — | — | 1.00 | 7.00 | — |
| 1934D | 28,446 | — | — | 5.00 | 20.00 | — |
| 1935 | 345,388 | — | — | 1.00 | 4.00 | — |
| 1935D | 47,000 | — | — | 1.00 | 7.00 | — |
| 1935S | 38,702 | — | — | 3.00 | 11.00 | — |
| 1936 | 309,638 | — | — | 1.00 | 2.00 | 200.00 |
| 1936D | 40,620 | — | — | 1.00 | 4.00 | — |
| 1936S | 29,130 | — | — | 1.00 | 3.00 | — |
| 1937 | 309,179 | — | — | 1.00 | 2.00 | 70.00 |
| 1937D | 56,430 | — | — | 1.00 | 2.00 | — |
| 1937S | 34,500 | — | — | 1.00 | 2.00 | — |
| 1938 | 157,697 | — | — | 1.00 | 2.00 | 50.00 |
| 1938D | 20,010 | — | — | 1.00 | 4.00 | — |
| 1938S | 15,180 | — | — | 1.00 | 4.00 | — |
| 1939 | 316,480 | — | — | — | 1.00 | 45.00 |
| 1939D | 15,160 | — | — | 1.00 | 2.00 | — |
| 1939S | 52,079 | — | — | 1.00 | 2.00 | — |
| 1940 | 586,826 | — | — | — | 1.00 | 25.00 |
| 1940D | 81,390 | — | — | 1.00 | 1.00 | — |
| 1940S | 112,940 | — | — | 1.00 | 1.00 | — |
| 1941 | 887,039 | — | — | — | 1.00 | 35.00 |
| 1941D | 128,700 | — | — | 1.00 | 3.00 | — |

|  | Mintage in Thousands | Unc. | Proof |
|---|---|---|---|
| 1941S | 92,360 | 2.00 | — |
| 1942 | 657,827 | 1.00 | 25.00 |
| 1942D | 206,688 | 1.00 | — |
| 1942S | 85,590 | 5.00 | — |
| 1943 Steel | 684,629 | 1.00 | — |
| 1943D Steel | 217,660 | 1.00 | — |
| 1943S Steel | 191,550 | 3.00 | — |
| 1944 Copper | 1,435,400 | 1.00 | — |

|  | Mintage in Thousands | Unc. | Proof |
|---|---|---|---|
| 1944D | 430,578 | — | — |
| 1944S | 282,760 | — | — |
| 1945 | 1,040,515 | 1.00 | — |
| 1945D | 226,268 | — | — |
| 1945S | 181,770 | — | — |
| 1946 | 991,655 | — | — |
| 1946D | 315,690 | — | — |
| 1946S | 198,100 | — | — |
| 1947 | 190,555 | 1.00 | — |
| 1947D | 194,750 | — | — |
| 1947S | 99,000 | — | — |
| 1948 | 317,570 | 1.00 | — |
| 1948D | 172,638 | — | — |
| 1948S | 81,735 | 1.00 | — |
| 1949 | 217,775 | 1.00 | — |
| 1949D | 153,133 | 1.00 | — |
| 1949S | 64,290 | 1.00 | — |
| 1950 | 272,686 | 1.00 | 35.00 |
| 1950D | 334,950 | 1.00 | — |
| 1950S | 118,550 | 1.00 | — |
| 1951 | 284,634 | 1.00 | 25.00 |
| 1951D | 625,355 | — | — |
| 1951S | 136,010 | 1.00 | — |
| 1952 | 186,857 | 1.00 | 20.00 |
| 1952D | 746,130 | — | — |
| 1952S | 137,800 | 1.00 | — |
| 1953 | 256,884 | — | 18.00 |
| 1953D | 700,515 | — | — |
| 1953S | 181,835 | — | — |
| 1954 | 71,873 | — | 6.00 |
| 1954D | 251,553 | — | — |
| 1954S | 96,190 | — | — |
| 1955 | 330,958 | — | 6.00 |

|  | Mintage in Thousands | Fine | Ex. Fine | Unc. | Proof |
|---|---|---|---|---|---|
| 1955 Double Die Obverse | — | 410.00 | 535.00 | 1,450.00 | — |
| 1955D | 563,258 | — | — | — | — |
| 1955S | 44,610 | — | — | 1.00 | — |
| 1956 | 421,414 | — | — | — | 3.00 |
| 1956D | 1,098,201 | — | — | — | — |
| 1957 | 283,788 | — | — | — | 2.00 |
| 1957D | 1,051,342 | — | — | — | — |
| 1958 | 253,401 | — | — | — | 2.00 |
| 1958D | 800,953 | — | — | — | — |

## MEMORIAL REVERSE TYPE

| | | | | | |
|---|---|---|---|---|---|
| 1959 | 610,864 | — | — | — | 2.00 |
| 1959D | 1,279,760 | — | — | — | — |
| 1960 Large Date, All Kinds | 588,097 | — | — | — | 1.00 |
| 1960 Small Date | — | — | 2.00 | 3.00 | 12.00 |
| 1960D Large Date, All Kinds | 1,580,884 | — | — | — | — |
| 190D Small Date | — | — | — | — | — |
| 1961 | 756,373 | — | — | — | 1.00 |
| 1961D | 1,753,267 | — | — | — | — |
| 1962 | 609,263 | — | — | — | 1.00 |
| 1962D | 1,793,148 | — | — | — | — |
| 1963 | 757,186 | — | — | — | 1.00 |
| 1963D | 1,774,020 | — | — | — | — |
| 1964 | 2,652,526 | — | — | — | 1.00 |

|  | Mintage in Thousands | Fine | Ex. Fine | Unc. | Proof |
|---|---|---|---|---|---|
| 1964D | 3,799,072 | — | — | — | — |
| 1965 | 1,497,225 | — | — | — | — |
| 1966 | 2,188,148 | — | — | — | — |
| 1967 | 3,048,667 | — | — | — | — |
| 1968 | 1,707,881 | — | — | — | — |
| 1968D | 2,886,270 | — | — | — | — |
| 1968S | 261,312 | — | — | — | 1.00 |
| 1969 | 1,136,910 | — | — | — | — |
| 1969D | 4,002,832 | — | — | — | — |
| 1969S | 547,310 | — | — | — | 1.00 |
| 1970 | 1,898,315 | — | — | — | — |
| 1970D | 2,891,439 | — | — | — | — |
| 1970S | 693,193 | — | — | — | 1.00 |
| 1971 | 1,919,490 | — | — | — | — |
| 1971D | 2,911,046 | — | — | — | — |
| 1971S | 528,354 | — | — | — | 1.00 |
| 1972 | 2,933,255 | — | — | — | — |
| 1972 Double Die Obverse | — | 115.00 | 130.00 | 220.00 | — |
| 1972D | 2,665,071 | — | — | — | — |
| 1972S | 380,200 | — | — | — | 1.00 |
| 1973 | 3,728,245 | — | — | — | — |
| 1973D | 3,549,577 | — | — | — | — |
| 1973S | 3,191,938 | — | — | — | 1.00 |
| 1974 | 4,232,141 | — | — | — | — |
| 1974D | 4,335,098 | — | — | — | — |
| 1974S | 412,039 | — | — | — | 1.00 |
| 1975 | 5,451,476 | — | — | — | — |
| 1975D | 4,505,245 | — | — | — | — |
| 1975S Proof only | 2,909 | — | — | — | 5.00 |
| 1976 P&D | 8,895,885 | — | — | — | — |
| 1976S Proof only | 4,150 | — | — | — | 3.00 |
| 1977 P&D | 8,663,992 | — | — | — | — |
| 1977S Proof only | 3,251 | — | — | — | 2.00 |
| 1978 P&D | 9,838,838 | — | — | — | — |
| 1978S Proof only | 3,128 | — | — | — | 2.00 |
| 1979S Type Two, Proof only, Sharp Mint Mark | — | — | — | — | — |
| 1979 P&D | 10,157,872 | — | — | — | — |
| 1979S Proof only | 3,677 | — | — | — | 3.00 |
| 1980 P&D | 12,554,803 | — | — | — | — |
| 1980S Proof only | — | — | — | — | — |
| 1981 P&D | 12,864,985 | — | — | — | — |
| 1981S Proof only | — | — | — | — | 2.00 |
| 1982 P&D | 15,138,259 | — | — | — | — |
| 1982S Proof only | — | — | — | — | 2.00 |
| 1983 P&D | — | — | — | — | — |
| 1983S Proof only | — | — | — | — | 4.00 |
| 1984 P&D | — | — | — | — | — |
| 1984S Proof only | — | — | — | — | 4.00 |
| 1985 P&D | — | — | — | — | — |
| 1985S Proof only | — | — | — | — | 4.00 |
| 1986 P&D | — | — | — | — | — |
| 1986S Proof only | — | — | — | — | 6.00 |
| 1987 P&D | — | — | — | — | — |
| 1987S Proof only | — | — | — | — | 3.00 |
| 1988 P&D | — | — | — | — | — |
| 1988S Proof only | — | — | — | — | 2.00 |
| 1989 Lincoln/MM | — | — | — | — | — |
| 1989S Lincoln/MM | — | — | — | — | 2.00 |
| 1990 Lincoln/MM | — | — | — | — | — |
| 1990S Lincoln/MM | — | — | — | — | 3.00 |

# 26.
# BRONZE TWO-CENT PIECES—
# 1864–1873

|  | Mintage in Thousands | Good | Fine | Unc. | Proof |
|---|---|---|---|---|---|
| 1864 Small Motto, All Kinds.... | 19,848 | 60.00 | 110.00 | 525.00 | 30,000.00 |
| 1864 Large Motto.............. | — | 11.00 | 20.00 | 85.00 | 750.00 |
| 1865.......................... | 13,460 | 11.00 | 20.00 | 85.00 | 500.00 |
| 1866.......................... | 3,177 | 11.00 | 20.00 | 90.00 | 500.00 |
| 1867.......................... | 2,939 | 13.00 | 20.00 | 100.00 | 500.00 |
| 1868.......................... | 2,804 | 12.00 | 20.00 | 135.00 | 500.00 |
| 1869.......................... | 1,547 | 11.00 | 20.00 | 125.00 | 500.00 |
| 1869 Recut Date ............... | — | 150.00 | 350.00 | 1,500.00 | — |
| 1870.......................... | 861 | 11.00 | 21.00 | 200.00 | 500.00 |
| 1871.......................... | 721 | 12.00 | 24.00 | 210.00 | 500.00 |
| 1872.......................... | 65 | 110.00 | 185.00 | 850.00 | 575.00 |
| 1873.......................... | 1 | 850.00 | 925.00 | — | 1,500.00 |

Note: Uncirculated two-cent pieces with full, original "mint red" color sell at a premium price.

# 27.
# NICKEL THREE-CENT PIECES— 1865–1889

|  | Mintage in Thousands | Good | Fine | Unc. | Proof-63 |
|---|---|---|---|---|---|
| 1865 | 11,382 | 11.00 | 12.00 | 100.00 | 1,750.00 |
| 1866 | 4,801 | 11.00 | 12.00 | 100.00 | 450.00 |
| 1867 | 3,915 | 11.00 | 12.00 | 100.00 | 400.00 |
| 1868 | 3,252 | 11.00 | 12.00 | 100.00 | 475.00 |
| 1869 | 1,604 | 11.00 | 12.00 | 110.00 | 375.00 |
| 1870 | 1,335 | 11.00 | 13.00 | 125.00 | 375.00 |
| 1871 | 604 | 11.00 | 12.00 | 130.00 | 400.00 |
| 1872 | 862 | 11.00 | 12.00 | 145.00 | 350.00 |
| 1873 | 1,173 | 11.00 | 13.00 | 115.00 | 350.00 |
| 1874 | 790 | 11.00 | 12.00 | 130.00 | 350.00 |
| 1875 | 228 | 11.00 | 13.00 | 150.00 | 400.00 |
| 1876 | 162 | 12.00 | 17.00 | 170.00 | 325.00 |
| 1877 | 1 | 850.00 | 900.00 | — | 1,250.00 |
| 1878 | 2 | 425.00 | 450.00 | — | 475.00 |
| 1879 | 41 | 45.00 | 65.00 | 250.00 | 300.00 |
| 1880 | 25 | 70.00 | 90.00 | 260.00 | 325.00 |
| 1881 | 1,681 | 11.00 | 12.00 | 120.00 | 325.00 |
| 1882 | 25 | 70.00 | 80.00 | 270.00 | 325.00 |
| 1883 | 11 | 135.00 | 180.00 | 475.00 | 325.00 |
| 1884 | 6 | 280.00 | 385.00 | 600.00 | 300.00 |
| 1885 | 5 | 350.00 | 500.00 | 700.00 | 350.00 |
| 1886 | 4 | 240.00 | 250.00 | — | 325.00 |
| 1887 over 6, All Kinds | 8 | 280.00 | 300.00 | — | 325.00 |
| 1887 | — | 225.00 | 250.00 | 425.00 | 325.00 |
| 1888 | 41 | 35.00 | 45.00 | 230.00 | 325.00 |
| 1889 | 22 | 63.00 | 90.00 | 260.00 | 325.00 |

# 28.
# NICKEL FIVE-CENT PIECES—
# 1866-Date

## SHIELD TYPE

         1866-1867                          1867-1883

|  | Mintage in Thousands | Good | Fine | Unc. | Proof |
|---|---|---|---|---|---|
| 1866 | 14,743 | 16.00 | 22.00 | 260.00 | 2,250.00 |
| 1867 Rays | 2,019 | 17.00 | 24.00 | 335.00 | 40,000.00 |
| 1867 Without Rays | 28,891 | 12.00 | 15.00 | 110.00 | 650.00 |
| 1868 | 28,817 | 12.00 | 15.00 | 110.00 | 450.00 |
| 1869 | 16,395 | 12.00 | 15.00 | 110.00 | 450.00 |
| 1870 | 4,806 | 12.00 | 17.00 | 140.00 | 425.00 |
| 1871 | 561 | 30.00 | 50.00 | 325.00 | 400.00 |
| 1872 | 6,036 | 12.00 | 17.00 | 160.00 | 350.00 |
| 1873 | 4,550 | 12.00 | 17.00 | 175.00 | 325.00 |
| 1874 | 3,538 | 12.00 | 24.00 | 180.00 | 350.00 |
| 1875 | 2,097 | 13.00 | 28.00 | 225.00 | 475.00 |
| 1876 | 2,530 | 12.00 | 24.00 | 160.00 | 350.00 |
| 1877 | 1 | 925.00 | 1,000.00 | — | 1,400.00 |
| 1878 | 2 | 425.00 | 450.00 | — | 500.00 |
| 1879 | 29 | 245.00 | 350.00 | 600.00 | 425.00 |
| 1880 | 20 | 280.00 | 365.00 | 675.00 | 350.00 |
| 1881 | 72 | 145.00 | 225.00 | 525.00 | 325.00 |
| 1882 | 11,476 | 12.00 | 15.00 | 110.00 | 325.00 |
| 1883 | 1,457 | 12.00 | 15.00 | 110.00 | 325.00 |
| 1883 over 2 | — | 70.00 | 135.00 | 500.00 | — |

Note: Choice, well-struck uncirculated shield nickels, especially 1866-74, are worth more than the listed prices.

## LIBERTY HEAD TYPE

       1883                       1883–1912

|  | Mintage in Thousands | Good | Fine | Unc. | Proof |
|---|---:|---:|---:|---:|---:|
| 1883 Without CENTS | 5,480 | 4.00 | 5.00 | 35.00 | 350.00 |
| 1883 With CENTS | 16,033 | 9.00 | 14.00 | 90.00 | 225.00 |
| 1884 | 11,274 | 12.00 | 16.00 | 150.00 | 250.00 |
| 1885 | 1,476 | 260.00 | 350.00 | 850.00 | 675.00 |
| 1886 | 3,330 | 90.00 | 150.00 | 525.00 | 275.00 |
| 1887 | 15,264 | 7.00 | 19.00 | 110.00 | 225.00 |
| 1888 | 10,720 | 13.00 | 22.00 | 160.00 | 225.00 |
| 1889 | 15,881 | 6.00 | 15.00 | 100.00 | 225.00 |
| 1890 | 16,259 | 6.00 | 15.00 | 110.00 | 225.00 |
| 1891 | 16,834 | 5.00 | 12.00 | 95.00 | 225.00 |
| 1892 | 11,700 | 5.00 | 13.00 | 110.00 | 225.00 |
| 1893 | 13,370 | 4.00 | 13.00 | 95.00 | 225.00 |
| 1894 | 5,413 | 7.00 | 50.00 | 200.00 | 225.00 |
| 1895 | 9,980 | 3.00 | 15.00 | 110.00 | 225.00 |
| 1896 | 8,843 | 5.00 | 18.00 | 135.00 | 225.00 |
| 1897 | 20,429 | 3.00 | 7.00 | 90.00 | 225.00 |
| 1898 | 12,532 | 2.00 | 7.00 | 100.00 | 225.00 |
| 1899 | 26,029 | 2.00 | 5.00 | 90.00 | 225.00 |
| 1900 | 27,256 | 1.00 | 5.00 | 80.00 | 225.00 |
| 1901 | 26,480 | 1.00 | 5.00 | 75.00 | 225.00 |
| 1902 | 31,490 | 1.00 | 4.00 | 75.00 | 225.00 |
| 1903 | 28,007 | 1.00 | 4.00 | 75.00 | 225.00 |
| 1904 | 21,405 | 1.00 | 4.00 | 75.00 | 250.00 |
| 1905 | 29,827 | 1.00 | 4.00 | 75.00 | 225.00 |
| 1906 | 38,614 | 1.00 | 3.00 | 75.00 | 225.00 |
| 1907 | 39,215 | 1.00 | 3.00 | 75.00 | 225.00 |
| 1908 | 22,686 | 1.00 | 3.00 | 75.00 | 225.00 |
| 1909 | 11,591 | 2.00 | 3.00 | 80.00 | 225.00 |
| 1910 | 30,169 | 1.00 | 3.00 | 75.00 | 225.00 |
| 1911 | 39,559 | 1.00 | 3.00 | 75.00 | 225.00 |
| 1912 | 26,237 | 1.00 | 3.00 | 75.00 | 225.00 |
| 1912D | 8,474 | 2.00 | 6.00 | 225.00 | — |
| 1912S | 238 | 45.00 | 110.00 | 825.00 | — |
| 1913 Liberty Head | (5 struck) | — | — | — | — |

## INDIAN HEAD OR BUFFALO TYPE

1913

1913–1938

|  | Mintage in Thousands | Good | Fine | Unc. | Matte Proof |
|---|---:|---:|---:|---:|---:|
| 1913 Var. 1 | 30,994 | 5.00 | 7.00 | 32.00 | 11,250.00 |
| 1913D Var. 1 | 5,337 | 9.00 | 13.00 | 50.00 | — |
| 1913S Var. 1 | 2,105 | 15.00 | 21.00 | 75.00 | — |
| 1913 Var. 2 | 29,859 | 7.00 | 9.00 | 35.00 | 875.00 |
| 1913D Var. 2 | 4,156 | 47.00 | 65.00 | 165.00 | — |
| 1913S Var. 2 | 1,209 | 105.00 | 165.00 | 375.00 | — |
| 1914 | 20,666 | 11.00 | 12.00 | 50.00 | 875.00 |
| 1914D | 3,912 | 40.00 | 65.00 | 265.00 | — |
| 1914S | 3,470 | 11.00 | 18.00 | 200.00 | — |
| 1915 | 20,987 | 4.00 | 6.00 | 45.00 | 875.00 |
| 1915D | 7,570 | 11.00 | 25.00 | 225.00 | — |
| 1915S | 1,505 | 15.00 | 45.00 | 500.00 | — |
| 1916 | 63,498 | 3.00 | 3.00 | 45.00 | 1,100.00 |
| 1916D | 13,333 | 8.00 | 13.00 | 165.00 | — |
| 1916S | 11,860 | 5.00 | 12.00 | 185.00 | — |
| 1917 | 51,224 | 2.00 | 4.00 | 65.00 | 7,500.00 |
| 1917D | 9,911 | 8.00 | 25.00 | 400.00 | — |
| 1917S | 4,193 | 9.00 | 30.00 | 475.00 | — |
| 1918 | 32,086 | 2.00 | 5.00 | 135.00 | — |
| 1918D over 7, All Kinds | 8,362 | 375.00 | 1,050.00 | 20,000.00 | — |
| 1918D Normal date | — | 8.00 | 30.00 | 450.00 | — |
| 1918S | 4,882 | 8.00 | 29.00 | 625.00 | — |
| 1919 | 60,868 | 1.00 | 2.00 | 55.00 | — |
| 1919D | 8,006 | 9.00 | 32.00 | 625.00 | — |
| 1919S | 7,521 | 5.00 | 28.00 | 600.00 | — |
| 1920 | 63,093 | 1.00 | 2.00 | 55.00 | — |
| 1920D | 9,418 | 6.00 | 25.00 | 625.00 | — |
| 1920S | 9,689 | 3.00 | 20.00 | 575.00 | — |
| 1921 | 10,663 | 2.00 | 3.00 | 135.00 | — |
| 1921S | 1,557 | 28.00 | 90.00 | 1,500.00 | — |
| 1923 | 35,715 | 1.00 | 3.00 | 55.00 | — |
| 1923S | 6,142 | 3.00 | 10.00 | 450.00 | — |
| 1924 | 21,620 | 1.00 | 2.00 | 75.00 | — |
| 1924D | 5,258 | 4.00 | 16.00 | 425.00 | — |
| 1924S | 1,437 | 7.00 | 65.00 | 2,250.00 | — |
| 1925 | 35,565 | 2.00 | 3.00 | 45.00 | — |
| 1925D | 4,450 | 6.00 | 30.00 | 385.00 | — |
| 1925S | 6,256 | 3.00 | 17.00 | 525.00 | — |

|  | Mintage in Thousands | Good | Fine | Unc. | Proof |
|---|---|---|---|---|---|
| 1926 | 44,693 | 1.00 | 2.00 | 32.00 | — |
| 1926D | 5,638 | 4.00 | 22.00 | 275.00 | — |
| 1926S | 970 | 9.00 | 50.00 | 3,500.00 | — |
| 1927 | 37,981 | 1.00 | 2.00 | 35.00 | — |
| 1927D | 5,730 | 2.00 | 6.00 | 165.00 | — |
| 1927S | 3,430 | 1.00 | 4.00 | 675.00 | — |
| 1928 | 23,411 | 1.00 | 2.00 | 35.00 | — |
| 1928D | 6,436 | 1.00 | 3.00 | 50.00 | — |
| 1928S | 6,936 | 1.00 | 2.00 | 275.00 | — |
| 1929 | 36,446 | 1.00 | 2.00 | 32.00 | — |
| 1929D | 8,370 | 1.00 | 2.00 | 60.00 | — |
| 1929S | 7,754 | 1.00 | 1.00 | 50.00 | — |
| 1930 | 22,849 | 1.00 | 1.00 | 30.00 | — |
| 1930S | 5,435 | 1.00 | 1.00 | 50.00 | — |
| 1931S | 1,200 | 4.00 | 5.00 | 45.00 | — |
| 1934 | 20,213 | 1.00 | 1.00 | 30.00 | — |
| 1934D | 7,480 | 1.00 | 1.00 | 47.00 | — |
| 1935 | 58,264 | 1.00 | 1.00 | 20.00 | — |
| 1935D | 12,092 | 1.00 | 2.00 | 40.00 | — |
| 1935S | 10,300 | 1.00 | 1.00 | 32.00 | — |
| 1936 | 119,001 | 1.00 | 1.00 | 20.00 | 725.00 |
| 1936D | 24,814 | 1.00 | 1.00 | 23.00 | — |
| 1936S | 14,930 | 1.00 | 1.00 | 23.00 | — |
| 1937 | 79,486 | 1.00 | 1.00 | 16.00 | 650.00 |
| 1937D, All Kinds | 17,826 | 1.00 | 1.00 | 20.00 | — |
| 1937D, 3-Legged Var. | — | 150.00 | 250.00 | 1,450.00 | — |
| 1937S | 5,635 | 1.00 | 1.00 | 17.00 | — |
| 1938D, All Kinds | 7,020 | 1.00 | 2.00 | 15.00 | — |
| 1938D/S | — | 3.00 | 7.00 | 45.00 | — |

## JEFFERSON TYPE

|  | Mintage in Thousands | Fine | Ex. Fine | Unc. | Proof |
|---|---|---|---|---|---|
| 1938 | 19,515 | — | 1.00 | 4.00 | 35.00 |
| 1938D | 5,376 | 1.00 | 2.00 | 4.00 | — |
| 1938S | 4,105 | 2.00 | 2.00 | 4.00 | — |
| 1939 | 120,628 | — | — | 2.00 | 40.00 |
| 1939D | 3,514 | 4.00 | 8.00 | 45.00 | — |
| 1939S | 6,630 | 1.00 | 3.00 | 18.00 | — |
| 1940 | 176,499 | — | — | 1.00 | 35.00 |
| 1940D | 43,540 | — | — | 2.00 | — |
| 1940S | 39,690 | — | 1.00 | 3.00 | — |
| 1941 | 203,284 | — | — | 1.00 | 35.00 |
| 1941D | 53,432 | — | — | 3.00 | — |
| 1941S | 43,445 | — | 1.00 | 4.00 | — |

|  | Mintage in Thousands | Fine | Ex. Fine | Unc. | Proof |
|---|---|---|---|---|---|
| 1942 | 49,819 | — | — | 6.00 | 35.00 |
| 1942D | 13,938 | — | 3.00 | 23.00 | — |
| 1942P Wartime Silver Nickels | 57,901 | 1.00 | 2.00 | 7.00 | 60.00 |
| 1942S | 32,900 | 1.00 | 2.00 | 6.00 | — |
| 1943P | 271,165 | 1.00 | 2.00 | 5.00 | — |
| 1943D | 15,294 | 1.00 | 2.00 | 3.00 | — |
| 1943S | 104,060 | 1.00 | 2.00 | 3.00 | — |
| 1944P | 119,150 | 1.00 | 2.00 | 6.00 | — |
| 1944D | 32,309 | 1.00 | 2.00 | 7.00 | — |
| 1944S | 21,640 | 1.00 | 2.00 | 4.00 | — |
| 1945P | 119,408 | 1.00 | 2.00 | 5.00 | — |
| 1945D | 37,158 | 1.00 | 2.00 | 5.00 | — |
| 1945S | 58,939 | 1.00 | 1.00 | 2.00 | — |
| 1946 Regular Nickels | 161,116 | — | — | 1.00 | — |
| 1946D | 45,292 | — | — | 1.00 | — |
| 1946S | 13,560 | — | — | 1.00 | — |
| 1947 | 95,000 | — | — | 1.00 | — |
| 1947D | 37,822 | — | — | 1.00 | — |
| 1947S | 24,720 | — | — | 1.00 | — |
| 1948 | 89,348 | — | — | 1.00 | — |
| 1948D | 44,734 | — | — | 1.00 | — |
| 1948S | 11,300 | — | — | 1.00 | — |
| 1949 | 60,652 | — | — | 2.00 | — |
| 1949D | 36,498 | — | — | 1.00 | — |
| 1949S | 9,716 | — | 1.00 | 2.00 | — |
| 1950 | 9,847 | — | — | 2.00 | 35.00 |
| 1950D | 2,630 | 5.00 | 6.00 | 8.00 | — |

|  | Mintage in Thousands | Unc. | Proof |
|---|---|---|---|
| 1951 | 28,610 | 1.00 | 20.00 |
| 1951D | 20,460 | 1.00 | — |
| 1951S | 7,776 | 2.00 | — |
| 1952 | 64,070 | 1.00 | 17.00 |
| 1952D | 30,638 | 2.00 | — |
| 1952S | 20,572 | 1.00 | — |
| 1953 | 46,773 | — | 15.00 |
| 1953D | 59,873 | — | — |
| 1953S | 19,211 | 1.00 | — |
| 1954 | 47,914 | — | 11.00 |
| 1954D | 117,183 | — | — |
| 1954S | 29,384 | — | — |
| 1955 | 8,266 | 1.00 | 7.00 |
| 1955D | 74,464 | — | — |
| 1956 | 35,885 | — | 3.00 |
| 1956D | 67,223 | — | — |
| 1957 | 39,656 | — | 1.00 |
| 1957D | 136,829 | — | — |
| 1958 | 17,964 | — | 2.00 |
| 1958D | 168,249 | — | — |
| 1959 | 28,397 | — | 1.00 |
| 1959D | 160,738 | — | — |
| 1960 | 57,108 | — | 1.00 |
| 1960D | 192,343 | — | — |
| 1961 | 76,668 | — | 1.00 |
| 1961D | 229,343 | — | — |
| 1962 | 100,602 | — | 1.00 |
| 1962D | 280,196 | — | — |

|  | Mintage in Thousands | Unc. | Proof |
|---|---:|:---:|---:|
| 1963 | 178,852 | — | 1.00 |
| 1963D | 276,829 | — | — |
| 1964 | 1,028,623 | — | 1.00 |
| 1964D | 1,787,297 | — | — |
| 1965 | 136,131 | — | — |
| 1966 | 156,208 | — | — |
| 1967 | 107,326 | — | — |
| 1968D | 91,228 | — | — |
| 1968S | 103,438 | — | 1.00 |
| 1969D | 202,808 | — | — |
| 1969S | 123,100 | — | 1.00 |
| 1970D | 515,485 | — | — |
| 1970S | 241,465 | — | 1.00 |
| 1971 | 106,884 | — | — |
| 1971D | 316,145 | — | — |
| 1971S Proof only | 3,224 | — | 2.00 |
| 1972 | 202,036 | — | — |
| 1972D | 351,695 | — | — |
| 1972S Proof only | 3,268 | — | 2.00 |
| 1973 | 384,396 | — | — |
| 1973D | 261,405 | — | — |
| 1973S Proof only | 2,770 | — | 2.00 |
| 1974 | 601,752 | — | — |
| 1974D | 277,373 | — | — |
| 1974S Proof only | 2,617 | — | 2.00 |
| 1975 | 181,772 | — | — |
| 1975D | 401,875 | — | — |
| 1975S Proof only | 2,909 | — | 2.00 |
| 1976 P-D | 931,088 | — | — |
| 1976S Proof only | 4,150 | — | 2.00 |
| 1977 P&D | 882,689 | — | — |
| 1977S Proof only | 3,251 | — | 2.00 |
| 1978 P&D | 704,402 | — | — |
| 1978S Proof only | 3,128 | — | 2.00 |
| 1979 P&D | 819,056 | — | — |
| 1979S Proof only | 3,677 | — | 1.00 |
| 1979S Type Two Proof only | — | — | 2.00 |
| 1980 P&D | — | — | — |
| 1980S Proof only | — | — | 1.00 |
| 1981 P&D | — | — | — |
| 1981S Proof only | — | — | 2.00 |
| 1982 P&D | — | — | — |
| 1982S Proof only | — | — | 3.00 |
| 1983 P&D | — | — | — |
| 1983S Proof only | — | — | 3.00 |
| 1984 P&D | — | — | — |
| 1984S Proof only | — | — | 5.00 |
| 1985P | — | — | — |
| 1985D | — | — | — |
| 1985S Proof only | — | — | 3.00 |
| 1986P | — | — | — |
| 1986D | — | — | — |
| 1986S Proof only | — | — | 7.00 |
| 1987P | — | — | — |
| 1987D | — | — | — |
| 1987S Proof only | — | — | 3.00 |
| 1988P | — | — | — |
| 1988D | — | — | — |
| 1988S Proof only | — | — | 4.00 |

# 29.
# SILVER THREE-CENT PIECES—
# 1851–1873

|  | Mintage in Thousands | Good | Fine | Unc. | Proof |
|---|---|---|---|---|---|
| 1851 | 5,447 | 17.00 | 23.00 | 165.00 | — |
| 1851O | 720 | 20.00 | 35.00 | 325.00 | — |
| 1852 | 18,664 | 17.00 | 23.00 | 165.00 | — |
| 1853 | 11,400 | 17.00 | 23.00 | 165.00 | — |
| 1854 | 671 | 18.00 | 25.00 | 375.00 | 17,500.00 |
| 1855 | 139 | 22.00 | 50.00 | 525.00 | 8,000.00 |
| 1856 | 1,458 | 18.00 | 25.00 | 325.00 | 5,500.00 |
| 1857 | 1,042 | 18.00 | 26.00 | 350.00 | 5,350.00 |
| 1858 | 1,604 | 18.00 | 25.00 | 285.00 | 4,000.00 |
| 1859 | 365 | 17.00 | 23.00 | 175.00 | 750.00 |
| 1860 | 287 | 17.00 | 25.00 | 175.00 | 750.00 |
| 1861 | 498 | 17.00 | 23.00 | 175.00 | 550.00 |
| 1862 | 344 | 17.00 | 25.00 | 175.00 | 550.00 |
| 1863 | 21 | 275.00 | 310.00 | 675.00 | 550.00 |
| 1864 | 12 | 275.00 | 310.00 | 625.00 | 550.00 |
| 1865 | 9 | 325.00 | 375.00 | 725.00 | 650.00 |
| 1866 | 23 | 275.00 | 310.00 | 625.00 | 550.00 |
| 1867 | 5 | 325.00 | 375.00 | 750.00 | 600.00 |
| 1868 | 4 | 325.00 | 375.00 | 775.00 | 550.00 |
| 1869 | 5 | 325.00 | 375.00 | 625.00 | 550.00 |
| 1870 | 4 | 275.00 | 325.00 | 725.00 | 550.00 |
| 1871 | 4 | 325.00 | 375.00 | 635.00 | 600.00 |
| 1872 | 2 | 350.00 | 400.00 | 850.00 | 700.00 |
| 1873 | 1 | 550.00 | 625.00 | — | 900.00 |

# 30.
# HALF DIMES—
# 1794–1873

## FLOWING HAIR TYPE

|  | Mintage in Thousands | Good | Fine | Unc. |
|---|---|---|---|---|
| 1794, All Kinds | 86 | 750.00 | 1,150.00 | 7,750.00 |
| 1795, All Kinds Total | — | 550.00 | 975.00 | 7,000.00 |

## DRAPED BUST TYPE

### 1796–1797　　　　　　　　1800–1805

| | | | | |
|---|---|---|---|---|
| 1796 over 5, All Kinds | 10 | 825.00 | 1,500.00 | 18,500.00 |
| 1796 Normal Date | — | 750.00 | 1,425.00 | 11,500.00 |
| 1796 LIKERTY | — | 750.00 | 1,425.00 | 12,750.00 |
| 1797 15 Stars, All Kinds | 45 | 700.00 | 1,375.00 | 7,750.00 |
| 1797 16 Stars | — | 700.00 | 1,375.00 | 8,250.00 |
| 1797 13 Stars | — | 700.00 | 1,375.00 | 16,500.00 |
| 1800, All Kinds | 24 | 400.00 | 825.00 | 5,850.00 |
| 1800 LIBEKTY | — | 400.00 | 825.00 | 6,000.00 |
| 1801 | 34 | 550.00 | 1,050.00 | 7,750.00 |
| 1802 | 13 | 12,500.00 | 27,500.00 | — |
| 1803 | 38 | 550.00 | 925.00 | 6,000.00 |
| 1805 | 16 | 675.00 | 1,050.00 | 13,500.00 |

## LIBERTY CAP TYPE

|  | Mintage in Thousands | Good | Fine | Unc. |
|---|---|---|---|---|
| 1829 | 1,230 | 23.00 | 35.00 | 350.00 |
| 1830 | 1,240 | 22.00 | 35.00 | 350.00 |
| 1831 | 1,243 | 20.00 | 32.00 | 350.00 |
| 1832 | 965 | 20.00 | 32.00 | 350.00 |
| 1833 | 1,370 | 21.00 | 33.00 | 350.00 |
| 1834 | 1,480 | 20.00 | 32.00 | 350.00 |
| 1835 | 2,760 | 20.00 | 32.00 | 350.00 |
| 1836 | 1,900 | 20.00 | 37.00 | 350.00 |
| 1837 | 2,276 | 22.00 | 32.00 | 375.00 |

## LIBERTY SEATED TYPE

|  | Mintage in Thousands | Good | Fine | Unc. |
|---|---|---|---|---|
| 1837 No Stars | (Included above) | 25.00 | 55.00 | 600.00 |

1837–1838          1838–1859          1860–1873

| | Mintage in Thousands | Good | Fine | Unc. |
|---|---|---|---|---|
| 1838O No Stars | 70 | 70.00 | 210.00 | 2,450.00 |
| 1838 No Drapery at Elbow | 2,255 | 9.00 | 15.00 | 275.00 |
| 1839 No Draper at Elbow | 1,069 | 10.00 | 15.00 | 275.00 |
| 1839O No Drapery at Elbow | 1,034 | 10.00 | 16.00 | 675.00 |
| 1840 No Drapery at Elbow | 1,344 | 10.00 | 15.00 | 275.00 |
| 1840O No Drapery at Elbow, All Kinds | 695 | 10.00 | 18.00 | 700.00 |
| 1840 Drapery at Elbow | 10 | 18.00 | 50.00 | 475.00 |
| 1840O Drapery at Elbow | 25 | 27.00 | 90.00 | 2,750.00 |
| 1841 | 1,150 | 9.00 | 13.00 | 175.00 |
| 1841O | 815 | 11.00 | 23.00 | 675.00 |
| 1842 | 815 | 9.00 | 13.00 | 175.00 |
| 1842O | 350 | 25.00 | 60.00 | 1,350.00 |
| 1843 | 1,165 | 10.00 | 14.00 | 175.00 |
| 1844 | 430 | 10.00 | 13.00 | 175.00 |
| 1844O | 220 | 65.00 | 185.00 | 6,500.00 |
| 1845 | 1,564 | 9.00 | 13.00 | 175.00 |
| 1846 | 27 | 210.00 | 475.00 | 9,000.00 |
| 1847 | 1,274 | 9.00 | 13.00 | 185.00 |
| 1848 | 668 | 10.00 | 13.00 | 250.00 |
| 1848O | 600 | 11.00 | 25.00 | 365.00 |
| 1849 over 48, All Kinds | 1,309 | 12.00 | 25.00 | 425.00 |
| 1849 over 46 | — | 10.00 | 20.00 | 450.00 |
| 1849 | — | 9.00 | 13.00 | 225.00 |
| 1849O | 140 | 22.00 | 75.00 | 2,250.00 |
| 1850 | 955 | 9.00 | 13.00 | 185.00 |

|  | Mintage in Thousands | Good | Fine | Unc. |
|---|---|---|---|---|
| 1850O | 690 | 10.00 | 23.00 | 800.00 |
| 1851 | 781 | 9.00 | 14.00 | 200.00 |
| 1851O | 860 | 10.00 | 25.00 | 525.00 |
| 1852 | 1,001 | 10.00 | 14.00 | 185.00 |
| 1852O | 260 | 23.00 | 65.00 | 850.00 |
| 1853 No Arrows | 135 | 25.00 | 60.00 | 650.00 |
| 1853O No Arrows | 160 | 135.00 | 300.00 | 6,000.00 |

|  | Mintage in Thousands | Good | Fine | Unc. | Proof |
|---|---|---|---|---|---|
| 1853 With Arrows | 13,210 | 9.00 | 13.00 | 210.00 | 20,000.00 |
| 1853O | 2,200 | 10.00 | 14.00 | 325.00 | — |
| 1854 | 5,740 | 9.00 | 13.00 | 210.00 | 10,000.00 |
| 1854O | 1,560 | 10.00 | 14.00 | 300.00 | — |
| 1855 | 1,750 | 9.00 | 13.00 | 225.00 | 10,000.00 |
| 1855O | 600 | 13.00 | 28.00 | 625.00 | — |
| 1856 No Arrows | 4,880 | 9.00 | 13.00 | 175.00 | 6,000.00 |
| 1856O | 1,100 | 10.00 | 16.00 | 600.00 | — |
| 1857 | 7,280 | 9.00 | 13.00 | 175.00 | 2,750.00 |
| 1857O | 1,380 | 10.00 | 17.00 | 360.00 | — |
| 1858 | 3,500 | 9.00 | 13.00 | 175.00 | 2,000.00 |
| 1858O | 1,660 | 10.00 | 55.00 | 275.00 | — |
| 1859 | 340 | 11.00 | 20.00 | 240.00 | — |
| 1859O | 560 | 11.00 | 23.00 | 260.00 | 1,500.00 |
| 1860 | 799 | 9.00 | 13.00 | 140.00 | — |
| 1860O | 1,060 | 9.00 | 13.00 | 210.00 | — |
| 1861 | 3,361 | 9.00 | 13.00 | 140.00 | — |
| 1862 | 1,493 | 9.00 | 13.00 | 140.00 | 600.00 |
| 1863 | 18 | 140.00 | 200.00 | 625.00 | 650.00 |
| 1863S | 100 | 20.00 | 33.00 | 700.00 | — |
| 1864 | 48 | 275.00 | 425.00 | 950.00 | 625.00 |
| 1864S | 90 | 35.00 | 80.00 | 675.00 | — |
| 1865 | 14 | 225.00 | 350.00 | 800.00 | 525.00 |
| 1865S | 120 | 22.00 | 40.00 | 875.00 | — |
| 1866 | 11 | 210.00 | 345.00 | 700.00 | 525.00 |
| 1866S | 120 | 22.00 | 37.00 | 450.00 | — |
| 1867 | 9 | 340.00 | 500.00 | 875.00 | 525.00 |
| 1867S | 120 | 19.00 | 29.00 | 625.00 | — |
| 1868 | 89 | 45.00 | 95.00 | 585.00 | 525.00 |
| 1868S | 280 | 11.00 | 20.00 | 325.00 | — |
| 1869 | 209 | 11.00 | 16.00 | 225.00 | 525.00 |
| 1869S | 230 | 10.00 | 15.00 | 350.00 | — |
| 1870 | 537 | 9.00 | 14.00 | 140.00 | 525.00 |
| 1871 | 1,874 | 9.00 | 14.00 | 140.00 | — |
| 1871S | 161 | 11.00 | 28.00 | 285.00 | 525.00 |
| 1872 | 2,948 | 9.00 | 14.00 | 140.00 | 525.00 |
| 1872S Mint Mark within Wreath | 837 | 9.00 | 14.00 | 140.00 | — |
| 1872 Mint Mark Below | — | 9.00 | 14.00 | 140.00 | 525.00 |
| 1873 | 713 | 9.00 | 15.00 | 140.00 | — |
| 1873S | 324 | 10.00 | 14.00 | 140.00 | — |

# 31.
# DIMES—
# 1796–Date

## DRAPED BUST TYPE

**1796–1797**  **1798–1807**

|  | Mintage in Thousands | Good | Fine | Unc. |
|---|---|---|---|---|
| 1796 | 22 | 1,000.00 | 1,900.00 | 8,250.00 |
| 1797 16 Stars, All Kinds | 25 | 1,150.00 | 2,000.00 | 8,750.00 |
| 1797 13 Stars | — | 1,100.00 | 2,000.00 | 8,750.00 |
| 1798 over 97, 13 Stars on Reverse, All Kinds | 28 | 1,000.00 | 2,750.00 | — |
| 1798 over 97, 16 Stars on Reverse | — | 475.00 | 800.00 | 4,850.00 |
| 1798 | — | 450.00 | 750.00 | 4,750.00 |
| 1800 | 22 | 450.00 | 750.00 | 5,500.00 |
| 1801 | 35 | 450.00 | 950.00 | — |
| 1802 | 11 | 675.00 | 1,300.00 | 12,500.00 |
| 1803 | 33 | 450.00 | 800.00 | 10,000.00 |
| 1804 13 Stars on Reverse, All Kinds | 8 | 1,000.00 | 2,100.00 | — |
| 1804 14 Stars on Reverse | — | 1,100.00 | 2,500.00 | — |
| 1805 | 121 | 350.00 | 625.00 | 4,000.00 |
| 1807 | 165 | 350.00 | 625.00 | 4,250.00 |

## LIBERTY CAP TYPE

| | | | | |
|---|---|---|---|---|
| 1809 | 51 | 100.00 | 265.00 | 2,850.00 |
| 1811 over 9 | 65 | 60.00 | 225.00 | 3,000.00 |
| 1814 | 422 | 27.00 | 55.00 | 1,100.00 |
| 1820 | 943 | 20.00 | 50.00 | 1,100.00 |

|  | Mintage in Thousands | Good | Fine | Unc. |
|---|---:|---:|---:|---:|
| 1821 | 1,187 | 20.00 | 45.00 | 1,100.00 |
| 1822 | 100 | 325.00 | 800.00 | 6,750.00 |
| 1823 over 22, All Kinds | 440 | 18.00 | 40.00 | 1,100.00 |
| 1824 over 22 | — | 23.00 | 65.00 | 1,650.00 |
| 1825 | 510 | 18.00 | 40.00 | 1,150.00 |
| 1827 | 1,215 | 18.00 | 40.00 | 1,100.00 |
| 1828 | 125 | 25.00 | 75.00 | 1,050.00 |
| 1829 | 770 | 18.00 | 30.00 | 775.00 |
| 1830 | 510 | 18.00 | 30.00 | 750.00 |
| 1831 | 771 | 18.00 | 30.00 | 750.00 |
| 1832 | 523 | 18.00 | 30.00 | 750.00 |
| 1833 | 485 | 18.00 | 30.00 | 750.00 |
| 1834 | 635 | 18.00 | 30.00 | 750.00 |
| 1835 | 1,410 | 18.00 | 30.00 | 750.00 |
| 1836 | 1,190 | 18.00 | 30.00 | 750.00 |
| 1837 | 1,042 | 18.00 | 30.00 | 775.00 |

## LIBERTY SEATED TYPE

No Stars        Stars

|  | Mintage | Good | Fine | Unc. |
|---|---:|---:|---:|---:|
| 1837 No Stars | (included above) | 27.00 | 75.00 | 1,100.00 |
| 1838O No Stars | 406 | 32.00 | 110.00 | 3,000.00 |
| 1838 With Stars, All Kinds | 1,993 | 11.00 | 45.00 | 350.00 |
| 1838 With Partial Drapery | — | 20.00 | 50.00 | 450.00 |
| 1839 | 1,053 | 10.00 | 16.00 | 350.00 |
| 1839O | 1,323 | 10.00 | 16.00 | 450.00 |
| 1840 | 981 | 10.00 | 13.00 | 350.00 |
| 1840O | 1,175 | 11.00 | 20.00 | 1,000.00 |
| 1841 | 1,623 | 10.00 | 13.00 | 325.00 |
| 1841O | 2,008 | 10.00 | 20.00 | 850.00 |
| 1842 | 1,888 | 10.00 | 13.00 | 300.00 |
| 1842O | 2,020 | 10.00 | 23.00 | 2,750.00 |
| 1843 | 1,370 | 10.00 | 14.00 | 350.00 |
| 1843O | 150 | 30.00 | 110.00 | 1,650.00 |
| 1844 | 73 | 200.00 | 425.00 | 2,350.00 |
| 1845 | 1,755 | 10.00 | 13.00 | 285.00 |
| 1845O | 230 | 16.00 | 55.00 | 1,700.00 |
| 1846 | 31 | 65.00 | 160.00 | 4,000.00 |
| 1847 | 245 | 13.00 | 30.00 |  |
| 1848 | 452 | 10.00 | 20.00 | 500.00 |
| 1849 | 839 | 10.00 | 16.00 | 325.00 |
| 1849O | 300 | 10.00 | 40.00 | 2,650.00 |
| 1850 | 1,932 | 10.00 | 13.00 | 300.00 |
| 1850O | 510 | 10.00 | 23.00 | 1,175.00 |
| 1851 | 1,027 | 10.00 | 13.00 | 375.00 |
| 1851O | 400 | 10.00 | 32.00 | 1,675.00 |

|  | Mintage in Thousands | Good | Fine | Unc. | Proof |
|---|---|---|---|---|---|
| 1852 | 1,536 | 10.00 | 13.00 | 300.00 | — |
| 1852O | 430 | 14.00 | 40.00 | 1,450.00 | — |
| 1853 No Arrows | 95 | 40.00 | 100.00 | 675.00 | — |
| 1853 With Arrows | 12,078 | 10.00 | 13.00 | 325.00 | 22,000.00 |
| 1853O | 1,100 | 11.00 | 14.00 | 1,175.00 | — |
| 1854 | 4,470 | 10.00 | 13.00 | 325.00 | 20,000.00 |
| 1854O | 1,770 | 10.00 | 13.00 | 350.00 | — |
| 1855 | 2,075 | 10.00 | 13.00 | 400.00 | 20,000.00 |
| 1856 No Arrows | 5,780 | 10.00 | 13.00 | 275.00 | 5,000.00 |
| 1856O | 1,180 | 11.00 | 14.00 | 725.00 | — |
| 1856S | 70 | 90.00 | 285.00 | 2,450.00 | — |
| 1857 | 5,580 | 10.00 | 13.00 | 275.00 | 3,250.00 |
| 1857O | 1,540 | 10.00 | 14.00 | 425.00 | — |
| 1858 | 1,540 | 10.00 | 13.00 | 285.00 | 1,900.00 |
| 1858O | 290 | 13.00 | 40.00 | 575.00 | — |
| 1858S | 60 | 80.00 | 160.00 | 2,500.00 | — |
| 1859 | 430 | 10.00 | 14.00 | 275.00 | 1,500.00 |
| 1859O | 480 | 10.00 | 14.00 | 375.00 | — |
| 1859S | 60 | 65.00 | 185.00 | 3,000.00 | — |
| 1860S | 140 | 22.00 | 55.00 | 1,850.00 | — |

## 1860–1891

|  | Mintage | Good | Fine | Unc. | Proof |
|---|---|---|---|---|---|
| 1860 | 607 | 10.00 | 14.00 | 185.00 | 525.00 |
| 1860O | 40 | 265.00 | 700.00 | 9,000.00 | — |
| 1861 | 1,884 | 10.00 | 13.00 | 150.00 | 550.00 |
| 1861S | 173 | 30.00 | 95.00 | 1,350.00 | — |
| 1862 | 848 | 10.00 | 13.00 | 160.00 | 600.00 |
| 1862S | 181 | 27.00 | 65.00 | 1,275.00 | — |
| 1863 | 14 | 240.00 | 450.00 | 925.00 | 600.00 |
| 1863S | 158 | 23.00 | 42.00 | 1,050.00 | — |
| 1864 | 11 | 170.00 | 335.00 | 850.00 | 675.00 |
| 1864S | 230 | 18.00 | 37.00 | 825.00 | — |
| 1865 | 11 | 210.00 | 430.00 | 975.00 | 700.00 |
| 1865S | 175 | 17.00 | 42.00 | 2,350.00 | — |
| 1866 | 9 | 235.00 | 500.00 | 1,100.00 | 525.00 |
| 1866S | 135 | 30.00 | 60.00 | 750.00 | — |
| 1867 | 7 | 335.00 | 685.00 | 1,200.00 | 650.00 |
| 1867S | 140 | 23.00 | 55.00 | 1,000.00 | — |
| 1868 | 465 | 10.00 | 21.00 | 325.00 | 550.00 |
| 1868S | 260 | 12.00 | 28.00 | 360.00 | — |
| 1869 | 257 | 13.00 | 30.00 | 400.00 | 500.00 |
| 1869S | 450 | 10.00 | 17.00 | 385.00 | — |
| 1870 | 472 | 10.00 | 13.00 | 225.00 | 500.00 |
| 1870S | 50 | 190.00 | 275.00 | 1,200.00 | — |
| 1871 | 908 | 10.00 | 13.00 | 260.00 | 500.00 |
| 1871CC | 20 | 750.00 | 1,750.00 | 16,000.00 | — |
| 1871S | 320 | 17.00 | 45.00 | 525.00 | — |
| 1872 | 2,396 | 10.00 | 12.00 | 150.00 | 500.00 |

| | Mintage in Thousands | Good | Fine | Unc. | Proof |
|---|---|---|---|---|---|
| 1872CC | 24 | 290.00 | 975.00 | 26,000.00 | — |
| 1872S | 190 | 13.00 | 70.00 | 1,300.00 | — |
| 1873 | 1,569 | 9.00 | 13.00 | 150.00 | 500.00 |
| 1873CC No Arrows (Unique) | 12 | — | — | — | — |
| 1973 Arrows at Date | 2,379 | 9 | 20.00 | 475.00 | 1,700.00 |
| 1873CC | 19 | 750.00 | 2,350.00 | 19,000.00 | — |
| 1873S | 455 | 12.00 | 28.00 | 900.00 | — |
| 1874 | 2,941 | 9.00 | 17.50 | 500.00 | 1,700.00 |
| 1874CC | 11 | 1,500.00 | 5,250.00 | 32,500.00 | — |
| 1874S | 240 | 18.00 | 55.00 | 775.00 | — |
| 1875 Arrows at Date Removed | 10,351 | 9.00 | 12.00 | 140.00 | 525.00 |
| 1875CC Under Wreath, All Kinds | 4,645 | 9.00 | 12.00 | 235.00 | — |
| 1875CC In Wreath | — | 9.00 | 14.00 | 210.00 | — |
| 1875S Under Wreath, All Kinds | 9,070 | 9.00 | 12.00 | 140.00 | — |
| 1875S In Wreath | — | 9.00 | 12.00 | 140.00 | — |
| 1876 | 11,461 | 9.00 | 12.00 | 135.00 | 500.00 |
| 1876CC | 8,270 | 9.00 | 12.00 | 210.00 | — |
| 1876S | 10,420 | 9.00 | 13.00 | 145.00 | — |
| 1877 | 7,311 | 9.00 | 12.00 | 140.00 | 500.00 |
| 1877CC | 7,700 | 9.00 | 12.00 | 180.00 | — |
| 1877S | 2,340 | 10.00 | 14.00 | 140.00 | — |
| 1878 | 1,679 | 9.00 | 12.00 | 145.00 | 500.00 |
| 1878CC | 200 | 45.00 | 100.00 | 1,000.00 | — |
| 1879 | 15 | 150.00 | 230.00 | 425.00 | 500.00 |
| 1880 | 37 | 95.00 | 200.00 | 500.00 | 525.00 |
| 1881 | 25 | 110.00 | 190.00 | 400.00 | 500.00 |
| 1882 | 3,911 | 9.00 | 12.00 | 135.00 | 500.00 |
| 1883 | 7,676 | 9.00 | 12.00 | 135.00 | 500.00 |
| 1884 | 3,366 | 9.00 | 12.00 | 135.00 | 500.00 |
| 1884S | 565 | 11.00 | 25.00 | 675.00 | — |
| 1885 | 2,533 | 9.00 | 12.00 | 145.00 | 500.00 |
| 1885S | 44 | 325.00 | 725.00 | 4,850.00 | — |
| 1886 | 6,378 | 9.00 | 12.00 | 135.00 | 500.00 |
| 1886S | 207 | 23.00 | 45.00 | 475.00 | — |
| 1887 | 11,284 | 9.00 | 12.00 | 135.00 | 500.00 |
| 1887S | 4,454 | 9.00 | 12.00 | 150.00 | — |
| 1888 | 5,496 | 9.00 | 12.00 | 135.00 | 500.00 |
| 1888S | 1,720 | 9.00 | 12.00 | 250.00 | — |
| 1889 | 7,381 | 9.00 | 12.00 | 135.00 | 500.00 |
| 1889S | 973 | 9.00 | 22.00 | 425.00 | — |
| 1890 | 9,912 | 9.00 | 12.00 | 135.00 | 500.00 |
| 1890S | 1,423 | 9.00 | 25.00 | 325.00 | — |
| 1891 | 15,311 | 9.00 | 12.00 | 135.00 | 500.00 |
| 1891O | 4,540 | 9.00 | 12.00 | 160.00 | — |
| 1891S | 3,196 | 9.00 | 12.00 | 150.00 | — |

## BARBER OR LIBERTY HEAD TYPE

|  | Mintage in Thousands | Good | Fine | Unc. | Proof |
|---|---|---|---|---|---|
| 1892 | 12,121 | 3.00 | 14.00 | 90.00 | 750.00 |
| 1892O | 3,842 | 6.00 | 25.00 | 145.00 | — |
| 1892S | 991 | 40.00 | 135.00 | 375.00 | — |
| 1893 | 3,341 | 6.00 | 15.00 | 145.00 | 750.00 |
| 1893O | 1,760 | 18.00 | 90.00 | 260.00 | — |
| 1893S | 2,491 | 8.00 | 23.00 | 230.00 | — |
| 1894 | 1,331 | 10.00 | 84.00 | 250.00 | 750.00 |
| 1894O | 720 | 40.00 | 160.00 | 1,100.00 | — |
| 1894S (Very rare) | 24 Pieces | — | — | — | — |
| 1895 | 691 | 60.00 | 280.00 | 625.00 | 750.00 |
| 1895O | 440 | 225.00 | 625.00 | 3,000.00 | — |
| 1895S | 1,120 | 26.00 | 105.00 | 475.00 | — |
| 1896 | 2,001 | 8.00 | 44.00 | 160.00 | 750.00 |
| 1896O | 610 | 50.00 | 215.00 | 800.00 | — |
| 1896S | 575 | 55.00 | 200.00 | 725.00 | — |
| 1897 | 10,869 | 2.00 | 6.00 | 120.00 | 750.00 |
| 1897O | 666 | 45.00 | 225.00 | 775.00 | — |
| 1897S | 1,343 | 11.00 | 72.00 | 425.00 | — |
| 1898 | 16,321 | 2.00 | 7.00 | 100.00 | 750.00 |
| 1898O | 2,130 | 6.00 | 65.00 | 450.00 | — |
| 1898S | 1,703 | 5.00 | 22.00 | 350.00 | — |
| 1899 | 19,581 | 2.00 | 6.00 | 100.00 | 750.00 |
| 1899O | 2,650 | 5.00 | 58.00 | 375.00 | — |
| 1899S | 1,867 | 5.00 | 15.00 | 300.00 | — |
| 1900 | 17,601 | 2.00 | 6.00 | 100.00 | 750.00 |
| 1900O | 2,010 | 7.00 | 75.00 | 525.00 | — |
| 1900S | 5,168 | 3.00 | 9.00 | 185.00 | — |
| 1901 | 18,860 | 2.00 | 5.00 | 100.00 | 750.00 |
| 1901O | 5,620 | 3.00 | 12.00 | 385.00 | — |
| 1901S | 593 | 47.00 | 280.00 | 825.00 | — |
| 1902 | 21,381 | 1.50 | 5.00 | 100.00 | 750.00 |
| 1902O | 4,500 | 3.00 | 13.00 | 350.00 | — |
| 1902S | 2,070 | 5.00 | 44.00 | 350.00 | — |
| 1903 | 19,501 | 1.50 | 4.00 | 110.00 | 750.00 |
| 1903O | 8,180 | 2.00 | 9.00 | 265.00 | — |
| 1903S | 613 | 43.00 | 320.00 | 1,050.00 | — |
| 1904 | 14,601 | 1.50 | 6.00 | 110.00 | 750.00 |
| 1904S | 800 | 30.00 | 120.00 | 625.00 | — |
| 1905 | 14,552 | 1.50 | 4.00 | 100.00 | 750.00 |
| 1905O | 3,400 | 3.00 | 27.00 | 250.00 | — |
| 1905S | 6,855 | 2.00 | 6.00 | 210.00 | — |
| 1906 | 19,958 | 1.50 | 4.00 | 100.00 | 750.00 |
| 1906D | 4,060 | 2.00 | 7.00 | 175.00 | — |
| 1906O | 2,610 | 3.00 | 41.00 | 180.00 | — |
| 1906S | 3,137 | 2.00 | 10.00 | 265.00 | — |
| 1907 | 22,221 | 1.50 | 3.00 | 100.00 | 750.00 |
| 1907D | 4,080 | 2.00 | 9.00 | 325.00 | — |
| 1907O | 5,058 | 2.00 | 25.00 | 225.00 | — |
| 1907S | 3,178 | 2.00 | 10.00 | 350.00 | — |
| 1908 | 10,601 | 1.50 | 3.00 | 100.00 | 750.00 |

|  | Mintage in Thousands | Good | Fine | Unc. | Proof |
|---|---|---|---|---|---|
| 1908D | 7,490 | 1.50 | 5.00 | 145.00 | — |
| 1908O | 1,789 | 3.00 | 36.00 | 285.00 | — |
| 1908S | 3,220 | 2.00 | 9.00 | 300.00 | — |
| 1909 | 10,241 | 1.50 | 4.00 | 100.00 | 750.00 |
| 1909D | 954 | 4.00 | 55.00 | 425.00 | — |
| 1909O | 2,287 | 2.00 | 9.00 | 210.00 | — |
| 1909S | 1,000 | 4.00 | 70.00 | 500.00 | — |
| 1910 | 11,521 | 1.50 | 7.00 | 100.00 | 750.00 |
| 1910D | 3,490 | 2.00 | 7.00 | 210.00 | — |
| 1910S | 1,240 | 3.00 | 45.00 | 375.00 | — |
| 1911 | 18,871 | 2.00 | 3.00 | 100.00 | 750.00 |
| 1911D | 17,209 | 2.00 | 3.00 | 100.00 | — |
| 1911S | 3,520 | 2.00 | 7.00 | 160.00 | — |
| 1912 | 19,351 | 1.50 | 3.00 | 100.00 | 825.00 |
| 1912D | 11,760 | 1.50 | 4.00 | 100.00 | — |
| 1912S | 3,420 | 1.50 | 5.00 | 160.00 | — |
| 1913 | 19,761 | 1.50 | 3.00 | 100.00 | 850.00 |
| 1913S | 510 | 8.00 | 65.00 | 390.00 | — |
| 1914 | 17,361 | 2.00 | 3.00 | 100.00 | 800.00 |
| 1914D | 11,908 | 1.50 | 4.00 | 100.00 | — |
| 1914S | 2,100 | 2.00 | 7.00 | 150.00 | — |
| 1915 | 5,620 | 1.50 | 3.00 | 100.00 | 850.00 |
| 1915S | 960 | 2.00 | 26.00 | 250.00 | — |
| 1916 | 18,490 | 1.50 | 3.00 | 100.00 | — |
| 1916S | 5,820 | 1.50 | 5.00 | 100.00 | — |

## MERCURY TYPE

|  | Mintage in Thousands | Good | Fine | Ex. Fine | Unc. |
|---|---|---|---|---|---|
| 1916 | 22,180 | 2.00 | 5.00 | 10.00 | 35.00 |
| 1916D | 264 | 525.00 | 1,200.00 | 2,600.00 | 5,000.00 |
| 1916S | 10,450 | 4.00 | 7.00 | 17.00 | 45.00 |
| 1917 | 55,230 | 1.00 | 3.00 | 8.00 | 45.00 |
| 1917D | 9,402 | 4.00 | 9.00 | 38.00 | 185.00 |
| 1917S | 27,330 | 1.00 | 3.00 | 10.00 | 90.00 |
| 1918 | 26,680 | 2.00 | 5.00 | 25.00 | 70.00 |
| 1918D | 22,675 | 2.00 | 4.00 | 23.00 | 135.00 |
| 1918S | 19,300 | 2.00 | 4.00 | 14.00 | 130.00 |
| 1919 | 35,740 | 1.00 | 3.00 | 11.00 | 60.00 |
| 1919D | 9,939 | 3.00 | 10.00 | 30.00 | 225.00 |
| 1919S | 8,850 | 3.00 | 8.00 | 30.00 | 225.00 |
| 1920 | 59,030 | 1.00 | 3.00 | 7.00 | 45.00 |
| 1920D | 19,171 | 2.00 | 4.00 | 15.00 | 175.00 |
| 1920S | 13,820 | 2.00 | 4.00 | 14.00 | 160.00 |
| 1921 | 1,230 | 27.00 | 75.00 | 425.00 | 1,050.00 |
| 1921D | 1,080 | 38.00 | 120.00 | 475.00 | 1,150.00 |
| 1923 | 50,130 | 1.00 | 2.00 | 7.00 | 30.00 |
| 1923S | 6,440 | 2.00 | 7.00 | 55.00 | 240.00 |

|  | Mintage in Thousands | Good | Fine | Ex. Fine | Unc. |
|---|---|---|---|---|---|
| 1924 | 24,010 | 1.00 | 3.00 | 12.00 | 50.00 |
| 1924D | 6,810 | 2.00 | 6.00 | 42.00 | 185.00 |
| 1924S | 7,120 | 2.00 | 4.00 | 42.00 | 250.00 |
| 1925 | 25,610 | 1.00 | 3.00 | 8.00 | 35.00 |
| 1925D | 5,117 | 4.00 | 13.00 | 95.00 | 400.00 |
| 1925S | 5,850 | 2.00 | 6.00 | 60.00 | 250.00 |
| 1926 | 32,160 | 1.00 | 2.00 | 6.00 | 35.00 |
| 1926D | 6,828 | 2.00 | 4.00 | 23.00 | 135.00 |
| 1926S | 1,520 | 6.00 | 21.00 | 190.00 | 875.00 |
| 1927 | 28,080 | 1.00 | 2.00 | 6.00 | 30.00 |
| 1927D | 4,812 | 2.00 | 6.00 | 55.00 | 200.00 |
| 1927S | 4,770 | 2.00 | 5.00 | 22.00 | 300.00 |
| 1928 | 19,480 | 1.00 | 2.00 | 5.00 | 30.00 |
| 1928D | 4,161 | 3.00 | 8.00 | 40.00 | 190.00 |
| 1928S | 7,400 | 2.00 | 3.00 | 16.00 | 145.00 |
| 1929 | 25,970 | 1.00 | 2.00 | 5.00 | 20.00 |
| 1929D | 5,034 | 2.00 | 4.00 | 15.00 | 28.00 |
| 1929S | 4,730 | 2.00 | 2.00 | 7.00 | 34.00 |
| 1930 | 6,770 | 1.00 | 2.00 | 7.00 | 30.00 |
| 1930S | 1,843 | 2.00 | 5.00 | 13.00 | 70.00 |
| 1931 | 3,150 | 2.00 | 3.00 | 9.00 | 40.00 |
| 1931D | 1,260 | 5.00 | 10.00 | 30.00 | 80.00 |
| 1931S | 1,800 | 2.00 | 4.00 | 12.00 | 75.00 |
| 1934 | 24,080 | 1.00 | 2.00 | 4.00 | 15.00 |
| 1934D | 6,772 | 1.00 | 3.00 | 10.00 | 32.00 |
| 1935 | 58,830 | 1.00 | 2.00 | 3.00 | 11.00 |
| 1935D | 10,447 | 1.00 | 2.00 | 9.00 | 35.00 |
| 1935S | 15,840 | 1.00 | 2.00 | 4.00 | 24.00 |

|  | Mintage in Thousands | Good | Fine | Ex. Fine | Unc. | Proof |
|---|---|---|---|---|---|---|
| 1936 | 87,504 | 1.00 | 2.00 | 3.00 | 9.00 | 650.00 |
| 1936D | 16,132 | 1.00 | 2.00 | 6.00 | 25.00 | — |
| 1936S | 9,210 | 1.00 | 2.00 | 4.00 | 20.00 | — |
| 1937 | 56,866 | 1.00 | 2.00 | 3.00 | 10.00 | 300.00 |
| 1937D | 14,146 | 1.00 | 2.00 | 4.00 | 21.00 | — |
| 1937S | 9,740 | 1.00 | 2.00 | 3.00 | 15.00 | — |
| 1938 | 22,199 | 1.00 | 2.00 | 3.00 | 14.00 | 190.00 |
| 1938D | 5,537 | 2.00 | 2.00 | 5.00 | 15.00 | — |
| 1938S | 8,090 | 1.00 | 2.00 | 3.00 | 18.00 | — |
| 1939 | 67,749 | 1.00 | 2.00 | 3.00 | 10.00 | 185.00 |
| 1939D | 24,934 | 1.00 | 2.00 | 3.00 | 9.00 | — |
| 1939S | 10,540 | 1.00 | 2.00 | 4.00 | 21.00 | — |
| 1940 | 65,362 | 1.00 | 1.00 | 2.00 | 7.00 | 115.00 |
| 1940D | 21,198 | 1.00 | 1.00 | 2.00 | 8.00 | — |
| 1940S | 21,560 | 1.00 | 1.00 | 2.00 | 9.00 | — |
| 1941 | 175,107 | 1.00 | 1.00 | 2.00 | 6.00 | 115.00 |
| 1941D | 45,634 | 1.00 | 1.00 | 2.00 | 8.00 | — |
| 1941S | 43,090 | 1.00 | 1.00 | 2.00 | 8.00 | — |
| 1942 over 41, All Kinds | 205,432 | 250.00 | 340.00 | 385.00 | 1,950.00 | — |
| 1942 | — | 1.00 | 1.00 | 2.00 | 6.00 | 115.00 |
| 1942D | — | 1.00 | 1.00 | 2.00 | 9.00 | — |
| 1942D 2 over 1 | 60,740 | 260.00 | 375.00 | 500.00 | 2,150.00 | — |
| 1942S | 49,300 | 1.00 | 1.00 | 2.00 | 10.00 | — |
| 1943 | 191,710 | 1.00 | 1.00 | 2.00 | 7.00 | — |
| 1943D | 71,949 | 1.00 | 1.00 | 2.00 | 7.00 | — |

|  | Mintage in Thousands | Good | Fine | Ex. Fine | Unc. |
|---|---|---|---|---|---|
| 1943S | 60,400 | 1.00 | 1.00 | 2.00 | 9.00 |
| 1944 | 231,410 | 1.00 | 1.00 | 2.00 | 7.00 |
| 1944D | 62,224 | 1.00 | 1.00 | 2.00 | 11.00 |
| 1944S | 49,490 | 1.00 | 1.00 | 2.00 | 9.00 |
| 1945 | 159,130 | 1.00 | 1.00 | 2.00 | 6.00 |
| 1945D | 40,245 | 1.00 | 1.00 | 2.00 | 7.00 |
| 1945S | 41,920 | 1.00 | 1.00 | 2.00 | 8.00 |

## ROOSEVELT TYPE

|  | Mintage in Thousands | Fine | Ex. Fine | Unc. |
|---|---|---|---|---|
| 1946 | 255,250 | — | 1.00 | 1.00 |
| 1946D | 61,044 | — | 1.00 | 1.00 |
| 1946S | 27,900 | — | 1.00 | 1.00 |
| 1947 | 121,520 | — | 1.00 | 2.00 |
| 1947D | 46,835 | — | 1.00 | 3.00 |
| 1947S | 34,840 | — | 1.00 | 2.00 |
| 1948 | 74,950 | — | 1.00 | 3.00 |
| 1948D | 52,841 | — | 1.00 | 3.00 |
| 1948S | 35,520 | — | 1.00 | 2.00 |
| 1949 | 30,940 | 1.00 | 2.00 | 13.00 |
| 1949D | 26,034 | 1.00 | 1.00 | 7.00 |
| 1949S | 13,510 | 1.00 | 4.00 | 23.00 |
| 1950 | 50,182 | — | 1.00 | 3.00 |
| 1950D | 46,803 | — | 1.00 | 2.00 |
| 1950S | 20,440 | 1.00 | 1.00 | 13.00 |
| 1951 | 103,938 | — | 1.00 | 1.00 |
| 1951D | 56,529 | — | 1.00 | 1.00 |
| 1951S | 31,630 | 1.00 | 1.00 | 10.00 |
| 1952 | 99,122 | — | 1.00 | 1.00 |
| 1952D | 122,100 | — | 1.00 | 1.00 |
| 1952S | 44,420 | 1.00 | 1.00 | 5.00 |
| 1953 | 53,619 | — | 1.00 | 1.00 |
| 1953D | 136,433 | — | 1.00 | 1.00 |
| 1953S | 39,180 | — | 1.00 | 1.00 |
| 1954 | 114,244 | — | 1.00 | 1.00 |
| 1954D | 106,397 | — | 1.00 | 1.00 |
| 1954S | 22,860 | — | 1.00 | 1.00 |
| 1955 | 12,828 | — | 1.00 | 1.00 |
| 1955D | 13,959 | — | 1.00 | 1.00 |
| 1955S | 18,510 | — | 1.00 | 1.00 |
| 1956 | 109,309 | — | 1.00 | 1.00 |
| 1956D | 108,015 | — | 1.00 | 1.00 |
| 1957 | 167,408 | — | 1.00 | 1.00 |
| 1957D | 133,354 | — | 1.00 | 1.00 |
| 1958 | 32,786 | — | 1.00 | 1.00 |
| 1958D | 136,565 | — | 1.00 | 1.00 |
| 1959 | 86,929 | — | 1.00 | 1.00 |
| 1959D | 164,920 | — | 1.00 | 1.00 |

|  | Mintage in Thousands | Fine | Ex. Fine | Unc. |
|---|---|---|---|---|
| 1960 | 72,082 | — | 1.00 | 1.00 |
| 1960D | 200,160 | — | 1.00 | 1.00 |
| 1961 | 96,758 | — | 1.00 | 1.00 |
| 1961D | 209,147 | — | 1.00 | 1.00 |
| 1962 | 75,668 | — | 1.00 | 1.00 |
| 1962D | 334,948 | — | 1.00 | 1.00 |
| 1963 | 126,726 | — | 1.00 | 1.00 |
| 1963D | 421,477 | — | 1.00 | 1.00 |
| 1964 | 933,311 | — | 1.00 | 1.00 |
| 1964D | 1,357,517 | — | 1.00 | 1.00 |
| 1965 | 1,652,141 | — | — | — |
| 1966 | 1,382,735 | — | — | — |
| 1967 | 2,244,007 | — | — | — |
| 1968 | 424,470 | — | — | — |
| 1968D | 480,748 | — | — | — |
| 1968S Proof only | 3,042 | — | — | — |
| 1969 | 145,790 | — | — | — |
| 1969D | 563,324 | — | — | — |
| 1969S Proof only | 2,935 | — | — | — |
| 1970 | 345,570 | — | — | — |
| 1970D | 754,942 | — | — | — |
| 1970S Proof only | 2,633 | — | — | — |
| 1971 | 162,690 | — | — | — |
| 1971D | 377,914 | — | — | — |
| 1971S Proof only | 3,224 | — | — | — |
| 1972 | 431,540 | — | — | — |
| 1972D | 330,290 | — | — | — |
| 1972S Proof only | 3,268 | — | — | — |
| 1973 | 315,670 | — | — | — |
| 1973D | 455,032 | — | — | — |
| 1973S Proof only | 2,770 | — | — | — |
| 1974 | 470,248 | — | — | — |
| 1974D | 521,083 | — | — | — |
| 1974S Proof only | 2,617 | — | — | — |
| 1975 | 585,678 | — | — | — |
| 1975D | 313,705 | — | — | — |
| 1975S Proof only | 2,909 | — | — | — |
| 1976 P-D | 1,263,983 | — | — | — |
| 1976S Proof only | 4,150 | — | — | — |
| 1977 P-D | 1,173,537 | — | — | — |
| 1977S Proof only | 3,251 | — | — | — |
| 1978 P-D | 946,828 | — | — | — |
| 1978S Proof only | 3,128 | — | — | — |
| 1979 P&D | 706,361 | — | — | — |
| 1979S Proof only | 3,677 | — | — | — |
| 1979S Type Two, Proof only, Sharp | — | — | — | — |
| 1980 P&D | 1,554,524 | — | — | — |
| 1980S Proof only | — | — | — | — |
| 1981 P&D | 1,388,934 | — | — | — |
| 1981S Proof only | — | — | — | — |
| 1982 P&D | 1,062,188 | — | — | 1.00 |
| 1982S Proof only | — | — | — | — |
| 1983 P&D | — | — | — | — |
| 1983S Proof only | — | — | — | — |
| 1984 P&D | — | — | — | — |
| 1984S Proof only | — | — | — | — |

## 32.
## TWENTY-CENT PIECES—
## 1875–1878

|  | Mintage in Thousands | Good | Fine | V. Fine | Unc. | Proof |
|---|---|---|---|---|---|---|
| 1875 | 40 | 55.00 | 80.00 | 115.00 | 650.00 | 2,850.00 |
| 1875CC | 133 | 55.00 | 85.00 | 130.00 | 725.00 | — |
| 1875S | 1,155 | 55.00 | 80.00 | 110.00 | 525.00 | — |
| 1876 | 16 | 100.00 | 165.00 | 225.00 | 675.00 | 2,850.00 |
| 1876CC (14 known) | 10 | — | — | — | — | — |
| 1877 | 1 | — | — | 1,575.00 | — | 3,500.00 |
| 1878 | 1 | — | — | 1,250.00 | — | 3,850.00 |

## 33.
## QUARTER-DOLLARS—
## 1796–Date

**DRAPED BUST TYPE**

1796                    1804–1807

|  | Mintage in Thousands | Good | Fine | Unc. |
|---|---|---|---|---|
| 1796 | 6 | 4,150.00 | 8,500.00 | 26,500.00 |
| 1804 | 7 | 1,200.00 | 2,150.00 | 45,000.00 |
| 1805 | 121 | 200.00 | 425.00 | 5,000.00 |
| 1806 over 5, All Kinds | 206 | 210.00 | 450.00 | 6,750.00 |
| 1806 | — | 200.00 | 400.00 | 4,850.00 |
| 1807 | 221 | 200.00 | 425.00 | 4,850.00 |

## LIBERTY HEAD TYPE

1815–1828  1831–1838

|  | Mintage in Thousands | Good | Fine | Unc. |
|---|---|---|---|---|
| 1815 | 89 | 55.00 | 135.00 | 2,450.00 |
| 1818 over 15, All Kinds | 361 | 55.00 | 135.00 | 2,450.00 |
| 1818 | — | 55.00 | 135.00 | 2,450.00 |
| 1819 | 144 | 55.00 | 125.00 | 2,450.00 |
| 1820 | 127 | 55.00 | 125.00 | 2,450.00 |
| 1821 | 217 | 55.00 | 125.00 | 2,450.00 |
| 1822, All Kinds | 64 | 60.00 | 160.00 | 3,000.00 |
| 1822 25 over 50c | — | 1,375.00 | 4,250.00 | 35,000.00 |
| 1823 over 22, All Kinds | 18 | 7,000.00 | 16,500.00 | — |
| 1824 over 2 | — | 90.00 | 260.00 | 6,000.00 |
| 1825 over 22, All Kinds | 168 | 75.00 | 165.00 | 2,750.00 |
| 1825 over 23 | — | 55.00 | 110.00 | 2,350.00 |
| 1825 over 24 | — | 55.00 | 110.00 | 2,350.00 |
| 1827 Original, curled base 2 in 25c, All Kinds | 4 | — | — | — |
| 1827 Restrike, square base 2 in 25c | — | — | — | — |
| 1828, All Kinds | 102 | 55.00 | 110.00 | 2,900.00 |
| 1828 25 over 50c | — | 135.00 | 450.00 | 8,000.00 |
| 1831 | 398 | 45.00 | 60.00 | 900.00 |
| 1832 | 320 | 45.00 | 60.00 | 900.00 |
| 1833 | 156 | 48.00 | 65.00 | 1,375.00 |
| 1834 | 286 | 45.00 | 60.00 | 900.00 |
| 1835 | 1,952 | 45.00 | 60.00 | 900.00 |
| 1836 | 472 | 45.00 | 60.00 | 900.00 |
| 1837 | 252 | 45.00 | 60.00 | 900.00 |
| 1838 | 832 | 45.00 | 60.00 | 950.00 |

# LIBERTY SEATED TYPE

### 1838–1865  1866–1891

| | Mintage in Thousands | Good | Fine | Unc. |
|---|---:|---:|---:|---:|
| 1838 No Drapery | (included above) | 15.00 | 30.00 | 1,450.00 |
| 1839 No Drapery | 491 | 16.00 | 30.00 | 1,450.00 |
| 1840O No Drapery | 390 | 15.00 | 40.00 | 1,550.00 |
| 1840 Drapery | 188 | 18.00 | 55.00 | 950.00 |
| 1840O Drapery | (included above) | 20.00 | 60.00 | 1,100.00 |
| 1841 | 120 | 45.00 | 80.00 | 800.00 |
| 1841O | 452 | 15.00 | 40.00 | 775.00 |
| 1842 | 88 | 65.00 | 140.00 | 1,050.00 |
| 1842O | 769 | 15.00 | 30.00 | 1,250.00 |
| 1843 | 646 | 15.00 | 30.00 | 500.00 |
| 1843O | 968 | 17.00 | 40.00 | 1,650.00 |
| 1844 | 421 | 15.00 | 30.00 | 500.00 |
| 1844O | 740 | 15.00 | 30.00 | 1,150.00 |
| 1845 | 922 | 16.00 | 27.00 | 500.00 |
| 1846 | 510 | 15.00 | 28.00 | 525.00 |
| 1847 | 734 | 15.00 | 28.00 | 500.00 |
| 1847O | 368 | 22.00 | 55.00 | 2,150.00 |
| 1848 | 146 | 25.00 | 75.00 | 1,250.00 |
| 1849 | 340 | 15.00 | 40.00 | 800.00 |
| 1849O | — | 360.00 | 800.00 | 7,500.00 |
| 1850 | 191 | 25.00 | 60.00 | 825.00 |
| 1850O | 412 | 18.00 | 55.00 | 1,375.00 |
| 1851 | 160 | 35.00 | 80.00 | 875.00 |
| 1851O | 88 | 150.00 | 400.00 | 5,000.00 |
| 1852 | 177 | 38.00 | 80.00 | 475.00 |
| 1852O | 96 | 150.00 | 350.00 | 10,000.00 |
| 1853 No Arrows or Rays, Recut Date | 44 | 235.00 | 475.00 | 2,500.00 |

| | Mintage in Thousands | Good | Fine | Unc. | Proof |
|---|---:|---:|---:|---:|---:|
| 1853 Arrows and Rays | 15,210 | 15.00 | 30.00 | 1,250.00 | — |
| 1853O | 1,332 | 15.00 | 35.00 | 3,500.00 | — |
| 1854 Arrows, no Rays | 12,380 | 15.00 | 30.00 | 550.00 | 15,000.00 |
| 1854O | 1,484 | 15.00 | 30.00 | 850.00 | — |
| 1855 | 2,857 | 15.00 | 30.00 | 3,250.00 | 17,500.00 |
| 1855O | 176 | 35.00 | 90.00 | 2,750.00 | — |
| 1855S | 396 | 30.00 | 60.00 | 2,250.00 | — |
| 1856 No Arrows | 7,264 | 15.00 | 30.00 | 350.00 | 7,000.00 |
| 1856O | 968 | 15.00 | 30.00 | 950.00 | — |
| 1856S | 286 | 45.00 | 80.00 | 2,200.00 | — |
| 1857 | 9,644 | 15.00 | 30.00 | 350.00 | 6,250.00 |
| 1857O | 1,180 | 15.00 | 30.00 | 1,250.00 | — |

|  | Mintage in Thousands | Good | Fine | Unc. | Proof |
|---|---|---|---|---|---|
| 1857S | 82 | 45.00 | 165.00 | 2,500.00 | — |
| 1858 | 7,368 | 15.00 | 25.00 | 325.00 | 2,250.00 |
| 1858O | 520 | 15.00 | 30.00 | 1,400.00 | — |
| 1858S | 121 | 35.00 | 135.00 | 6,000.00 | — |
| 1859 | 1,344 | 15.00 | 25.00 | 450.00 | 1,900.00 |
| 1859O | 260 | 16.00 | 35.00 | 1,350.00 | — |
| 1859S | 80 | 80.00 | 175.00 | 2,850.00 | — |
| 1860 | 805 | 15.00 | 25.00 | 425.00 | 1,850.00 |
| 1860O | 388 | 15.00 | 35.00 | 1,150.00 | — |
| 1860S | 56 | 140.00 | 350.00 | 8,500.00 | — |
| 1861 | 4,855 | 15.00 | 25.00 | 325.00 | 1,850.00 |
| 1861S | 96 | 45.00 | 165.00 | 5,000.00 | — |
| 1862 | 933 | 15.00 | 25.00 | 325.00 | 1,850.00 |
| 1862S | 67 | 50.00 | 110.00 | 2,225.00 | — |
| 1863 | 192 | 25.00 | 55.00 | 485.00 | 1,850.00 |
| 1864 | 94 | 50.00 | 90.00 | 625.00 | 1,850.00 |
| 1864S | 20 | 250.00 | 575.00 | 6,500.00 | — |
| 1865 | 59 | 55.00 | 95.00 | 650.00 | 1,850.00 |
| 1865S | 41 | 70.00 | 165.00 | 1,150.00 | — |
| 1866 | 18 | 300.00 | 500.00 | 1,550.00 | 850.00 |
| 1866S | 28 | 160.00 | 460.00 | 2,500.00 | — |
| 1867 | 21 | 160.00 | 325.00 | 825.00 | 875.00 |
| 1867S | 48 | 115.00 | 325.00 | 2,250.00 | — |
| 1868 | 30 | 95.00 | 175.00 | 725.00 | 900.00 |
| 1868S | 96 | 65.00 | 135.00 | 2,000.00 | — |
| 1869 | 17 | 200.00 | 325.00 | 1,350.00 | 850.00 |
| 1869S | 76 | 75.00 | 165.00 | 2,350.00 | — |
| 1870 | 87 | 40.00 | 95.00 | 775.00 | 850.00 |
| 1870CC | 8 | 1,750.00 | 5,850.00 | 25,000.00 | — |
| 1871 | 119 | 30.00 | 55.00 | 525.00 | 825.00 |
| 1871CC | 11 | 1,350.00 | 3,750.00 | 27,500.00 | — |
| 1871S | 31 | 250.00 | 425.00 | 2,400.00 | — |
| 1872 | 183 | 25.00 | 50.00 | 475.00 | 800.00 |
| 1872CC | 23 | 450.00 | 1,050.00 | 11,500.00 | — |
| 1872S | 83 | 675.00 | 925.00 | 6,000.00 | — |
| 1873 No Arrows | 213 | 30.00 | 55.00 | 400.00 | 800.00 |
| 1873 Arrows | 1,272 | 15.00 | 31.00 | 850.00 | 2,750.00 |
| 1873CC | 12 | 1,350.00 | 3,500.00 | 37,500.00 | — |
| 1873S | 156 | 20.00 | 55.00 | 1,275.00 | — |
| 1874 | 472 | 15.00 | 30.00 | 825.00 | 2,750.00 |
| 1874S | 392 | 16.00 | 55.00 | 875.00 | — |
| 1875 Arrows Removed | 4,294 | 15.00 | 25.00 | 250.00 | 800.00 |
| 1875CC | 140 | 55.00 | 145.00 | 1,500.00 | — |
| 1875S | 680 | 27.00 | 65.00 | 650.00 | — |
| 1876 | 17,817 | 15.00 | 25.00 | 250.00 | 775.00 |
| 1876CC | 4,944 | 15.00 | 25.00 | 375.00 | — |
| 1876S | 8,596 | 15.00 | 25.00 | 250.00 | — |
| 1877 | 10,912 | 15.00 | 25.00 | 250.00 | 800.00 |
| 1877CC | 4,192 | 15.00 | 25.00 | 350.00 | — |
| 1877S | 8,996 | 15.00 | 25.00 | 250.00 | — |
| 1878 | 2,261 | 15.00 | 25.00 | 250.00 | 800.00 |
| 1878CC | 996 | 20.00 | 50.00 | 475.00 | — |
| 1878S | 140 | 90.00 | 225.00 | 1,350.00 | — |
| 1879 | 15 | 110.00 | 185.00 | 475.00 | 725.00 |
| 1880 | 15 | 110.00 | 185.00 | 500.00 | 725.00 |
| 1881 | 13 | 120.00 | 225.00 | 525.00 | 725.00 |
| 1882 | 16 | 125.00 | 200.00 | 535.00 | 725.00 |
| 1883 | 15 | 120.00 | 190.00 | 525.00 | 725.00 |
| 1884 | 9 | 225.00 | 325.00 | 565.00 | 725.00 |

|  | Mintage in Thousands | Good | Fine | Unc. | Proof |
|---|---:|---:|---:|---:|---:|
| 1885 | 15 | 125.00 | 210.00 | 525.00 | 750.00 |
| 1886 | 6 | 250.00 | 400.00 | 725.00 | 750.00 |
| 1887 | 11 | 200.00 | 315.00 | 625.00 | 725.00 |
| 1888 | 11 | 185.00 | 285.00 | 585.00 | 725.00 |
| 1888S | 1,216 | 15.00 | 25.00 | 275.00 | — |
| 1889 | 13 | 125.00 | 195.00 | 525.00 | 725.00 |
| 1890 | 81 | 50.00 | 80.00 | 475.00 | 725.00 |
| 1891 | 3,921 | 15.00 | 25.00 | 250.00 | 750.00 |
| 1891O | 68 | 120.00 | 265.00 | 2,650.00 | — |
| 1891S | 2,216 | 15.00 | 27.00 | 250.00 | |

## BARBER OR LIBERTY HEAD TYPE

|  | Mintage in Thousands | Good | Fine | Ex. Fine | Unc. | Proof |
|---|---:|---:|---:|---:|---:|---:|
| 1892 | 8,237 | 5.00 | 20.00 | 75.00 | 175.00 | 800.00 |
| 1892O | 2,640 | 6.00 | 26.00 | 80.00 | 275.00 | — |
| 1892S | 964 | 15.00 | 55.00 | 125.00 | 425.00 | — |
| 1893 | 5,445 | 5.00 | 21.00 | 75.00 | 210.00 | 800.00 |
| 1893O | 3,396 | 5.00 | 25.00 | 80.00 | 275.00 | — |
| 1893S | 1,455 | 8.00 | 40.00 | 125.00 | 450.00 | — |
| 1894 | 3,433 | 5.00 | 23.00 | 80.00 | 225.00 | 800.00 |
| 1894O | 2,852 | 5.00 | 33.00 | 95.00 | 350.00 | — |
| 1894S | 2,649 | 6.00 | 28.00 | 95.00 | 300.00 | — |
| 1895 | 4,441 | 5.00 | 22.00 | 75.00 | 235.00 | 800.00 |
| 1895O | 2,816 | 7.00 | 35.00 | 100.00 | 400.00 | — |
| 1895S | 1,765 | 8.00 | 40.00 | 100.00 | 385.00 | — |
| 1896 | 3,875 | 5.00 | 22.00 | 75.00 | 235.00 | 800.00 |
| 1896O | 1,484 | 8.00 | 70.00 | 350.00 | 900.00 | — |
| 1896S | 188 | 280.00 | 575.00 | 1,675.00 | 4,250.00 | |
| 1897 | 8,141 | 4.00 | 22.00 | 75.00 | 175.00 | 800.00 |
| 1897O | 1,415 | 8.00 | 75.00 | 350.00 | 775.00 | — |
| 1897S | 542 | 16.00 | 150.00 | 350.00 | 900.00 | — |
| 1898 | 11,101 | 4.00 | 19.00 | 75.00 | 175.00 | 800.00 |
| 1898O | 1,868 | 7.00 | 55.00 | 230.00 | 450.00 | — |
| 1898S | 1,021 | 5.00 | 40.00 | 80.00 | 345.00 | — |
| 1899 | 12,625 | 4.00 | 19.00 | 75.00 | 170.00 | 800.00 |
| 1899O | 2,644 | 5.00 | 30.00 | 100.00 | 400.00 | — |
| 1899S | 708 | 9.00 | 45.00 | 110.00 | 450.00 | — |
| 1900 | 10,017 | 5.00 | 19.00 | 70.00 | 170.00 | 800.00 |
| 1900O | 3,416 | 7.00 | 50.00 | 140.00 | 550.00 | — |
| 1900S | 1,859 | 6.00 | 36.00 | 75.00 | 400.00 | — |
| 1901 | 8,893 | 6.00 | 20.00 | 70.00 | 170.00 | 800.00 |
| 1901O | 1,612 | 24.00 | 85.00 | 350.00 | 775.00 | — |
| 1901S | 73 | 1,750.00 | 4,500.00 | 7,500.00 | 15,000.00 | — |
| 1902 | 12,198 | 4.00 | 16.00 | 65.00 | 170.00 | 800.00 |

|        | Mintage in Thousands | Good   | Fine    | Ex. Fine | Unc.    | Proof  |
|--------|---------------------|--------|---------|----------|---------|--------|
| 1902O  | 4,748               | 5.00   | 35.00   | 100.00   | 400.00  | —      |
| 1902S  | 1,525               | 9.00   | 36.00   | 85.00    | 375.00  | —      |
| 1903   | 9,670               | 4.00   | 18.00   | 65.00    | 175.00  | 800.00 |
| 1903O  | 3,500               | 6.00   | 32.00   | 85.00    | 425.00  | —      |
| 1903S  | 1,036               | 8.00   | 38.00   | 100.00   | 450.00  | —      |
| 1904   | 9,589               | 4.00   | 18.00   | 65.00    | 170.00  | 800.00 |
| 1904O  | 2,456               | 7.00   | 45.00   | 175.00   | 775.00  | —      |
| 1905   | 4,968               | 4.00   | 24.00   | 65.00    | 185.00  | 800.00 |
| 1905O  | 1,230               | 10.00  | 65.00   | 200.00   | 475.00  | —      |
| 1905S  | 1,884               | 7.00   | 36.00   | 90.00    | 325.00  | —      |
| 1906   | 3,656               | 4.00   | 18.00   | 70.00    | 160.00  | 800.00 |
| 1906D  | 3,280               | 4.00   | 24.00   | 70.00    | 240.00  | —      |
| 1906O  | 2,056               | 4.00   | 32.00   | 85.00    | 200.00  | —      |
| 1907   | 7,193               | 4.00   | 18.00   | 65.00    | 170.00  | 800.00 |
| 1907D  | 3,484               | 4.00   | 24.00   | 80.00    | 275.00  | —      |
| 1907O  | 4,560               | 4.00   | 18.00   | 65.00    | 225.00  | —      |
| 1907S  | 1,360               | 6.00   | 37.00   | 100.00   | 450.00  | —      |
| 1908   | 4,233               | 4.00   | 19.00   | 65.00    | 205.00  | 800.00 |
| 1908D  | 5,788               | 4.00   | 18.00   | 70.00    | 225.00  | —      |
| 1908O  | 6,244               | 4.00   | 18.00   | 70.00    | 190.00  | —      |
| 1908S  | 784                 | 10.00  | 65.00   | 215.00   | 700.00  | —      |
| 1909   | 9,269               | 4.00   | 18.00   | 65.00    | 170.00  | 800.00 |
| 1909D  | 5,114               | 4.00   | 18.00   | 65.00    | 190.00  | —      |
| 1909O  | 712                 | 12.00  | 75.00   | 265.00   | 750.00  | —      |
| 1909S  | 1,348               | 4.00   | 28.00   | 65.00    | 285.00  | —      |
| 1910   | 2,245               | 4.00   | 23.00   | 65.00    | 190.00  | 800.00 |
| 1910D  | 1,500               | 5.00   | 36.00   | 100.00   | 350.00  | —      |
| 1911   | 3,721               | 4.00   | 18.00   | 75.00    | 170.00  | 800.00 |
| 1911D  | 934                 | 6.00   | 70.00   | 265.00   | 650.00  | —      |
| 1911S  | 988                 | 6.00   | 45.00   | 130.00   | 375.00  | —      |
| 1912   | 4,401               | 5.00   | 18.00   | 65.00    | 170.00  | 900.00 |
| 1912S  | 708                 | 6.00   | 40.00   | 100.00   | 385.00  | —      |
| 1913   | 485                 | 10.00  | 60.00   | 360.00   | 850.00  | 900.00 |
| 1913D  | 1,451               | 6.00   | 30.00   | 80.00    | 260.00  | —      |
| 1913S  | 40                  | 485.00 | 1,800.00| 3,300.00 | 4,750.00| —      |
| 1914   | 6,245               | 4.00   | 16.00   | 65.00    | 170.00  | 850.00 |
| 1914D  | 3,046               | 4.00   | 16.00   | 65.00    | 170.00  | —      |
| 1914S  | 264                 | 50.00  | 135.00  | 370.00   | 850.00  | —      |
| 1915   | 3,480               | 4.00   | 17.00   | 65.00    | 170.00  | 900.00 |
| 1915D  | 3,694               | 4.00   | 17.00   | 65.00    | 170.00  | —      |
| 1915S  | 708                 | 4.00   | 25.00   | 75.00    | 250.00  | —      |
| 1916   | 1,788               | 4.00   | 17.00   | 60.00    | 170.00  | —      |
| 1916D  | 6,541               | 4.00   | 16.00   | 60.00    | 170.00  | —      |

## STANDING LIBERTY TYPE

**1916–1917**       **1917–1930**

|  | Mintage in Thousands | Good | Fine | Ex. Fine | Unc. |
|---|---|---|---|---|---|
| 1916 | 52 | 1,450.00 | 2,200.00 | 3,100.00 | 5,250.00 |
| 1917 Type 1 | 8,792 | 15.00 | 35.00 | 65.00 | 185.00 |
| 1917D | 1,509 | 17.00 | 35.00 | 85.00 | 235.00 |
| 1917S | 1,952 | 16.00 | 37.00 | 125.00 | 260.00 |
| 1917 Type 2 | 13,880 | 14.00 | 21.00 | 40.00 | 135.00 |
| 1917D | 6,224 | 28.00 | 60.00 | 90.00 | 185.00 |
| 1917S | 5,552 | 24.00 | 40.00 | 75.00 | 175.00 |
| 1918 | 14,240 | 15.00 | 22.00 | 47.00 | 140.00 |
| 1918D | 7,380 | 28.00 | 43.00 | 80.00 | 225.00 |
| 1918S, All Kinds | 11,072 | 17.00 | 30.00 | 45.00 | 190.00 |
| 1918S over 7 | — | 1,200.00 | 1,850.00 | 4,500.00 | 13,500.00 |
| 1919 | 11,324 | 29.00 | 43.00 | 65.00 | 140.00 |
| 1919D | 1,944 | 80.00 | 125.00 | 285.00 | 675.00 |
| 1919S | 1,836 | 80.00 | 130.00 | 340.00 | 750.00 |
| 1920 | 27,860 | 15.00 | 20.00 | 40.00 | 130.00 |
| 1920D | 3,586 | 45.00 | 65.00 | 100.00 | 285.00 |
| 1920S | 6,380. | 21.00 | 28.00 | 55.00 | 275.00 |
| 1921 | 1,916 | 100.00 | 135.00 | 265.00 | 450.00 |
| 1923 | 9,716 | 15.00 | 25.00 | 37.00 | 125.00 |
| 1923S | 1,360 | 180.00 | 250.00 | 425.00 | 625.00 |
| 1924 | 10,920 | 13.00 | 21.00 | 35.00 | 125.00 |
| 1924D | 3,112 | 36.00 | 55.00 | 90.00 | 150.00 |
| 1924S | 2,860 | 22.00 | 32.00 | 90.00 | 350.00 |
| 1925 | 12,280 | 3.00 | 6.00 | 30.00 | 125.00 |
| 1926 | 11,316 | 3.00 | 6.00 | 30.00 | 125.00 |
| 1926D | 1,716 | 6.00 | 14.00 | 50.00 | 135.00 |
| 1926S | 2,700 | 3.00 | 13.00 | 100.00 | 350.00 |
| 1927 | 11,912 | 3.00 | 6.00 | 30.00 | 125.00 |
| 1927D | 976 | 7.00 | 19.00 | 85.00 | 150.00 |
| 1927S | 396 | 10.00 | 50.00 | 1,000.00 | 3,650.00 |
| 1928 | 6,336 | 3.00 | 6.00 | 30.00 | 125.00 |
| 1928D | 1,628 | 4.00 | 7.00 | 40.00 | 135.00 |
| 1928S | 2,644 | 3.00 | 7.00 | 30.00 | 135.00 |
| 1929 | 11,140 | 3.00 | 6.00 | 30.00 | 125.00 |
| 1929D | 1,358 | 4.00 | 7.00 | 30.00 | 135.00 |
| 1929S | 1,764 | 3.00 | 6.00 | 30.00 | 135.00 |
| 1930 | 5,632 | 3.00 | 6.00 | 30.00 | 125.00 |
| 1930S | 1,556 | 3.00 | 6.00 | 30.00 | 125.00 |

## WASHINGTON HEAD TYPE

|  | Mintage in Thousands | V. Good | Fine | Ex. Fine | Unc. | Proof |
|---|---|---|---|---|---|---|
| 1932 | 5,404 | 4.00 | 5.00 | 9.00 | 30.00 | — |
| 1932D | 437 | 50.00 | 57.00 | 160.00 | 550.00 | — |
| 1932S | 408 | 53.00 | 55.00 | 85.00 | 290.00 | — |
| 1934 | 31,912 | 2.00 | 3.00 | 4.00 | 23.00 | — |
| 1934D | 3,527 | 5.00 | 7.00 | 19.00 | 195.00 | — |
| 1935 | 32,484 | 2.00 | 3.00 | 5.00 | 21.00 | — |
| 1935D | 5,780 | 4.00 | 5.00 | 20.00 | 205.00 | — |
| 1935S | 5,660 | 3.00 | 5.00 | 15.00 | 59.00 | — |
| 1936 | 41,304 | 2.00 | 3.00 | 5.00 | 20.00 | 675.00 |

|  | Mintage in Thousands | V. Good | Fine | Ex. Fine | Unc. | Proof |
|---|---|---|---|---|---|---|
| 1936D | 5,374 | 4.00 | 5.00 | 42.00 | 325.00 | — |
| 1936S | 3,828 | 3.00 | 4.00 | 15.00 | 56.00 | — |
| 1937 | 19,702 | 3.00 | 4.00 | 6.00 | 23.00 | 285.00 |
| 1937D | 7,190 | 3.00 | 4.00 | 13.00 | 40.00 | — |
| 1937S | 1,652 | 4.00 | 5.00 | 21.00 | 100.00 | — |
| 1938 | 9,480 | 4.00 | 5.00 | 15.00 | 59.00 | 130.00 |
| 1938S | 2,832 | 5.00 | 5.00 | 15.00 | 59.00 | — |
| 1939 | 33,549 | 3.00 | 3.00 | 4.00 | 16.00 | 130.00 |
| 1939D | 7,992 | 3.00 | 4.00 | 9.00 | 32.00 | — |
| 1939S | 2,628 | 4.00 | 4.00 | 15.00 | 65.00 | — |
| 1940 | 35,715 | 2.00 | 3.00 | 4.00 | 12.00 | 125.00 |
| 1940D | 2,798 | 3.00 | 7.00 | 18.00 | 63.00 | — |
| 1940S | 8,244 | 3.00 | 5.00 | 7.00 | 16.00 | — |
| 1941 | 79,047 | 1.00 | 2.00 | 3.00 | 8.00 | 70.00 |
| 1941D | 16,715 | 1.00 | 2.00 | 4.00 | 20.00 | — |
| 1941S | 16,080 | 1.00 | 2.00 | 3.00 | 16.00 | — |
| 1942 | 102,117 | 1.00 | 2.00 | 3.00 | 5.00 | 70.00 |
| 1942D | 17,487 | 1.00 | 2.00 | 3.00 | 10.00 | — |
| 1942S | 19,384 | 1.00 | 2.00 | 8.00 | 50.00 | — |
| 1943 | 99,700 | 1.00 | 2.00 | 3.00 | 5.00 | — |
| 1943D | 16,096 | 1.00 | 2.00 | 4.00 | 20.00 | — |
| 1943S | 21,700 | 1.00 | 2.00 | 6.00 | 25.00 | — |
| 1944 | 104,956 | 1.00 | 2.00 | 3.00 | 4.00 | — |
| 1944D | 14,601 | 1.00 | 2.00 | 3.00 | 11.00 | — |
| 1944S | 12,560 | 1.00 | 2.00 | 3.00 | 12.00 | — |
| 1945 | 74,372 | 1.00 | 2.00 | 3.00 | 4.00 | — |
| 1945D | 12,342 | 1.00 | 2.00 | 3.00 | 10.00 | — |
| 1945S | 17,004 | 1.00 | 2.00 | 3.00 | 6.00 | — |
| 1946 | 53,436 | 1.00 | 2.00 | 2.00 | 5.00 | — |
| 1946D | 9,073 | 1.00 | 2.00 | 2.00 | 4.00 | — |
| 1946S | 4,204 | 1.00 | 2.00 | 2.00 | 4.00 | — |
| 1947 | 22,556 | 1.00 | 2.00 | 3.00 | 7.00 | — |
| 1947D | 15,338 | 1.00 | 2.00 | 2.00 | 6.00 | — |
| 1947S | 5,532 | 1.00 | 2.00 | 2.00 | 5.00 | — |
| 1948 | 35,196 | 1.00 | 2.00 | 2.00 | 4.00 | — |
| 1948D | 16,767 | 1.00 | 2.00 | 2.00 | 5.00 | — |
| 1948S | 15,960 | 1.00 | 2.00 | 2.00 | 5.00 | — |
| 1949 | 9,312 | 1.00 | 2.00 | 6.00 | 19.00 | — |
| 1949D | 10,068 | 1.00 | 2.00 | 3.00 | 11.00 | — |
| 1950 | 24,972 | 1.00 | 2.00 | 3.00 | 5.00 | 50.00 |
| 1950D | 21,076 | 1.00 | 2.00 | 3.00 | 5.00 | — |
| 1950S | 10,284 | 1.00 | 2.00 | 3.00 | 7.00 | — |
| 1951 | 43,506 | 1.00 | 1.00 | 2.00 | 5.00 | 40.00 |
| 1951D | 35,355 | 1.00 | 1.00 | 2.00 | 3.00 | — |
| 1951S | 9,048 | 1.00 | 1.00 | 3.00 | 13.00 | — |
| 1952 | 38,862 | 1.00 | 1.00 | 2.00 | 3.00 | 35.00 |
| 1952D | 49,795 | 1.00 | 1.00 | 2.00 | 3.00 | — |
| 1952S | 13,708 | 1.00 | 1.00 | 3.00 | 9.00 | — |
| 1953 | 18,665 | 1.00 | 1.00 | 2.00 | 3.00 | 24.00 |
| 1953D | 56,112 | 1.00 | 1.00 | 2.00 | 2.00 | — |
| 1953S | 14,016 | 1.00 | 1.00 | 2.00 | 4.00 | — |
| 1954 | 54,646 | 1.00 | 1.00 | 2.00 | 2.00 | 10.00 |
| 1954D | 46,306 | 1.00 | 1.00 | 2.00 | 2.00 | — |
| 1954S | 11,835 | 1.00 | 1.00 | 2.00 | 2.00 | — |
| 1955 | 18,558 | 1.00 | 1.00 | 2.00 | 2.00 | 9.00 |
| 1955D | 3,182 | 1.00 | 1.00 | 2.00 | 3.00 | — |
| 1956 | 44,813 | 1.00 | 1.00 | 2.00 | 2.00 | 7.00 |
| 1956D | 32,335 | 1.00 | 1.00 | 2.00 | 3.00 | — |
| 1957 | 47,780 | 1.00 | 1.00 | 2.00 | 3.00 | 4.00 |
| 1957D | 77,924 | 1.00 | 1.00 | 2.00 | 2.00 | — |
| 1958 | 7,236 | 1.00 | 1.00 | 2.00 | 3.00 | 6.00 |

|  | Mintage in Thousands | V. Good | Fine | Ex. Fine | Unc. | Proof |
|---|---|---|---|---|---|---|
| 1958D | 78,125 | 1.00 | 1.00 | 1.00 | 2.00 | — |
| 1959 | 25,533 | 1.00 | 1.00 | 1.00 | 2.00 | 4.00 |
| 1959D | 62,054 | 1.00 | 1.00 | 1.00 | 2.00 | — |
| 1960 | 30,856 | 1.00 | 1.00 | 1.00 | 3.00 | 3.00 |
| 1960D | 63,000 | 1.00 | 1.00 | 1.00 | 2.00 | — |
| 1961 | 40,064 | 1.00 | 1.00 | 1.00 | 3.00 | 2.00 |
| 1961D | 83,657 | 1.00 | 1.00 | 1.00 | 2.00 | — |
| 1962 | 39,374 | 1.00 | 1.00 | 1.00 | 2.00 | 2.00 |
| 1962D | 127,555 | 1.00 | 1.00 | 1.00 | 2.00 | — |
| 1963 | 77,392 | 1.00 | 1.00 | 1.00 | 2.00 | 2.00 |
| 1963D | 135,288 | 1.00 | 1.00 | 1.00 | 2.00 | — |
| 1964 | 564,341 | 1.00 | 1.00 | 1.00 | 2.00 | 2.00 |
| 1964D | 704,136 | 1.00 | 1.00 | 1.00 | 2.00 | — |
| 1965 | 1,819,718 | — | — | — | 1.00 | — |
| 1966 | 821,102 | — | — | — | 1.00 | — |
| 1967 | 1,524,032 | — | — | — | 1.00 | — |
| 1968 | 220,732 | — | — | — | 1.00 | — |
| 1968D | 101,534 | — | — | — | 1.00 | — |
| 1968S Proof only | 3,042 | — | — | — | — | 1.00 |
| 1969 | 176,212 | — | — | — | 1.00 | — |
| 1969D | 114,372 | — | — | — | 1.00 | — |
| 1969S Proof only | 2,935 | — | — | — | — | 1.00 |
| 1970 | 136,420 | — | — | — | 1.00 | — |
| 1970D | 417,341 | — | — | — | 1.00 | — |
| 1970S Proof only | 2,633 | — | — | — | — | 1.00 |
| 1971 | 109,284 | — | — | — | 1.00 | — |
| 1971D | 258,634 | — | — | — | 1.00 | — |
| 1971S Proof only | 3,224 | — | — | — | — | 1.00 |
| 1972 | 215,048 | — | — | — | 1.00 | — |
| 1972D | 311,068 | — | — | — | 1.00 | — |
| 1972S Proof only | 3,268 | — | — | — | — | 1.00 |
| 1973 | 346,924 | — | — | — | 1.00 | — |
| 1973D | 232,977 | — | — | — | 1.00 | — |
| 1973S Proof only | 2,770 | — | — | — | — | 1.00 |
| 1974 | 801,456 | — | — | — | 1.00 | — |
| 1974D | 353,160 | — | — | — | 1.00 | — |
| 1974S Proof only | 2,617 | — | — | — | — | 1.00 |
| 1976 P-D | 725,081 | — | — | — | 1.00 | — |
| 1976S Proof only | 4,150 | — | — | — | — | 1.00 |
| 1976S Silver Proof | 4,000,000 | — | — | — | 3.00 | 2.00 |
| 1977S Proof only | 3,251 | — | — | — | — | 1.00 |
| 1977 P-D | 725,081 | — | — | — | — | — |
| 1978 P-D | 808,825 | — | — | — | — | — |
| 1978S Proof only | 3,128 | — | — | — | — | 1.00 |
| 1979 P-D | 1,005,498 | — | — | — | — | — |
| 1979S Proof only | 3,677 | — | — | — | — | 1.00 |
| 1979S Type Two, Proof only, Sharp Mint Mark | — | — | — | — | — | 2.00 |
| 1980 P&D | — | — | — | — | — | — |
| 1980S Proof only | — | — | — | — | — | 1.00 |
| 1981 P&D | — | — | — | — | — | — |
| 1981S Proof only | — | — | — | — | — | 1.00 |
| 1982 P&D | — | — | — | — | 2.00 | — |
| 1982S Proof only | — | — | — | — | — | 2.00 |
| 1983 P&D | — | — | — | — | 5.00 | — |
| 1983S Proof only | — | — | — | — | — | 2.00 |
| 1984 P&D | — | — | — | — | 2.00 | — |
| 1984S Proof only | — | — | — | — | — | 1.00 |
| 1985 P&D | — | — | — | — | 3.00 | — |
| 1985S | — | — | — | — | — | 1.00 |

|        | Mintage in Thousands | V. Good | Fine | Ex. Fine | Unc. | Proof |
|--------|---------------------:|:-------:|:----:|:--------:|:----:|:-----:|
| 1986P  | — | — | — | — | 3.00 | — |
| 1986S  | — | — | — | — | — | 3.00 |
| 1987P  | — | — | — | — | — | — |
| 1987S  | — | — | — | — | — | 2.00 |
| 1988P  | — | — | — | — | 3.00 | — |
| 1988S  | — | — | — | — | — | 2.00 |
| 1989P  | — | — | — | — | 2.00 | — |
| 1989S  | — | — | — | — | — | 2.00 |
| 1990P  | — | — | — | — | 2.00 | — |
| 1990S  | — | — | — | — | — | 3.00 |

(Note: No 1975 dated quarters were minted.)

## 34.
# HALF DOLLARS—
### FLOWING HAIR TYPE

|        | Mintage in Thousands | Good | Fine | V. Fine | Unc. |
|--------|---------------------:|-----:|-----:|--------:|-----:|
| 1794   | 23  | 1,300.00 | 3,250.00 | 5,850.00 | 50,000.00 |
| 1795   | 300 |   485.00 | 1,000.00 | 1,950.00 | 20,000.00 |

### DRAPED BUST TYPE

**1796–1797**    **1801–1807**

| | | | | | |
|---|---:|---:|---:|---:|---:|
| 1796 15 Stars, All Kinds | 4 | 11,500.00 | 18,750.00 | 27,500.00 | 100,000.00 |
| 1796 16 Stars | — | 13,500.00 | 22,500.00 | 32,500.00 | 125,000.00 |
| 1797, All Kinds | — | 11,000.00 | 18,750.00 | 28,500.00 | 85,000.00 |

|  | Mintage in Thousands | Good | Fine | V. Fine | Unc. |
|---|---|---|---|---|---|
| 1801 | 30 | 225.00 | 500.00 | 900.00 | 16,000.00 |
| 1802 | 30 | 200.00 | 450.00 | 825.00 | 13,500.00 |
| 1803 | 188 | 160.00 | 250.00 | 450.00 | 7,000.00 |
| 1805 over 4, All Kinds | 212 | 170.00 | 525.00 | 700.00 | 20,000.00 |
| 1805 | — | 150.00 | 225.00 | 325.00 | 7,000.00 |
| 1806 over 5, All Kinds | 840 | 150.00 | 300.00 | 375.00 | 7,000.00 |
| 1806 over Inverted 6 | — | 170.00 | 600.00 | 925.00 | 11,000.00 |
| 1806 | — | 150.00 | 225.00 | 350.00 | 6,750.00 |
| 1807 | 301 | 150.00 | 225.00 | 325.00 | 6,500.00 |

## TURBAN HEAD TYPE

1807–1836          1836–1839

|  | Mintage in Thousands | Good | Fine | Unc. | Proof |
|---|---|---|---|---|---|
| 1807, All Kinds | 751 | 65.00 | 175.00 | 3,750.00 | — |
| 1807 50 over 20 | — | 50.00 | 110.00 | 3,500.00 | — |
| 1808 over 7, All Kinds | 1,369 | 50.00 | 85.00 | 2,400.00 | — |
| 1808 | — | 50.00 | 65.00 | 1,500.00 | — |
| 1809 | 1,406 | 50.00 | 65.00 | 1,650.00 | — |
| 1810 | 1,276 | 50.00 | 65.00 | 1,650.00 | — |
| 1811 | 1,204 | 50.00 | 65.00 | 1,000.00 | — |
| 1812 over 11, All Kinds | 1,628 | 45.00 | 90.00 | 2,750.00 | — |
| 1812 | — | 45.00 | 65.00 | 850.00 | — |
| 1813 | 1,242 | 45.00 | 65.00 | 1,175.00 | — |
| 1814 over 13, All Kinds | 1,039 | 50.00 | 90.00 | 2,350.00 | — |
| 1814 | — | 45.00 | 65.00 | 1,000.00 | — |
| 1815 over 12 | 47 | 750.00 | 1,250.00 | 10,000.00 | — |
| 1817 over 13, All Kinds | 1,216 | 75.00 | 160.00 | 3,650.00 | — |
| 1817 over 14 (Rare) | — | 45,000.00 | 110,000.00 | — | — |
| 1817 | — | 45.00 | 60.00 | 1,000.00 | — |
| 1818 over 17, All Kinds | 1,960 | 45.00 | 60.00 | 1,500.00 | — |
| 1818 | — | 45.00 | 60.00 | 875.00 | — |
| 1819 over 18, All Kinds | 2,208 | 45.00 | 65.00 | 1,375.00 | — |
| 1819 | — | 45.00 | 55.00 | 850.00 | — |
| 1820 over 19, All Kinds | 251 | 50.00 | 75.00 | 1,600.00 | — |
| 1820 | — | 45.00 | 70.00 | 1,150.00 | — |
| 1821 | 1,306 | 45.00 | 65.00 | 1,050.00 | — |
| 1822, All Kinds | 1,560 | 45.00 | 55.00 | 550.00 | — |
| 1822 over 1 | — | 50.00 | 80.00 | 1,150.00 | — |
| 1823 Broken 3, All Kinds | 1,694 | 50.00 | 85.00 | 1,300.00 | — |
| 1823 | — | 45.00 | 55.00 | 700.00 | — |
| 1824 over 21, All Kinds | 3,505 | 45.00 | 60.00 | 1,000.00 | — |
| 1824 over Various Dates | — | 50.00 | 75.00 | 1,150.00 | — |

|  | Mintage in Thousands | Good | Fine | V. Fine | Unc. |
|---|---|---|---|---|---|
| 1824 | — | 45.00 | 50.00 | 55.00 | 450.00 |
| 1825 | 2,943 | 45.00 | 50.00 | 55.00 | 475.00 |
| 1826 | 4,004 | 45.00 | 50.00 | 55.00 | 450.00 |
| 1827 over 6, All Kinds | 5,493 | 45.00 | 55.00 | 75.00 | 1,000.00 |
| 1827 | — | 45.00 | 50.00 | 55.00 | 450.00 |
| 1828 | 3,075 | 45.00 | 50.00 | 55.00 | 500.00 |
| 1829 over 27, All Kinds | — | 45.00 | 60.00 | 75.00 | 1,250.00 |
| 1829, All Kinds | 3,712 | 45.00 | 50.00 | 55.00 | 450.00 |
| 1830 | 4,765 | 45.00 | 50.00 | 55.00 | 450.00 |
| 1831 | 5,874 | 45.00 | 50.00 | 55.00 | 450.00 |
| 1832 | 4,797 | 45.00 | 50.00 | 55.00 | 450.00 |
| 1833 | 5,206 | 45.00 | 50.00 | 55.00 | 450.00 |
| 1834 | 6,412 | 45.00 | 50.00 | 55.00 | 450.00 |
| 1835 | 5,352 | 45.00 | 50.00 | 55.00 | 450.00 |
| 1836 (Lettered Edge), All Kinds | 6,545 | 45.00 | 50.00 | 55.00 | 450.00 |
| 1836 50 over 00 | — | 50.00 | 65.00 | 110.00 | 1,600.00 |
| 1836 Reeded Edge | 1 | 625.00 | 1,050.00 | 1,175.00 | 6,750.00 |
| 1837 | 3,630 | 45.00 | 55.00 | 85.00 | 750.00 |
| 1838 | 3,546 | 45.00 | 55.00 | 85.00 | 750.00 |
| 1838O (Very rare) | 20 Pieces | — | — | — | 120,000.00 |
| 1839 | 3,335 | 45.00 | 60.00 | 85.00 | 1,000.00 |
| 1839O | 179 | 120.00 | 235.00 | 325.00 | 2,650.00 |

## LIBERTY SEATED TYPE

**1839–1865**  **1866–1891**

|  | Mintage | Good | Fine | V. Fine | Unc. |
|---|---|---|---|---|---|
| 1939 No Drapery from Elbow | (included above) | 45.00 | 120.00 | 350.00 | 5,000.00 |
| 1839 With Drapery | (included above) | 25.00 | 55.00 | 85.00 | 525.00 |
| 1840 | 1,435 | 27.00 | 55.00 | 75.00 | 450.00 |
| 1840O | 855 | 25.00 | 50.00 | 85.00 | 525.00 |
| 1841 | 310 | 37.00 | 85.00 | 135.00 | 1,300.00 |
| 1841O | 401 | 20.00 | 50.00 | 80.00 | 650.00 |
| 1842 | 2,013 | 27.00 | 50.00 | 70.00 | 525.00 |
| 1842O | 957 | 20.00 | 45.00 | 60.00 | 1,250.00 |
| 1843 | 3,844 | 20.00 | 45.00 | 60.00 | 450.00 |
| 1843O | 2,268 | 20.00 | 45.00 | 60.00 | 450.00 |
| 1844 | 1,766 | 20.00 | 45.00 | 55.00 | 450.00 |
| 1844O | 2,005 | 20.00 | 45.00 | 55.00 | 525.00 |
| 1845 | 589 | 27.00 | 60.00 | 120.00 | 750.00 |
| 1845O, All Kinds | 2,094 | 20.00 | 45.00 | 60.00 | 525.00 |
| 1845O, No Drapery | — | 28.00 | 75.00 | 110.00 | 1,300.00 |
| 1846, All Kinds | 2,210 | 22.00 | 45.00 | 60.00 | 500.00 |
| 1846 over Horizontal 6 | — | 135.00 | 235.00 | 360.00 | 3,750.00 |
| 1846O | 2,304 | 22.00 | 45.00 | 55.00 | 1,100.00 |

|  | Mintage in Thousands | Good | Fine | V. Fine | Unc. |
|---|---|---|---|---|---|
| 1847 over 46, All Kinds | 1,156 | 1,750.00 | 3,000.00 | 4,250.00 | — |
| 1847 | — | 20.00 | 45.00 | 60.00 | 500.00 |
| 1847O | 2,584 | 20.00 | 45.00 | 60.00 | 675.00 |
| 1848 | 580 | 40.00 | 85.00 | 150.00 | 1,250.00 |
| 1848O | 3,180 | 20.00 | 45.00 | 65.00 | 750.00 |
| 1849 | 1,252 | 30.00 | 60.00 | 85.00 | 900.00 |
| 1849O | 2,310 | 22.00 | 45.00 | 65.00 | 775.00 |
| 1850 | 227 | 210.00 | 425.00 | 525.00 | 1,750.00 |
| 1850O | 2,456 | 22.00 | 45.00 | 65.00 | 550.00 |
| 1851 | 201 | 285.00 | 450.00 | 525.00 | 1,650.00 |
| 1851O | 402 | 25.00 | 60.00 | 80.00 | 525.00 |
| 1852 | 77 | 350.00 | 575.00 | 775.00 | 1,475.00 |
| 1852O | 144 | 60.00 | 150.00 | 250.00 | 2,000.00 |
| 1853O No Rays & Arrows (Very rare) | — | — | — | — | — |
| 1853 Arrows & Rays | 3,533 | 20.00 | 55.00 | 90.00 | 1,650.00 |
| 1853O | 1,328 | 22.00 | 65.00 | 150.00 | 2,500.00 |

|  | Mintage in Thousands | Good | Fine | V. Fine | Unc. | Proof |
|---|---|---|---|---|---|---|
| 1854 Arrows at Date | 2,982 | 20.00 | 45.00 | 65.00 | 650.00 | — |
| 1854O | 5,240 | 20.00 | 45.00 | 70.00 | 650.00 | — |
| 1855 | 760 | 20.00 | 45.00 | 67.00 | 775.00 | 22,500.00 |
| 1855 over 54 | — | 75.00 | 175.00 | 275.00 | 2,500.00 | — |
| 1855O | 3,688 | 20.00 | 45.00 | 65.00 | 650.00 | — |
| 1855S | 130 | 300.00 | 675.00 | 1,300.00 | — | — |
| 1856 No Arrows | 938 | 20.00 | 45.00 | 55.00 | 425.00 | 8,750.00 |
| 1856O | 2,658 | 20.00 | 45.00 | 55.00 | 450.00 | — |
| 1856S | 211 | 45.00 | 130.00 | 275.00 | 3,750.00 | — |
| 1857 | 1,988 | 20.00 | 45.00 | 55.00 | 450.00 | 5,500.00 |
| 1857O | 818 | 20.00 | 45.00 | 55.00 | 1,275.00 | — |
| 1857S | 158 | 55.00 | 135.00 | 240.00 | 4,250.00 | — |
| 1858 | 4,226 | 20.00 | 45.00 | 55.00 | 450.00 | 5,250.00 |
| 1858O | 7,294 | 20.00 | 45.00 | 55.00 | 450.00 | — |
| 1858S | 476 | 22.00 | 55.00 | 125.00 | 1,150.00 | — |
| 1859 | 748 | 30.00 | 60.00 | 85.00 | 485.00 | 2,350.00 |
| 1859O | 2,834 | 20.00 | 45.00 | 55.00 | 450.00 | — |
| 1859S | 566 | 22.00 | 55.00 | 95.00 | 975.00 | — |
| 1860 | 304 | 22.00 | 45.00 | 57.00 | 625.00 | 2,300.00 |
| 1860O | 1,290 | 20.00 | 45.00 | 55.00 | 450.00 | — |
| 1860S | 472 | 21.00 | 45.00 | 55.00 | 875.00 | — |
| 1861 | 2,888 | 20.00 | 45.00 | 55.00 | 450.00 | 2,300.00 |
| 1861O | 2,533 | 20.00 | 45.00 | 55.00 | 450.00 | — |
| 1861S | 940 | 20.00 | 45.00 | 55.00 | 725.00 | — |
| 1862 | 254 | 30.00 | 65.00 | 115.00 | 550.00 | 2,300.00 |
| 1862S | 1,325 | 20.00 | 45.00 | 55.00 | 625.00 | — |
| 1863 | 504 | 22.00 | 55.00 | 75.00 | 550.00 | 2,500.00 |
| 1863S | 916 | 20.00 | 45.00 | 55.00 | 600.00 | — |
| 1864 | 380 | 25.00 | 60.00 | 95.00 | 475.00 | 2,300.00 |
| 1864S | 658 | 20.00 | 45.00 | 60.00 | 925.00 | — |
| 1865 | 512 | 25.00 | 55.00 | 85.00 | 500.00 | 2,300.00 |
| 1865S | 675 | 20.00 | 45.00 | 55.00 | 650.00 | — |
| 1866 Motto | 746 | 22.00 | 45.00 | 65.00 | 575.00 | 1,250.00 |
| 1866S No Motto, All Kinds | 1,054 | 75.00 | 200.00 | 375.00 | 4,250.00 | — |
| 1866S Motto | — | 20.00 | 45.00 | 55.00 | 650.00 | — |
| 1867 | 450 | 27.00 | 65.00 | 115.00 | 575.00 | 1,300.00 |
| 1867S | 1,196 | 20.00 | 45.00 | 55.00 | 650.00 | — |
| 1868 | 418 | 42.00 | 90.00 | 130.00 | 600.00 | 1,250.00 |

|  | Mintage in Thousands | Good | Fine | V. Fine | Unc. | Proof |
|---|---|---|---|---|---|---|
| 1868S | 1,160 | 20.00 | 45.00 | 65.00 | 625.00 | — |
| 1869 | 796 | 22.00 | 50.00 | 67.00 | 500.00 | 1,250.00 |
| 1869S | 656 | 20.00 | 45.00 | 70.00 | 1,000.00 | — |
| 1870 | 635 | 23.00 | 47.00 | 70.00 | 500.00 | 1,250.00 |
| 1870CC | 55 | 500.00 | 1,500.00 | 3,600.00 | 35,000.00 | — |
| 1870S | 1,004 | 20.00 | 45.00 | 75.00 | 1,050.00 | — |
| 1871 | 1,205 | 20.00 | 45.00 | 60.00 | 450.00 | 1,250.00 |
| 1871CC | 150 | 130.00 | 310.00 | 585.00 | 11,000.00 | — |
| 1871S | 2,178 | 20.00 | 45.00 | 55.00 | 575.00 | — |
| 1872 | 882 | 20.00 | 45.00 | 55.00 | 600.00 | 1,250.00 |
| 1872CC | 252 | 65.00 | 200.00 | 350.00 | 4,750.00 | — |
| 1872S | 580 | 30.00 | 70.00 | 125.00 | 1,200.00 | — |
| 1873 | 802 | 27.00 | 65.00 | 100.00 | 675.00 | 1,250.00 |
| 1873CC | 123 | 130.00 | 325.00 | 600.00 | 11,000.00 | — |
| 1873 Arrows | 1,816 | 21.00 | 50.00 | 100.00 | 1,150.00 | 2,850.00 |
| 1873S | 228 | 55.00 | 130.00 | 250.00 | 2,750.00 | — |
| 1873CC | 215 | 135.00 | 360.00 | 775.00 | 6,850.00 | — |
| 1874 | 2,360 | 21.00 | 50.00 | 100.00 | 1,150.00 | 2,750.00 |
| 1874CC | 59 | 265.00 | 685.00 | 1,250.00 | 12,000.00 | — |
| 1874S | 394 | 32.00 | 85.00 | 190.00 | 2,000.00 | — |
| 1875 No Arrows | 6,028 | 20.00 | 45.00 | 55.00 | 450.00 | 1,250.00 |
| 1875CC | 1,008 | 27.00 | 55.00 | 80.00 | 675.00 | — |
| 1875S | 3,200 | 20.00 | 45.00 | 65.00 | 360.00 | — |
| 1876 | 8,419 | 20.00 | 42.00 | 55.00 | 360.00 | 1,250.00 |
| 1876CC | 1,956 | 22.00 | 50.00 | 70.00 | 675.00 | — |
| 1876S | 4,528 | 20.00 | 42.00 | 55.00 | 360.00 | — |
| 1877 | 8,305 | 20.00 | 42.00 | 50.00 | 360.00 | 1,250.00 |
| 1877CC | 1,420 | 22.00 | 45.00 | 70.00 | 700.00 | — |
| 1877S | 5,356 | 20.00 | 42.00 | 50.00 | 360.00 | — |
| 1878 | 1,378 | 25.00 | 55.00 | 85.00 | 485.00 | 1,250.00 |
| 1878CC | 62 | 300.00 | 485.00 | 875.00 | 5,500.00 | — |
| 1878S | 12 | 6,500.00 | 9,250.00 | 11,750.00 | 32,500.00 | — |
| 1879 | 6 | 225.00 | 300.00 | 350.00 | 700.00 | 1,250.00 |
| 1880 | 10 | 180.00 | 250.00 | 285.00 | 625.00 | 1,250.00 |
| 1881 | 11 | 180.00 | 250.00 | 285.00 | 600.00 | 1,250.00 |
| 1882 | 6 | 225.00 | 325.00 | 350.00 | 700.00 | 1,250.00 |
| 1883 | 9 | 200.00 | 275.00 | 325.00 | 675.00 | 1,250.00 |
| 1884 | 5 | 290.00 | 350.00 | 375.00 | 725.00 | 1,250.00 |
| 1885 | 6 | 275.00 | 315.00 | 325.00 | 725.00 | 1,250.00 |
| 1886 | 6 | 310.00 | 410.00 | 460.00 | 750.00 | 1,250.00 |
| 1887 | 6 | 410.00 | 550.00 | 580.00 | 875.00 | 1,250.00 |
| 1888 | 13 | 185.00 | 240.00 | 285.00 | 575.00 | 1,250.00 |
| 1889 | 13 | 185.00 | 240.00 | 300.00 | 575.00 | 1,250.00 |
| 1890 | 13 | 195.00 | 240.00 | 310.00 | 585.00 | 1,250.00 |
| 1891 | 201 | 45.00 | 100.00 | 115.00 | 435.00 | 1,250.00 |

## BARBER OR LIBERTY HEAD TYPE

|  | Mintage in Thousands | Good | Fine | V. Fine | Unc. | Proof |
|---|---|---|---|---|---|---|
| 1892 | 935 | 21.00 | 48.00 | 90.00 | 400.00 | 1,250.00 |
| 1892O | 390 | 145.00 | 275.00 | 295.00 | 875.00 | — |
| 1892S | 1,029 | 130.00 | 235.00 | 280.00 | 950.00 | — |
| 1893 | 1,827 | 14.00 | 45.00 | 80.00 | 550.00 | 1,250.00 |
| 1893O | 1,389 | 23.00 | 70.00 | 125.00 | 550.00 | — |
| 1893S | 740 | 100.00 | 175.00 | 285.00 | 1,250.00 | — |
| 1894 | 1,149 | 18.00 | 68.00 | 100.00 | 500.00 | 1,250.00 |
| 1894O | 2,138 | 13.00 | 63.00 | 95.00 | 525.00 | — |
| 1894S | 4,049 | 12.00 | 48.00 | 80.00 | 500.00 | — |
| 1895 | 1,835 | 10.00 | 50.00 | 85.00 | 550.00 | 1,250.00 |
| 1895O | 1,766 | 13.00 | 55.00 | 100.00 | 625.00 | — |
| 1895S | 1,108 | 18.00 | 68.00 | 125.00 | 600.00 | — |
| 1896 | 951 | 16.00 | 55.00 | 90.00 | 550.00 | 1,250.00 |
| 1896O | 924 | 24.00 | 95.00 | 145.00 | 1,300.00 | — |
| 1896S | 1,141 | 65.00 | 125.00 | 200.00 | 1,250.00 | — |
| 1897 | 2,481 | 8.00 | 35.00 | 75.00 | 475.00 | 1,250.00 |
| 1897O | 632 | 55.00 | 350.00 | 650.00 | 1,500.00 | — |
| 1897S | 934 | 110.00 | 260.00 | 400.00 | 1,350.00 | — |
| 1898 | 2,957 | 8.00 | 30.00 | 71.00 | 425.00 | 1,250.00 |
| 1898O | 874 | 18.00 | 100.00 | 160.00 | 900.00 | — |
| 1898S | 2,359 | 10.00 | 42.00 | 86.00 | 875.00 | — |
| 1899 | 5,539 | 9.00 | 26.00 | 71.00 | 425.00 | 1,250.00 |
| 1899O | 1,724 | 10.00 | 45.00 | 90.00 | 575.00 | — |
| 1899S | 1,686 | 13.00 | 50.00 | 88.00 | 775.00 | — |
| 1900 | 4,763 | 7.00 | 28.00 | 71.00 | 400.00 | 1,250.00 |
| 1900O | 2,744 | 8.00 | 40.00 | 90.00 | 875.00 | — |
| 1900S | 2,560 | 8.00 | 42.00 | 95.00 | 675.00 | — |
| 1901 | 4,269 | 7.00 | 28.00 | 71.00 | 425.00 | 1,250.00 |
| 1901O | 1,124 | 9.00 | 53.00 | 115.00 | 1,375.00 | — |
| 1901S | 847 | 17.00 | 110.00 | 225.00 | 1,500.00 | — |
| 1902 | 4,923 | 7.00 | 28.00 | 71.00 | 400.00 | 1,250.00 |
| 1902O | 2,526 | 8.00 | 38.00 | 80.00 | 775.00 | — |
| 1902S | 1,461 | 8.00 | 48.00 | 90.00 | 725.00 | — |
| 1903 | 2,279 | 7.00 | 37.00 | 78.00 | 500.00 | 1,250.00 |
| 1903O | 2,100 | 8.00 | 43.00 | 75.00 | 700.00 | — |
| 1903S | 1,921 | 8.00 | 43.00 | 75.00 | 650.00 | — |
| 1904 | 2,993 | 7.00 | 28.00 | 65.00 | 450.00 | 1,250.00 |
| 1904O | 1,118 | 11.00 | 50.00 | 110.00 | 1,150.00 | — |
| 1904S | 553 | 16.00 | 135.00 | 325.00 | 1,900.00 | — |
| 1905 | 663 | 12.00 | 52.00 | 78.00 | 575.00 | 1,250.00 |
| 1905O | 505 | 15.00 | 75.00 | 130.00 | 750.00 | — |
| 1905S | 2,494 | 7.00 | 38.00 | 79.00 | 675.00 | — |
| 1906 | 2,639 | 7.00 | 27.00 | 65.00 | 425.00 | 1,250.00 |
| 1906D | 4,028 | 7.00 | 30.00 | 65.00 | 425.00 | — |

|  | Mintage in Thousands | Good | Fine | V. Fine | Unc. | Proof |
|---|---|---|---|---|---|---|
| 1906O | 2,446 | 7.00 | 35.00 | 75.00 | 600.00 | — |
| 1906S | 1,740 | 7.00 | 42.00 | 75.00 | 600.00 | — |
| 1907 | 2,599 | 7.00 | 26.00 | 65.00 | 410.00 | 1,250.00 |
| 1907D | 3,856 | 7.00 | 27.00 | 65.00 | 425.00 | — |
| 1907O | 3,947 | 7.00 | 27.00 | 70.00 | 585.00 | — |
| 1907S | 1,250 | 7.00 | 65.00 | 125.00 | 975.00 | — |
| 1908 | 1,355 | 7.00 | 30.00 | 70.00 | 425.00 | 1,250.00 |
| 1908D | 3,280 | 7.00 | 30.00 | 70.00 | 425.00 | — |
| 1908O | 5,360 | 7.00 | 30.00 | 70.00 | 550.00 | — |
| 1908S | 1,645 | 7.00 | 45.00 | 78.00 | 775.00 | — |
| 1909 | 2,369 | 7.00 | 30.00 | 65.00 | 400.00 | 1,250.00 |
| 1909O | 925 | 9.00 | 45.00 | 70.00 | 750.00 | — |
| 1909S | 1,764 | 7.00 | 33.00 | 75.00 | 600.00 | — |
| 1910 | 419 | 11.00 | 64.00 | 120.00 | 650.00 | 1,250.00 |
| 1910S | 1,948 | 7.00 | 32.00 | 70.00 | 675.00 | — |
| 1911 | 1,407 | 7.00 | 28.00 | 65.00 | 425.00 | 1,250.00 |
| 1911D | 695 | 7.00 | 35.00 | 70.00 | 550.00 | — |
| 1911S | 1,272 | 7.00 | 35.00 | 75.00 | 575.00 | — |
| 1912 | 1,551 | 7.00 | 26.00 | 65.00 | 425.00 | 1,250.00 |
| 1912D | 2,301 | 7.00 | 26.00 | 65.00 | 450.00 | — |
| 1912S | 1,370 | 7.00 | 30.00 | 70.00 | 550.00 | — |
| 1913 | 189 | 20.00 | 115.00 | 175.00 | 925.00 | 1,250.00 |
| 1913D | 534 | 7.00 | 35.00 | 70.00 | 475.00 | — |
| 1913S | 604 | 7.00 | 44.00 | 80.00 | 650.00 | — |
| 1914 | 125 | 27.00 | 160.00 | 310.00 | 925.00 | 1,350.00 |
| 1914S | 992 | 7.00 | 34.00 | 70.00 | 575.00 | — |
| 1915 | 138 | 20.00 | 90.00 | 200.00 | 1,000.00 | 1,250.00 |
| 1915D | 1,170 | 7.00 | 27.00 | 65.00 | 385.00 | — |
| 1915S | 1,604 | 7.00 | 30.00 | 65.00 | 415.00 | — |

## LIBERTY WALKING TYPE

|  | Mintage in Thousands | Good | Fine | Ex. Fine | Unc. |
|---|---|---|---|---|---|
| 1916 | 608 | 25.00 | 57.00 | 160.00 | 300.00 |
| 1916D on Obverse | 1,014 | 20.00 | 40.00 | 145.00 | 400.00 |
| 1916S on Obverse | 508 | 80.00 | 135.00 | 525.00 | 1,150.00 |
| 1917 | 12,292 | 5.00 | 11.00 | 35.00 | 125.00 |
| 1917D on Obverse | 765 | 14.00 | 40.00 | 165.00 | 575.00 |
| 1917D on Reverse | 1,940 | 9.00 | 28.00 | 230.00 | 800.00 |
| 1917S on Obverse | 952 | 17.00 | 55.00 | 665.00 | 2,450.00 |
| 1917S on Reverse | 5,554 | 7.00 | 14.00 | 55.00 | 475.00 |
| 1918 | 6,634 | 7.00 | 17.00 | 145.00 | 600.00 |
| 1918D | 3,853 | 8.00 | 22.00 | 155.00 | 1,000.00 |
| 1918S | 10,282 | 7.00 | 14.00 | 60.00 | 550.00 |

|  | Mintage in Thousands | Good | Fine | Ex. Fine | Unc. |
|---|---|---|---|---|---|
| 1919 | 962 | 17.00 | 50.00 | 450.00 | 1,250.00 |
| 1919D | 1,165 | 13.00 | 55.00 | 575.00 | 2,850.00 |
| 1919S | 1,552 | 14.00 | 40.00 | 700.00 | 2,450.00 |
| 1920 | 6,372 | 6.00 | 13.00 | 65.00 | 360.00 |
| 1920D | 1,551 | 9.00 | 35.00 | 375.00 | 1,450.00 |
| 1920S | 4,624 | 6.00 | 15.00 | 200.00 | 875.00 |
| 1921 | 246 | 95.00 | 190.00 | 1,400.00 | 3,150.00 |
| 1921D | 208 | 140.00 | 260.00 | 2,000.00 | 3,150.00 |
| 1921S | 548 | 25.00 | 100.00 | 4,150.00 | 10,000.00 |
| 1923S | 2,178 | 9.00 | 24.00 | 210.00 | 1,350.00 |
| 1927S | 2,392 | 5.00 | 11.00 | 90.00 | 850.00 |
| 1928S | 1,940 | 5.00 | 13.00 | 100.00 | 825.00 |
| 1929D | 1,001 | 6.00 | 13.00 | 75.00 | 350.00 |
| 1929S | 1,902 | 5.00 | 10.00 | 80.00 | 400.00 |
| 1933S | 1,786 | 5.00 | 10.00 | 45.00 | 625.00 |
| 1934 | 6,964 | 3.00 | 4.00 | 11.00 | 65.00 |
| 1934D | 2,361 | 5.00 | 6.00 | 25.00 | 165.00 |
| 1934S | 3,652 | 3.00 | 5.00 | 25.00 | 385.00 |
| 1935 | 9,162 | 3.00 | 4.00 | 9.00 | 50.00 |
| 1935D | 3,004 | 4.00 | 5.00 | 25.00 | 160.00 |
| 1935S | 3,854 | 3.00 | 5.00 | 25.00 | 240.00 |

|  | Mintage in Thousands | Good | Fine | Ex. Fine | Unc. | Proof |
|---|---|---|---|---|---|---|
| 1936 | 12,618 | 3.00 | 4.00 | 9.00 | 45.00 | 1,500.00 |
| 1936D | 4,252 | 3.00 | 5.00 | 17.00 | 90.00 | — |
| 1936S | 3,884 | 3.00 | 5.00 | 20.00 | 150.00 | 500.00 |
| 1937 | 9,528 | 3.00 | 4.00 | 9.00 | 45.00 | 850.00 |
| 1937D | 1,676 | 5.00 | 7.00 | 28.00 | 160.00 | — |
| 1937S | 2,090 | 4.00 | 6.00 | 18.00 | 140.00 | — |
| 1938 | 4,118 | 3.00 | 5.00 | 11.00 | 80.00 | 425.00 |
| 1938D | 492 | 22.00 | 28.00 | 90.00 | 390.00 | — |
| 1939 | 6,821 | 3.00 | 4.00 | 10.00 | 45.00 | 425.00 |
| 1939D | 4,267 | 3.00 | 5.00 | 11.00 | 45.00 | — |
| 1939S | 2,552 | 4.00 | 6.00 | 13.00 | 110.00 | — |
| 1940 | 9,167 | 3.00 | 4.00 | 8.00 | 40.00 | 375.00 |
| 1940S | 4,550 | 3.00 | 4.00 | 9.00 | 40.00 | — |
| 1941 | 24,207 | 3.00 | 4.00 | 7.00 | 40.00 | 325.00 |
| 1941D | 11,248 | 3.00 | 4.00 | 6.00 | 40.00 | — |
| 1941S | 8,098 | 3.00 | 4.00 | 7.00 | 80.00 | — |
| 1942 | 47,839 | 3.00 | 4.00 | 6.00 | 40.00 | 325.00 |
| 1942D | 10,974 | 3.00 | 4.00 | 6.00 | 50.00 | — |
| 1942S | 12,708 | 3.00 | 4.00 | 7.00 | 45.00 | — |

|  | Mintage in Thousands | Good | Fine | Ex. Fine | Unc. |
|---|---|---|---|---|---|
| 1943 | 53,190 | 3.00 | 4.00 | 6.00 | 40.00 |
| 1943D | 11,346 | 3.00 | 4.00 | 6.00 | 50.00 |
| 1943S | 13,450 | 3.00 | 4.00 | 6.00 | 40.00 |
| 1944 | 28,206 | 3.00 | 4.00 | 6.00 | 40.00 |
| 1944D | 9,769 | 3.00 | 4.00 | 6.00 | 40.00 |
| 1944S | 9,904 | 3.00 | 4.00 | 6.00 | 40.00 |
| 1945 | 31,502 | 3.00 | 4.00 | 6.00 | 40.00 |
| 1945D | 9,967 | 3.00 | 4.00 | 6.00 | 40.00 |
| 1945S | 10,156 | 3.00 | 4.00 | 6.00 | 40.00 |
| 1946 | 12,118 | 3.00 | 4.00 | 6.00 | 40.00 |
| 1946D | 2,151 | 3.00 | 6.00 | 10.00 | 40.00 |

|  | Mintage in Thousands | Good | Fine | Ex. Fine | Unc. |
|---|---|---|---|---|---|
| 1946S | 3,724 | 3.00 | 4.00 | 6.00 | 40.00 |
| 1947 | 4,094 | 3.00 | 4.00 | 8.00 | 45.00 |
| 1947D | 3,901 | 3.00 | 4.00 | 8.00 | 40.00 |

## FRANKLIN TYPE

|  | Mintage in Thousands | Ex. Fine | Unc. | Proof |
|---|---|---|---|---|
| 1948 | 3,007 | 5.00 | 16.00 | — |
| 1948D | 4,029 | 5.00 | 12.00 | — |
| 1949 | 5,614 | 9.00 | 35.00 | — |
| 1949D | 4,121 | 12.00 | 37.00 | — |
| 1949S | 3,748 | 14.00 | 50.00 | — |
| 1950 | 7,794 | 6.00 | 23.00 | 250.00 |
| 1950D | 8,032 | 7.00 | 22.00 | — |
| 1951 | 16,860 | 4.00 | 12.00 | 200.00 |
| 1951D | 9,475 | 8.00 | 22.00 | — |
| 1951S | 13,696 | 6.00 | 22.00 | — |
| 1952 | 21,274 | 3.00 | 10.00 | 115.00 |
| 1952D | 25,396 | 3.00 | 8.00 | — |
| 1952S | 5,526 | 7.00 | 35.00 | — |
| 1953 | 2,797 | 5.00 | 16.00 | 70.00 |
| 1953D | 20,900 | 4.00 | 8.00 | — |
| 1953S | 4,148 | 6.00 | 16.00 | — |
| 1954 | 13,422 | 4.00 | 8.00 | 40.00 |
| 1954D | 25,446 | 4.00 | 8.00 | — |
| 1954S | 4,993 | 4.00 | 8.00 | — |
| 1955 | 2,876 | 6.00 | 8.00 | 40.00 |
| 1956 | 4,701 | 4.00 | 7.00 | 15.00 |
| 1957 | 6,362 | 3.00 | 7.00 | 13.00 |
| 1957D | 19,967 | 3.00 | 6.00 | — |
| 1958 | 4,918 | 3.00 | 6.00 | 13.00 |
| 1958D | 23,962 | 3.00 | 6.00 | — |
| 1959 | 7,349 | 3.00 | 6.00 | 12.00 |
| 1959D | 13,054 | 3.00 | 6.00 | — |
| 1960 | 7,716 | 3.00 | 6.00 | 12.00 |
| 1960D | 18,216 | 3.00 | 6.00 | — |
| 1961 | 11,318 | 3.00 | 6.00 | 9.00 |
| 1961D | 20,276 | 3.00 | 6.00 | — |
| 1962 | 12,932 | 3.00 | 6.00 | 9.00 |
| 1962D | 35,473 | 3.00 | 6.00 | — |
| 1963 | 25,240 | 3.00 | 6.00 | 9.00 |
| 1963D | 67,069 | 3.00 | 6.00 | — |

# KENNEDY TYPE

| | Mintage in Thousands | Unc. | Proof |
|---|---|---|---|
| 1964 | 277,255 | 3.00 | 6.00 |
| 1964D | 156,205 | 3.00 | — |
| 1965 | 65,879 | 1.00 | — |
| 1966 | 108,985 | 1.00 | — |
| 1967 | 295,047 | 1.00 | — |
| 1968D | 246,952 | 1.00 | — |
| 1968S Proof only | 3,042 | — | 4.00 |
| 1969D | 129,882 | 1.00 | — |
| 1969S Proof only | 2,935 | — | 4.00 |
| 1970D | 2,150 | 10.00 | — |
| 1970S Proof only | 2,633 | — | 10.00 |
| 1971 | 155,164 | 1.00 | — |
| 1971D | 302,097 | 1.00 | — |
| 1971S Proof only | 3,224 | — | 3.00 |
| 1972 | 153,180 | 1.00 | — |
| 1972D | 141,890 | 1.00 | — |
| 1972S Proof only | 3,268 | — | 3.00 |
| 1973 | 64,964 | 2.00 | — |
| 1973D | 83,171 | 1.00 | — |
| 1973S Proof only | 2,770 | — | 3.00 |
| 1974 | 201,596 | 1.00 | — |
| 1974D | 79,066 | 1.00 | — |
| 1974S Proof only | 2,617 | — | 3.00 |
| 1976 P-D* | 521,873 | 1.00 | — |
| 1976S Proof only* | 7,059 | — | 2.00 |
| 1976S Silver Proof* | 4,000,000 | 4.00 | 6.00 |
| 1977 P-D | 75,047 | 2.00 | — |
| 1977S Proof only | 3,251 | — | 3.00 |
| 1978 P-D | 28,116 | 2.00 | — |
| 1978S Proof only | 3,128 | — | 2.00 |
| 1979 P-D | 84,127 | 1.00 | — |
| 1979S Proof only | — | — | 2.00 |
| 1979S Type Two, Proof only, Sharp Mint Mark | — | — | 15.00 |
| 1980 P-D | 77,590 | 1.00 | — |
| 1980S Proof only | — | — | 2.00 |
| 1981 P-D | 57,384 | 2.00 | — |
| 1981S Proof only | — | — | 2.00 |
| 1982 P-D | 23,959 | 2.00 | — |
| 1982S Proof only | — | — | 3.00 |
| 1983 P-D | 66,611 | 3.00 | — |
| 1983S Proof only | — | — | 3.00 |
| 1984 P-D | — | 1.00 | — |
| 1984S Proof only | — | — | 7.00 |
| 1985 P-D | — | 1.00 | — |
| 1985S Proof only | — | — | 4.00 |
| 1986 P-D | — | 3.00 | — |
| 1986S | — | — | 10.00 |
| 1987 P-D | — | 4.00 | — |
| 1987S | — | — | 4.00 |
| 1988 P-D | — | 2.00 | — |
| 1988S | — | — | 5.00 |
| 1989P-D | — | 2.00 | — |
| 1989S Proof only | — | — | 4.00 |
| 1990P-D | — | 2.00 | — |
| 1990S Proof only | — | — | 5.00 |

*Bicentennial coinage dated 1776-1976, with reverses showing Independence Hall in Philadelphia. No 1975 dated half dollars were struck.

# 35.
# SILVER DOLLARS—
# 1794–Date

## FLOWING HAIR TYPE

|  | Mintage in Thousands | Good | Fine | V. Fine | Unc. |
|---|---|---|---|---|---|
| 1794 | 2 | 13,500.00 | 30,000.00 | 55,000.00 | — |
| 1795 | 160 | 800.00 | 1,300.00 | 2,450.00 | 22,500.00 |

## DRAPED BUST TYPE

1795–1798     1798–1804

| | | | | | |
|---|---|---|---|---|---|
| 1795 | 43 | 675.00 | 1,150.00 | 1,750.00 | 22,500.00 |
| 1796 | 73 | 675.00 | 1,150.00 | 1,650.00 | 22,500.00 |
| 1797 9 Stars Left, 7 Right, All Kinds | 8 | 625.00 | 1,100.00 | 1,650.00 | 22,500.00 |
| 1797 10 Stars Left, 6 Right | — | 625.00 | 1,100.00 | 1,650.00 | 22,500.00 |
| 1798 13 Stars, All Kinds | 328 | 800.00 | 1,300.00 | 2,150.00 | 25,000.00 |
| 1798 15 Stars | — | 1,000.00 | 2,000.00 | 2,500.00 | 28,500.00 |
| 1798 Large Eagle | — | 400.00 | 600.00 | 800.00 | 11,500.00 |
| 1799 over 98, All Kinds | 424 | 410.00 | 610.00 | 825.00 | 12,500.00 |
| 1799 Stars 7 Left, 6 Right, All Kinds | — | 400.00 | 600.00 | 800.00 | 11,500.00 |

|  | Mintage in Thousands | Good | Fine | V. Fine | Unc. |
|---|---|---|---|---|---|
| 1799 Stars 8 Left, 5 Right, All Kinds | — | 500.00 | 800.00 | 1,100.00 | 15,000.00 |
| 1800 | 221 | 400.00 | 600.00 | 800.00 | 11,500.00 |
| 1801 | 54 | 425.00 | 650.00 | 900.00 | 16,000.00 |
| 1802 over 1, All Kinds | — | 400.00 | 600.00 | 975.00 | 11,500.00 |
| 1802, All Kinds | — | 425.00 | 675.00 | 925.00 | 12,000.00 |
| 1803 | 86 | 425.00 | 600.00 | 825.00 | 12,000.00 |
| 1804 (Very rare) | — | — | — | — | — |

## GOBRECHT PATTERNS

|  | Mintage in Thousands | Proof |
|---|---|---|
| 1836 C. Gobrecht E in field below base. Reverse Eagle in field of stars (Rare) | — | 25,000.00 |
| 1836 Obverse as above Reverse. Eagle flying in plain field (Rare) | 1 | 25,000.00 |

|  | Mintage in Thousands | V. Fine | Proof |
|---|---|---|---|
| 1836 C. Gobrecht on base | (inc. above) | 3,500.00 | 9,500.00 |
| 1838 | about 100 Pieces | 5,500.00 | 16,000.00 |
| 1839 | about 300 Pieces | — | 13,500.00 |

## LIBERTY SEATED TYPE

1840–1865         1866–1873

|       | Mintage in Thousands | V. Good | V. Fine | Unc. | Proof |
|---|---|---|---|---|---|
| 1840 | 61 | 180.00 | 300.00 | 1,750.00 | — |
| 1841 | 173 | 130.00 | 220.00 | 1,600.00 | — |
| 1842 | 185 | 130.00 | 220.00 | 1,100.00 | — |
| 1843 | 165 | 130.00 | 220.00 | 1,250.00 | — |
| 1844 | 20 | 225.00 | 375.00 | 2,750.00 | — |
| 1845 | 25 | 250.00 | 325.00 | 5,500.00 | — |
| 1846 | 111 | 130.00 | 220.00 | 1,450.00 | — |
| 1846O | 59 | 165.00 | 325.00 | 3,000.00 | — |
| 1847 | 141 | 130.00 | 220.00 | 1,100.00 | — |
| 1848 | 15 | 275.00 | 500.00 | 3,250.00 | — |
| 1849 | 63 | 160.00 | 260.00 | 1,650.00 | — |
| 1850 | 8 | 450.00 | 775.00 | 4,750.00 | — |
| 1850O | 40 | 225.00 | 675.00 | 7,750.00 | — |
| 1851 | 1 | 1,250.00 | 3,500.00 | 20,000.00 | 27,500.00 |
| 1852 | 1 | 1,200.00 | 3,150.00 | 21,500.00 | 25,000.00 |
| 1853 | 46 | 185.00 | 375.00 | 2,750.00 | — |
| 1854 | 33 | 1,200.00 | 2,450.00 | 7,000.00 | 16,000.00 |
| 1855 | 26 | 975.00 | 1,950.00 | 7,750.00 | 16,000.00 |
| 1856 | 64 | 340.00 | 550.00 | 3,650.00 | 11,000.00 |
| 1857 | 94 | 335.00 | 575.00 | 2,650.00 | 10,000.00 |
| 1858 | About 300 Pieces | 3,000.00 | 4,000.00 | — | 12,000.00 |
| 1859 | 257 | 240.00 | 400.00 | 1,375.00 | 3,500.00 |
| 1859O | 360 | 130.00 | 220.00 | 1,000.00 | — |
| 1859S | 20 | 300.00 | 550.00 | 10,000.00 | — |
| 1860 | 219 | 210.00 | 400.00 | 1,150.00 | 3,500.00 |
| 1860O | 515 | 130.00 | 220.00 | 1,000.00 | — |
| 1861 | 79 | 575.00 | 825.00 | 2,950.00 | 3,750.00 |
| 1862 | 12 | 475.00 | 750.00 | 2,850.00 | 3,600.00 |
| 1863 | 28 | 250.00 | 425.00 | 2,650.00 | 3,600.00 |
| 1864 | 31 | 225.00 | 425.00 | 2,650.00 | 3,500.00 |
| 1865 | 47 | 210.00 | 400.00 | 2,500.00 | 3,250.00 |
| 1866 | 50 | 210.00 | 390.00 | 1,750.00 | 2,950.00 |
| 1867 | 48 | 200.00 | 375.00 | 1,750.00 | 2,800.00 |
| 1868 | 163 | 175.00 | 350.00 | 1,950.00 | 2,750.00 |
| 1869 | 424 | 160.00 | 275.00 | 1,825.00 | 2,750.00 |
| 1870 | 416 | 130.00 | 220.00 | 1,500.00 | 2,750.00 |

|  | Mintage in Thousands | V. Good | V. Fine | Unc. | Proof |
|---|---|---|---|---|---|
| 1870CC | 12 | 350.00 | 750.00 | 13,500.00 | — |
| 1870S (Rare) | — | — | 99,500.00 | — | — |
| 1871 | 1,075 | 130.00 | 220.00 | 1,000.00 | 2,750.00 |
| 1871CC | 1 | 2,100.00 | 5,000.00 | 55,000.00 | — |
| 1872 | 1,106 | 130.00 | 220.00 | 1,000.00 | 2,750.00 |
| 1872CC | 3 | 1,200.00 | 2,650.00 | 21,000.00 | — |
| 1872S | 9 | 290.00 | 575.00 | 10,000.00 | — |
| 1873 | 294 | 140.00 | 250.00 | 1,275.00 | 2,750.00 |
| 1873CC | 2 | 4,500.00 | 8,500.00 | 75,000.00 | — |
| 1873S (Unknown) | 1 | — | — | — | — |

## MORGAN OR LIBERTY HEAD TYPE

|  | Mintage in Thousands | Ex. Fine | Unc. | Proof |
|---|---|---|---|---|
| 1878 8 Tail Feathers | 750 | 25.00 | 100.00 | 2,250.00 |
| 1878 7 Tail Feathers over 8 Tail Feathers | | 30.00 | 110.00 | — |
| 1878 7 Tail Feathers Reverse of 1878 | 9,760 | 19.00 | 50.00 | 2,500.00 |
| 1878 7 Tail Feathers Reverse of 1879 | — | 19.00 | 60.00 | 30,000.00 |
| 1878CC | 2,212 | 50.00 | 130.00 | — |
| 1878S | 9,774 | 17.00 | 35.00 | — |
| 1879 | 14,807 | 15.00 | 30.00 | 1,600.00 |
| 1879CC | 756 | 300.00 | 1,500.00 | — |
| 1879O | 2,887 | 15.00 | 75.00 | — |
| 1879S | 9,110 | 15.00 | 30.00 | — |
| 1880 | 12,601 | 15.00 | 30.00 | 1,600.00 |
| 1880CC | 591 | 100.00 | 225.00 | — |
| 1880O | 5,305 | 15.00 | 65.00 | — |
| 1880S | 8,990 | 15.00 | 25.00 | — |
| 1881 | 9,164 | 15.00 | 30.00 | 1,600.00 |
| 1881CC | 296 | 130.00 | 210.00 | — |
| 1881O | 5,708 | 15.00 | 25.00 | — |
| 1881S | 12,760 | 15.00 | 25.00 | — |
| 1882 | 11,101 | 15.00 | 25.00 | 1,600.00 |
| 1882CC | 1,133 | 55.00 | 90.00 | — |
| 1882O | 6,090 | 15.00 | 25.00 | — |
| 1882S | 9,250 | 15.00 | 25.00 | — |
| 1883 | 12,291 | 15.00 | 25.00 | 1,600.00 |
| 1883CC | 1,204 | 50.00 | 90.00 | — |
| 1883O | 8,725 | 15.00 | 23.00 | — |
| 1883S | 6,250 | 30.00 | 375.00 | — |

|  | Mintage in Thousands | Ex. Fine | Unc. | Proof |
|---|---|---|---|---|
| 1884 | 14,071 | 15.00 | 25.00 | 1,600.00 |
| 1884CC | 1,136 | 55.00 | 90.00 | — |
| 1884O | 9,730 | 15.00 | 23.00 | — |
| 1884S | 3,200 | 40.00 | 3,600.00 | — |
| 1885 | 17,788 | 15.00 | 23.00 | 1,600.00 |
| 1885CC | 228 | 215.00 | 245.00 | — |
| 1885O | 9,185 | 15.00 | 23.00 | — |
| 1885S | 1,497 | 20.00 | 125.00 | — |
| 1886 | 19,964 | 15.00 | 23.00 | 1,600.00 |
| 1886O | 10,710 | 17.00 | 325.00 | — |
| 1886S | 750 | 45.00 | 165.00 | — |
| 1887 | 20,291 | 15.00 | 23.00 | 1,600.00 |
| 1887O | 11,550 | 15.00 | 50.00 | — |
| 1887S | 1,771 | 20.00 | 75.00 | — |
| 1888 | 19,184 | 15.00 | 23.00 | 1,600.00 |
| 1888O | 12,150 | 15.00 | 28.00 | — |
| 1888S | 657 | 40.00 | 165.00 | — |
| 1889 | 21,737 | 15.00 | 25.00 | 1,600.00 |
| 1889CC | 350 | 1,250.00 | 8,500.00 | — |
| 1889O | 11,875 | 15.00 | 110.00 | — |
| 1889S | 700 | 35.00 | 135.00 | — |
| 1890 | 16,803 | 15.00 | 25.00 | 1,700.00 |
| 1890CC | 2,309 | 55.00 | 300.00 | — |
| 1890O | 10,701 | 15.00 | 45.00 | — |
| 1890S | 8,230 | 15.00 | 50.00 | — |
| 1891 | 8,694 | 15.00 | 45.00 | 1,600.00 |
| 1891CC | 1,608 | 55.00 | 280.00 | — |
| 1891O | 7,955 | 15.00 | 100.00 | — |
| 1891S | 5,296 | 15.00 | 55.00 | — |
| 1892 | 1,037 | 25.00 | 150.00 | 1,575.00 |
| 1892CC | 1,352 | 120.00 | 450.00 | — |
| 1892O | 2,742 | 20.00 | 110.00 | — |
| 1892S | 1,200 | 175.00 | 17,500.00 | — |
| 1893 | 390 | 165.00 | 350.00 | 1,600.00 |
| 1893CC | 677 | 575.00 | 1,500.00 | — |
| 1893O | 300 | 225.00 | 1,700.00 | — |
| 1893S | 100 | 4,750.00 | 50,000.00 | — |
| 1894 | 111 | 400.00 | 1,000.00 | 1,600.00 |
| 1894O | 1,723 | 50.00 | 550.00 | — |
| 1894S | 1,260 | 110.00 | 450.00 | — |
| 1895 | 13 | 16,500.00 | — | 22,500.00 |
| 1895O | 450 | 325.00 | 11,000.00 | — |
| 1895S | 400 | 450.00 | 1,850.00 | — |
| 1896 | 9,977 | 15.00 | 23.00 | 1,600.00 |
| 1896O | 4,900 | 18.00 | 775.00 | — |
| 1896S | 5,000 | 150.00 | 775.00 | — |
| 1897 | 2,823 | 15.00 | 25.00 | 1,750.00 |
| 1897O | 4,004 | 22.00 | 650.00 | — |
| 1897S | 5,825 | 15.00 | 45.00 | — |
| 1898 | 5,885 | 15.00 | 23.00 | 1,575.00 |
| 1898O | 4,440 | 15.00 | 26.00 | — |
| 1898S | 4,102 | 30.00 | 175.00 | — |
| 1899 | 331 | 50.00 | 90.00 | 1,575.00 |
| 1899O | 12,290 | 15.00 | 26.00 | — |
| 1899S | 2,562 | 30.00 | 200.00 | — |
| 1900 | 8,831 | 16.00 | 26.00 | 1,600.00 |
| 1900O | 12,590 | 16.00 | 30.00 | — |
| 1900S | 3,540 | 30.00 | 180.00 | — |
| 1901 | 6,963 | 55.00 | 1,750.00 | 1,800.00 |

|  | Mintage in Thousands | Ex. Fine | Unc. | Proof |
|---|---|---|---|---|
| 1901O | 13,320 | 15.00 | 25.00 | — |
| 1901S | 2,284 | 50.00 | 285.00 | — |
| 1902 | 7,995 | 15.00 | 40.00 | 1,600.00 |
| 1902O | 8,636 | 15.00 | 23.00 | — |
| 1902S | 1,530 | 100.00 | 225.00 | — |
| 1903 | 4,653 | 20.00 | 35.00 | 1,575.00 |
| 1903O | 4,450 | 145.00 | 220.00 | — |
| 1903S | 1,241 | 300.00 | 2,750.00 | — |
| 1904 | 2,789 | 15.00 | 70.00 | 1,575.00 |
| 1904O | 3,720 | 15.00 | 23.00 | — |
| 1904S | 2,304 | 200.00 | 1,100.00 | — |
| 1921 | 44,690 | 11.00 | 16.00 | 3,250.00 |
| 1921D | 20,345 | 12.00 | 30.00 | — |
| 1921S | 21,695 | 12.00 | 27.00 | — |

## PEACE TYPE

|  | Mintage in Thousands | Ex. Fine | Unc. |
|---|---|---|---|
| 1921 | 1,006 | 55.00 | 150.00 |
| 1922 | 51,737 | 10.00 | 16.00 |
| 1922D | 15,063 | 10.00 | 17.00 |
| 1922S | 17,475 | 10.00 | 17.00 |
| 1923 | 30,800 | 10.00 | 16.00 |
| 1923D | 6,811 | 10.00 | 45.00 |
| 1923S | 13,020 | 10.00 | 22.00 |
| 1924 | 11,811 | 10.00 | 16.00 |
| 1924S | 1,728 | 22.00 | 185.00 |
| 1925 | 10,198 | 10.00 | 16.00 |
| 1925S | 1,610 | 13.00 | 65.00 |
| 1926 | 1,939 | 11.00 | 23.00 |
| 1926D | 2,349 | 12.00 | 60.00 |
| 1926S | 6,980 | 11.00 | 40.00 |
| 1927 | 848 | 27.00 | 60.00 |
| 1927D | 1,269 | 25.00 | 140.00 |
| 1927S | 866 | 24.00 | 120.00 |
| 1928 | 361 | 155.00 | 230.00 |
| 1928S | 1,632 | 24.00 | 115.00 |
| 1934 | 954 | 20.00 | 75.00 |
| 1934D | 1,570 | 20.00 | 90.00 |
| 1934S | 1,011 | 150.00 | 1,250.00 |

|  | Mintage in Thousands | Ex. Fine | Unc. |
|---|---|---|---|
| 1935 | 1,576 | 16.00 | 55.00 |
| 1935S | 1,964 | 23.00 | 150.00 |

## EISENHOWER DOLLAR

|  | Mintage in Thousands | Unc. | Proof |
|---|---|---|---|
| 1971 Copper Nickel | 47,799 | 3.00 | — |
| 1971D Copper Nickel | 68,587 | 3.00 | — |
| 1971S Silver | 11,134 | 5.00 | 6.00 |
| 1972 Copper Nickel | 75,890 | 2.00 | — |
| 1972D Copper Nickel | 92,549 | 2.00 | — |
| 1972S Silver | 4,005 | 5.00 | 6.00 |
| 1973 Copper Nickel | 2,000 | 5.00 | — |
| 1973D Copper Nickel | 2,000 | 5.00 | — |
| 1973S Copper Nickel | 2,770 | — | 5.00 |
| 1973S Silver | 2,889 | 6.00 | 17.00 |
| 1974 Copper Nickel | 27,366 | 3.00 | — |
| 1974D Copper Nickel | 45,517 | 2.00 | — |
| 1974S Copper Nickel | 2,617 | — | — |
| 1974S Silver | 3,215 | 5.00 | 6.00 |
| 1976 Copper Nickel* | 117,338 | 2.00 | — |
| 1976D Copper Nickel* | 103,228 | 2.00 | — |
| 1976S Silver* | 15,000 | 10.00 | 10.00 |
| 1976S Copper Nickel* | 6,995 | — | 6.00 |
| 1977 Copper Nickel | 12,596 | 4.00 | — |
| 1977D Copper Nickel | 32,983 | 2.00 | — |
| 1977S Copper Nickel | 3,251 | — | 5.00 |
| 1978 | 25,702 | 2.00 | — |
| 1978D | 23,013 | 4.00 | — |
| 1978S Copper Nickel | 3,128 | — | 6.00 |

## ANTHONY DOLLAR

| | | | |
|---|---|---|---|
| 1979P | 360,222 | 2.00 | — |
| 1979D | 288,016 | 2.00 | — |
| 1979S | 113,253 | 2.00 | 6.00 |
| 1979S Type Two, Proof only, Sharp Mint Mark | 3,667 | — | 70.00 |
| 1980P | 27,610 | 2.00 | — |
| 1980D | 41,629 | 2.00 | — |
| 1980S | 23,969 | 2.00 | 5.00 |
| 1981P-D | 6,250 | 4.00 | — |
| 1981S | 7,555 | 4.00 | 6.00 |

*Bicentennial coinage dated 1776–1976, with reverses showing the Liberty Bell superimposed on the moon. No 1975 dated dollars were struck.

# 36.
# TRADE DOLLARS—
# 1873–1885

|  | Mintage in Thousands | V. Good | Fine | Ex. Fine | Unc. | Proof |
|---|---:|---:|---:|---:|---:|---:|
| 1873 . . . . . . . . . . . . . . . | 398 | 75.00 | 100.00 | 180.00 | 450.00 | 2,250.00 |
| 1873CC . . . . . . . . . . . . | 125 | 90.00 | 170.00 | 550.00 | 2,850.00 | — |
| 1873S . . . . . . . . . . . . . . | 703 | 75.00 | 105.00 | 215.00 | 875.00 | — |
| 1874 . . . . . . . . . . . . . . . | 988 | 75.00 | 100.00 | 160.00 | 450.00 | 2,150.00 |
| 1874CC . . . . . . . . . . . . | 1,373 | 85.00 | 105.00 | 250.00 | 1,300.00 | — |
| 1874S . . . . . . . . . . . . . . | 2,549 | 75.00 | 100.00 | 160.00 | 425.00 | — |
| 1875 . . . . . . . . . . . . . . . | 219 | 150.00 | 285.00 | 450.00 | 1,325.00 | 2,150.00 |
| 1875CC . . . . . . . . . . . . | 1,574 | 85.00 | 120.00 | 230.00 | 725.00 | — |
| 1875S . . . . . . . . . . . . . . | 4,487 | 75.00 | 100.00 | 160.00 | 425.00 | — |
| 1876 . . . . . . . . . . . . . . . | 456 | 75.00 | 105.00 | 160.00 | 425.00 | 2,150.00 |
| 1876CC . . . . . . . . . . . . | 509 | 80.00 | 125.00 | 325.00 | 2,750.00 | — |
| 1876S . . . . . . . . . . . . . . | 5,227 | 75.00 | 100.00 | 160.00 | 425.00 | — |
| 1877 . . . . . . . . . . . . . . . | 3,040 | 75.00 | 100.00 | 160.00 | 450.00 | 2,150.00 |
| 1877CC . . . . . . . . . . . . | 534 | 140.00 | 195.00 | 450.00 | 1,100.00 | — |
| 1877S . . . . . . . . . . . . . . | 9,519 | 75.00 | 100.00 | 160.00 | 425.00 | — |
| 1878 . . . . . . . . . . . . . . . | 1 | 650.00 | 750.00 | 975.00 | — | 2,150.00 |
| 1878CC . . . . . . . . . . . . | 97 | 375.00 | 575.00 | 1,675.00 | 11,000.00 | — |
| 1878S . . . . . . . . . . . . . . | 4,162 | 75.00 | 100.00 | 160.00 | 450.00 | — |
| 1879 . . . . . . . . . . . . . . . | 2 | 575.00 | 700.00 | 850.00 | — | 2,150.00 |
| 1880 . . . . . . . . . . . . . . . | 2 | 575.00 | 700.00 | 850.00 | — | 2,150.00 |
| 1881 . . . . . . . . . . . . . . . | 1 | 625.00 | 750.00 | 925.00 | — | 2,150.00 |
| 1882 . . . . . . . . . . . . . . . | 1 | 600.00 | 725.00 | 900.00 | — | 2,150.00 |
| 1883 . . . . . . . . . . . . . . . | 1 | 650.00 | 750.00 | 925.00 | — | 2,150.00 |
| 1884 Only 10 Struck | — | — | — | — | — | 200,000.00 |
| 1885 Only 5 Struck . . | — | — | — | — | — | 600,000.00 |

Note: Trade dollars with oriental counterstamps ("Gin" marks) are worth considerably less than quoted values.

# 37.
# SILVER COMMEMORATIVE COINS
## (Half Dollars unless otherwise specified)

| | Mintage in Thousands | Ex. Fine | Unc. |
|---|---|---|---|
| 1892 Columbian Exposition | 950 | 12.00 | 25.00 |
| 1893 Columbian Exposition | 1,550 | 12.00 | 25.00 |
| 1893 Isabella Quarter | 24 | 215.00 | 350.00 |
| 1900 Lafayette Dollar | 36 | 225.00 | 475.00 |
| 1915S Panama-Pacific Exposition | 27 | 160.00 | 400.00 |
| 1918 Illinois Centennial | 100 | 65.00 | 95.00 |
| 1920 Maine Centennial | 50 | 65.00 | 125.00 |
| 1920 Pilgrim Tercentenary | 152 | 45.00 | 75.00 |
| 1921 Pilgrim Tercentenary (1921) on obverse | 20 | 80.00 | 130.00 |
| 1921 Missouri Centennial (with star) | 5 | 260.00 | 600.00 |
| 1921 Missouri Centennial (no star) | 15 | 170.00 | 500.00 |
| 1921 Alabama Centennial (with 2 × 2) | 6 | 120.00 | 375.00 |
| 1921 Alabama Centennial (no 2 × 2) | 59 | 70.00 | 250.00 |
| 1922 Grant Memorial (with star) | 4 | 500.00 | 1,000.00 |
| 1922 Grant Memorial (no star) | 67 | 65.00 | 125.00 |
| 1923S Monroe Doctrine Centennial | 274 | 23.00 | 60.00 |
| 1924 Huguenot-Walloon Tercentenary | 142 | 70.00 | 110.00 |
| 1925 Lexington-Concord Sesquicentennial | 162 | 45.00 | 80.00 |
| 1925 Stone Mountain Memorial | 1,315 | 33.00 | 50.00 |
| 1925S California Diamond Jubilee | 87 | 80.00 | 130.00 |
| 1925 Fort Vancouver Centennial | 15 | 200.00 | 300.00 |
| 1926 Sesquicentennial of American Independence | 141 | 45.00 | 90.00 |
| 1926 Oregon Trail Memorial | 48 | 75.00 | 100.00 |
| 1926 Oregon Trail Memorial, S Mint | 83 | 75.00 | 100.00 |
| 1928 Oregon Trail Memorial | 6 | 135.00 | 160.00 |
| 1933D Oregon Trail Memorial | 5 | 210.00 | 230.00 |
| 1934D Oregon Trail Memorial | 7 | 115.00 | 150.00 |
| 1936 Oregon Trail Memorial | 10 | 95.00 | 115.00 |
| 1936S Oregon Trail Memorial | 5 | 100.00 | 135.00 |
| 1937D Oregon Trail Memorial | 12 | 110.00 | 130.00 |
| 1938P-D-S Oregon Trail Memorial (set of three) | Each 6 | 425.00 | 500.00 |
| 1939P-D-S Oregon Trail Memorial (set of three) | Each 3 | 850.00 | 1,100.00 |
| 1927 Vermont Sesquicentennial | 28 | 130.00 | 160.00 |
| 1928 Hawaiian Sesquicentennial | 10 | 925.00 | 1,500.00 |
| 1934 Maryland Tercentenary | 25 | 95.00 | 135.00 |
| 1934 Texas Centennial | 61 | 75.00 | 95.00 |
| 1935P-D-S Texas Centennial (set of three) | Each 10 | 220.00 | 270.00 |
| 1936P-D-S Texas Centennial (set of three) | Each 9 | 220.00 | 280.00 |
| 1937P-D-S Texas Centennial (set of three) | Each 7 | 235.00 | 290.00 |
| 1938P-D-S Texas Centennial (set of three) | Each 4 | 425.00 | 675.00 |
| 1934 Daniel Boone Bicentennial | 10 | 58.00 | 75.00 |
| 1935P-D-S Daniel Boone Bicentennial (set of three) | Each 5 | 185.00 | 235.00 |
| 1935P-D-S Daniel Boone Bicentennial (set of three)* | Each 2 | 475.00 | 675.00 |
| 1936P-D-S Daniel Boone Bicentennial (set of three) | Each 5 | 185.00 | 225.00 |
| 1937P-D-S Daniel Boone Bicentennial (set of three) | Each 3 | 375.00 | 600.00 |
| 1938P-D-S Daniel Boone Bicentennial (set of three) | Each 2 | 625.00 | 800.00 |
| 1935 Connecticut Tercentenary | 25 | 150.00 | 180.00 |
| 1935P-D-S Arkansas Centennial (set of three) | Each 6 | 180.00 | 210.00 |
| 1936P-D-S Arkansas Centennial (set of three) | Each 10 | 180.00 | 210.00 |
| 1937P-D-S Arkansas Centennial (set of three) | Each 6 | 190.00 | 240.00 |
| 1938P-D-S Arkansas Centennial (set of three) | Each 3 | 230.00 | 350.00 |

|  | Mintage in Thousands | Ex. Fine | Unc. |
|---|---|---|---|
| 1939P-D-S Arkansas Centennial (set of three) | Each 2 | 450.00 | 650.00 |
| 1935 Hudson, N.Y. Sesquicentennial | 10 | 400.00 | 465.00 |
| 1935S California-Pacific Exposition | 70 | 50.00 | 60.00 |
| 1936D California-Pacific Exposition | 30 | 53.00 | 65.00 |
| 1935 Old Spanish Trail | 10 | 685.00 | 750.00 |
| 1936P-D-S Rhode Island Tercentenary (set of three) | Each 15 | 180.00 | 225.00 |
| 1936 Cleveland, Great Lakes Exposition | 56 | 55.00 | 63.00 |
| 1936 Wisconsin Territorial Centennial | 25 | 135.00 | 150.00 |
| 1936P-D-S Cincinnati Musical Center (set of three) | Each 5 | 560.00 | 650.00 |
| 1936 Long Island Tercentenary | 82 | 48.00 | 65.00 |
| 1936 York County, Maine Tercentenary | 25 | 130.00 | 150.00 |
| 1936 Bridgeport, Conn. Centennial | 25 | 85.00 | 110.00 |
| 1936 Lynchburg, Va. Sesquicentennial | 20 | 130.00 | 150.00 |
| 1936 Elgin, Illinois Centennial | 20 | 145.00 | 165.00 |
| 1936 Albany, N.Y. Charter | 18 | 175.00 | 210.00 |
| 1936S San Francisco-Oakland Bay Bridge | 71 | 85.00 | 110.00 |
| 1936P-D-S Columbia, S.C. Sesquicentennial (set of three) | Each 8 | 450.00 | 500.00 |
| 1936 Arkansas Centennial-Robinson | 25 | 90.00 | 100.00 |
| 1936 Delaware Tercentenary | 21 | 175.00 | 210.00 |
| 1936 Battle of Gettysburg (1863–1938) | 27 | 235.00 | 265.00 |
| 1936 Norfolk, Va. Bicentennial | 17 | 325.00 | 385.00 |
| 1937 Roanoke Island, N.C. (1587–1937) | 29 | 135.00 | 170.00 |
| 1937 Battle of Antietam (1862–1937) | 18 | 375.00 | 425.00 |
| 1938 New Rochelle, N.Y. (1688–1938) | 15 | 225.00 | 270.00 |
| 1946 Iowa Centennial | 100 | 55.00 | 70.00 |
| 1946 Booker T. Washington Memorial (set of three) | +1001 | 30.00 | 45.00 |
| 1947 Booker T. Washington Memorial (set of three) | Each 100 | 33.00 | 65.00 |
| 1948 Booker T. Washington Memorial (set of three) | Each 8 | 48.00 | 105.00 |
| 1949 Booker T. Washington Memorial (set of three) | Each 6 | 115.00 | 175.00 |
| 1950 Booker T. Washington Memorial (set of three) | Each 6+ | 48.00 | 95.00 |
| 1951 Booker T. Washington Memorial (set of three) | Each 7+ | 50.00 | 110.00 |
| 1951 Washington Carver (set of three) | Each 10 | 35.00 | 75.00 |
| 1952 Washington Carver (set of three) | Each 8 | 35.00 | 95.00 |
| 1953 Washington Carver (set of three) | Each 8 | 35.00 | 95.00 |
| 1954 Washington Carver (set of three) | Each 12 | 32.00 | 80.00 |

*Small "1934" added on Reverse.
+ Additional quantities struck, beyond sets of three.

|  | Unc. | Proof |
|---|---|---|
| 1982D Geo. Washington—250th Anniversary | 5.00 | — |
| 1982S Geo. Washington—250th Anniversary | — | 5.00 |
| 1983P Los Angeles XIII Olympiad Dollar | 10.00 | — |
| 1983D Los Angeles XIII Olympiad Dollar | 10.00 | — |
| 1983S Los Angeles XIII Olympiad Dollar | 10.00 | 11.00 |
| 1984P Los Angeles XIII Olympiad Dollar | 15.00 | — |
| 1984D Los Angeles XIII Olympiad Dollar | 25.00 | — |
| 1984S Los Angeles XIII Olympiad Dollar | 25.00 | 12.00 |
| 1986D Statue of Liberty | 5.00 | — |
| 1986S Statue of Liberty | — | 5.00 |
| 1986 Silver American Eagle | 12.00 | 22.00 |
| 1987 Constitution Bicentennial Dollar | 10.00 | 12.00 |
| 1987 Silver American Eagle | 10.00 | 22.00 |
| 1988 Olympiad Dollar | 10.00 | 10.00 |
| 1988 Silver American Eagle | 10.00 | 40.00 |
| 1989S Silver Congressional | 10.00 | 6.00 |
| 1989S Silver American Eagle | — | 22.00 |

## 38.

## GOLD COMMEMORATIVE COINS
(Dollar unless otherwise specified)

|  | Mintage in Thousands | Ex. Fine | Unc. |
|---|---|---|---|
| 1903 Louisiana Purchase (Jefferson) | 18 | 300.00 | 500.00 |
| 1903 Louisiana Purchase (McKinley) | 18 | 285.00 | 450.00 |
| 1904 Lewis and Clark Exposition | 10 | 425.00 | 875.00 |
| 1905 Lewis and Clark Exposition | 10 | 425.00 | 1,000.00 |
| 1915S Panama-Pacific Exposition | 15 | 285.00 | 375.00 |
| 1915S Panama-Pacific Exposition ($2.50) | 7 | 975.00 | 1,500.00 |
| 1915S Panama-Pacific Exposition ($50 round) | 483 Pieces | 22,500.00 | 27,500.00 |
| 1915S Panama-Pacific Exposition ($50 octagonal) | 645 Pieces | 19,000.00 | 24,000.00 |
| 1916 McKinley Memorial | 10 | 245.00 | 400.00 |
| 1917 McKinley Memorial | 10 | 300.00 | 575.00 |
| 1922 Grant Memorial (with star) | 5 | 1,000.00 | 1,350.00 |
| 1922 Grant Memorial (no star) | 5 | 975.00 | 1,150.00 |
| 1926 Philadelphia Sesquicentennial ($2.50) | 46 | 230.00 | 325.00 |

|  | Unc. | Proof |
|---|---|---|
| 1984 Los Angeles Olympic Gold Eagle ($10) | — | — |
| 1986W Statue of Liberty | 135.00 | 135.00 |
| 1987W Constitution Bicentennial | 135.00 | 135.00 |
| 1988W Olympiad—1988 | 135.00 | 135.00 |
| 1989W Gold Congressional | 135.00 | 135.00 |

## 39.
## PROOF SETS
### EACH SET CONTAINS A HALF, QUARTER, DIME, NICKEL AND CENT, SPECIALLY STRUCK AT THE MINT WITH MIRROR-LIKE FINISH (ALSO A DOLLAR FROM 1973 ONWARDS)

| Date and Number of Sets Coined | Proof |
|---|---|
| 1936 (3,837) | 3,800.00 |
| 1937 (5,542) | 2,250.00 |
| 1938 (8,045) | 950.00 |
| 1939 (8,795) | 1,000.00 |
| 1940 (11,246) | 775.00 |
| 1941 (15,287) | 650.00 |
| 1942 (21,120) 6 pieces | 725.00 |
| 1950 (51,386) | 390.00 |
| 1951 (57,500) | 335.00 |
| 1952 (81,980) | 170.00 |
| 1953 (128,800) | 135.00 |
| 1954 (233,300) | 70.00 |
| 1955 (378,200) | 65.00 |
| 1956 (669,384) | 30.00 |
| 1957 (1,247,952) | 16.00 |
| 1958 (875,652) | 25.00 |
| 1959 (1,149,291) | 19.00 |
| 1960 (1,691,602) | 12.00 |
| 1960 with sm. dr. ct. | 23.00 |
| 1961 (3,028,244) | 9.00 |
| 1962 (3,218,039) | 9.00 |
| 1963 (3,075,045) | 9.00 |
| 1964 (3,950,962) | 9.00 |
| 1968S (3,041,509) | 6.00 |
| 1969S (2,934,631) | 5.00 |
| 1970S (2,632,810) | 10.00 |
| 1971S (3,224,138) | 5.00 |
| 1972S (3,267,667) | 6.00 |
| 1973S (2,769,624) | 10.00 |
| 1974S (2,617,350) | 12.00 |
| 1975S (2,909,369) | 12.00 |
| 1976S (4,149,730) | 13.00 |
| 1977S (3,251,152) | 11.00 |
| 1978S (3,127,781) | 11.00 |
| 1979S Type I | 12.00 |
| 1979S Type II (each mintmark is sharp and well defined) (3,677,175) | 80.00 |
| 1980S (3,554,806) | 8.00 |
| 1981S (4,063,083) | 9.00 |
| 1982S (3,857,479) | 5.00 |
| 1983S (3,138,765) | 6.00 |
| 1983S "P" 10¢ (included above) | 385.00 |
| 1984S (2,748,430) | 8.00 |
| 1985S (3,362,821) | 5.00 |
| 1986S (2,411,180) | 17.00 |
| 1987S (3,792,233) | 5.00 |
| 1988S (3,031,287) | 8.00 |
| 1989S (3,009,107) | 9.00 |
| 1990S (2,793,433) | 12.00 |
| 1991S (2,610,833) | 22.00 |
| 1992S | 10.00 |
| 1993S | 21.00 |

## 40.
## GOLD, GOLD, THAT MAGIC WORD

Since the dawn of civilization, gold has been hunted by man! Treasured beyond belief, its beautiful color, durability, ease of transportation and scarcity have led man to go to unbelievable lengths to secure it. Its demand made it the first basic commodity in trade. Ancient Egyptians cherished it; King Croesus first struck coins out of it; Greek and Romans buried their hoards of it in earthen jars. The Incas in South America hoarded it, erected statues and made idols out of it. Man throughout all parts of the world sought it.

In ancient times, armies sacked cities for gold and other treasures. During the middle ages, walled castles were built to protect such valuables. Vikings sacked England; pirates roved the seas; outlaws robbed; Spain conquered and pilfered Central and South America. All for gold and treasures.

The discovery of gold in 1849 in California hastened the population of the far west, caused murders, stage coach and train robberies. All in the name of the magic word GOLD.

Up until 1933, we had been on the gold standard, with the price of gold set by government edict at about twenty dollars per ounce. A twenty-dollar gold piece contained nearly one ounce of gold (with, of course, some alloy to harden the coin for circulation). When the dollar was devalued in 1933 the price of a twenty-dollar gold piece immediately was set at thirty-five dollars. This price gradually increased through the years until it reached the sixty-dollar figure.

The recent lowering of the value of the dollar again has caused an unbelievable boom in gold prices. Is this the top? Will it go higher? That is the question.

Let's analyze the situation. The currencies of the world, always under the pressure of inflation, have been subjected to various degrees of inflation, reducing their purchasing power. There has to be some basic medium by which valuations can be determined. Gold has always been accepted as this medium. This would make gold rise in value. Now, the population of the world is much greater than it ever was, hence we have more demand for gold, but gold supply is limited. Another reason why gold should rise in value.

How high will gold go? Who knows? But it will be determined by the rate of inflation of currencies and demand; today demand is high.

# 41.
# GOLD DOLLARS—
# 1849–1889

## LIBERTY HEAD TYPE

|  | Mintage in Thousands | V. Fine | Unc. |
|---|---|---|---|
| 1849 | 689 | 135.00 | 500.00 |
| 1849C | 12 | 500.00 | 8,250.00 |
| 1849D | 22 | 450.00 | 4,500.00 |
| 1849O | 215 | 150.00 | 775.00 |
| 1850 | 482 | 140.00 | 475.00 |
| 1850C | 7 | 575.00 | 8,750.00 |
| 1850D | 8 | 575.00 | 9,250.00 |
| 1850O | 14 | 260.00 | 3,250.00 |
| 1851 | 3,318 | 135.00 | 325.00 |
| 1851C | 41 | 450.00 | 2,450.00 |
| 1851D | 10 | 500.00 | 4,850.00 |
| 1851O | 290 | 165.00 | 750.00 |
| 1852 | 2,045 | 135.00 | 325.00 |
| 1852C | 9 | 425.00 | 4,500.00 |
| 1852D | 6 | 675.00 | 7,850.00 |
| 1852O | 140 | 145.00 | 1,475.00 |
| 1853 | 4,076 | 135.00 | 325.00 |
| 1853C | 12 | 550.00 | 6,750.00 |
| 1853D | 7 | 675.00 | 10,000.00 |
| 1853O | 290 | 160.00 | 675.00 |
| 1854 Small Planchet | 737 | 135.00 | 325.00 |
| 1854D | 3 | 900.00 | 15,000.00 |
| 1854S | 15 | 300.00 | 2,350.00 |

## INDIAN HEADDRESS TYPE

|  | Mintage in Thousands | V. Fine | Unc. |
|---|---|---|---|
| 1954 Large Planchet | 903 | 285.00 | 2,475.00 |
| 1855 | 758 | 285.00 | 2,475.00 |
| 1855C | 10 | 1,350.00 | 16,500.00 |
| 1855D | 2 | 2,650.00 | 28,500.00 |
| 1855O | 55 | 450.00 | 6,000.00 |
| 1856S | 25 | 650.00 | 7,750.00 |

## LARGER INDIAN HEADDRESS TYPE

|  | Mintage in Thousands | V. Fine | Unc. | Proof |
|---|---|---|---|---|
| 1856 | 1,763 | 140.00 | 325.00 | — |
| 1856D | 1 | 3,600.00 | 25,000.00 | — |
| 1857 | 775 | 140.00 | 325.00 | — |
| 1857C | 13 | 625.00 | 12,500.00 | — |
| 1857D | 4 | 875.00 | 12,500.00 | — |
| 1857S | 10 | 500.00 | 6,500.00 | — |
| 1858 | 118 | 140.00 | 375.00 | 5,000.00 |
| 1858D | 3 | 775.00 | 10,000.00 | — |
| 1858S | 10 | 385.00 | 6,250.00 | — |
| 1859 | 168 | 140.00 | 375.00 | 4,500.00 |
| 1859C | 5 | 550.00 | 15,000.00 | — |
| 1859D | 5 | 775.00 | 10,500.00 | — |
| 1859S | 15 | 250.00 | 5,500.00 | — |
| 1860 | 37 | 140.00 | 425.00 | 4,250.00 |
| 1860D | 2 | 2,450.00 | 26,500.00 | — |
| 1860S | 13 | 335.00 | 2,750.00 | — |
| 1861 | 527 | 140.00 | 325.00 | 4,750.00 |
| 1861D | — | 6,250.00 | 36,500.00 | — |
| 1862 | 1,361 | 140.00 | 325.00 | 4,900.00 |
| 1863 | 6 | 450.00 | 4,250.00 | 4,750.00 |
| 1864 | 6 | 350.00 | 1,250.00 | 6,000.00 |
| 1865 | 4 | 350.00 | 1,600.00 | 4,750.00 |
| 1866 | 7 | 350.00 | 1,100.00 | 4,750.00 |
| 1867 | 5 | 385.00 | 1,200.00 | 4,900.00 |
| 1868 | 11 | 295.00 | 1,100.00 | 5,250.00 |
| 1869 | 6 | 360.00 | 1,200.00 | 6,000.00 |

|  | Mintage in Thousands | V. Fine | Unc. | Proof |
|---|---|---|---|---|
| 1870 | 6 | 285.00 | 900.00 | 5,000.00 |
| 1870S | 3 | 475.00 | 2,650.00 | — |
| 1871 | 4 | 285.00 | 725.00 | 4,500.00 |
| 1872 | 4 | 290.00 | 900.00 | 5,500.00 |
| 1873 | 125 | 140.00 | 325.00 | 8,500.00 |
| 1874 | 199 | 140.00 | 325.00 | 7,500.00 |
| 1875 | 420 Pieces | 2,500.00 | 6,500.00 | 13,500.00 |
| 1876 | 3 | 275.00 | 650.00 | 4,500.00 |
| 1877 | 4 | 190.00 | 675.00 | 5,250.00 |
| 1878 | 3 | 230.00 | 650.00 | 4,500.00 |
| 1879 | 3 | 190.00 | 575.00 | 4,850.00 |
| 1880 | 2 | 160.00 | 500.00 | 4,500.00 |
| 1881 | 8 | 160.00 | 500.00 | 4,300.00 |
| 1882 | 5 | 175.00 | 500.00 | 4,150.00 |
| 1883 | 11 | 160.00 | 500.00 | 4,150.00 |
| 1884 | 6 | 155.00 | 500.00 | 4,150.00 |
| 1885 | 12 | 160.00 | 500.00 | 4,150.00 |
| 1886 | 6 | 160.00 | 500.00 | 4,150.00 |
| 1887 | 9 | 160.00 | 500.00 | 4,150.00 |
| 1888 | 16 | 160.00 | 500.00 | 4,150.00 |
| 1889 | 31 | 160.00 | 400.00 | 4,150.00 |

# 42.
# QUARTER EAGLES
# 1796–1929

## ($2.50 GOLD PIECES)
## LIBERTY CAP TYPE

         1796                           1796–1807

|  | Mintage in Thousands | V. Fine | Unc. |
|---|---|---|---|
| 1796 No Stars | 1 | 20,000.00 | 200,000.00 |
| 1796 Stars | 432 Pieces | 13,500.00 | 150,000.00 |
| 1797 | 427 Pieces | 11,000.00 | 90,000.00 |
| 1798 | 1 | 3,850.00 | 55,000.00 |
| 1802 over 1 | 3 | 3,750.00 | 17,000.00 |
| 1804 | 3 | 3,850.00 | 25,000.00 |
| 1805 | 2 | 3,750.00 | 23,000.00 |
| 1806 over 4 | 2 | 3,950.00 | 25,000.00 |
| 1806 over 5 | 2 | 7,750.00 | 75,000.00 |
| 1807 | 7 | 3,950.00 | 17,000.00 |

## TURBAN HEAD TYPE

| | | | |
|---|---|---|---|
| 1808 | 3 | 15,000.00 | 50,000.00 |
| 1821 | 6 | 3,900.00 | 17,000.00 |
| 1824 over 21 | 3 | 3,900.00 | 14,500.00 |
| 1825 | 4 | 3,700.00 | 12,000.00 |
| 1826 over 25 | 1 | 4,400.00 | 28,500.00 |
| 1827 | 3 | 5,250.00 | 16,500.00 |
| 1829 | 3 | 3,650.00 | 10,500.00 |
| 1830 | 5 | 3,650.00 | 10,500.00 |
| 1831 | 5 | 3,650.00 | 10,500.00 |
| 1832 | 4 | 3,650.00 | 10,500.00 |
| 1833 | 4 | 3,650.00 | 11,500.00 |
| 1834 With Motto | 4 | 9,250.00 | 30,000.00 |

## CLASSIC HEAD TYPE

|  | Mintage in Thousands | Ex. Fine | Unc. |
|---|---|---|---|
| 1834 No Motto | 112 | 450.00 | 2,000.00 |
| 1835 | 131 | 450.00 | 2,400.00 |
| 1836 | 548 | 450.00 | 2,000.00 |
| 1837 | 45 | 475.00 | 2,800.00 |
| 1838 | 47 | 475.00 | 2,000.00 |
| 1838C | 8 | 2,150.00 | 26,500.00 |
| 1839 | 27 | 675.00 | 4,750.00 |
| 1839C | 18 | 2,150.00 | 25,000.00 |
| 1839D | 14 | 3,150.00 | 25,000.00 |
| 1839O | 18 | 950.00 | 6,500.00 |

## CORONET TYPE

|  | Mintage in Thousands | Ex. Fine | Unc. |
|---|---|---|---|
| 1840 | 19 | 900.00 | 6,500.00 |
| 1840C | 13 | 1,250.00 | 17,500.00 |
| 1840D | 4 | 7,750.00 | 35,000.00 |
| 1840O | 34 | 850.00 | 12,000.00 |
| 1841 Proof (Ex. rare) | — | 75,000.00 | — |
| 1841C | 10 | 1,250.00 | 20,000.00 |
| 1841D | 4 | 3,500.00 | 25,000.00 |
| 1842 | 3 | 2,650.00 | 18,500.00 |
| 1842C | 7 | 2,750.00 | 24,500.00 |
| 1842D | 5 | 3,250.00 | 35,000.00 |
| 1842O | 20 | 1,100.00 | 13,000.00 |
| 1843 | 101 | 210.00 | 1,250.00 |
| 1843C | 26 | 1,150.00 | 8,000.00 |
| 1843D | 36 | 1,300.00 | 9,750.00 |
| 1843O | 364 | 230.00 | 1,650.00 |
| 1844 | 7 | 875.00 | 7,250.00 |
| 1844C | 12 | 1,850.00 | 22,000.00 |
| 1844D | 17 | 1,275.00 | 7,250.00 |
| 1845 | 91 | 290.00 | 1,175.00 |

|  | Mintage in Thousands | Ex. Fine | Unc. | Proof |
|---|---|---|---|---|
| 1845D | 19 | 1,350.00 | 16,000.00 | — |
| 1845O | 4 | 2,100.00 | 16,000.00 | — |
| 1846 | 22 | 550.00 | 5,750.00 | — |
| 1846C | 5 | 2,100.00 | 22,000.00 | — |
| 1846D | 19 | 1,100.00 | 13,750.00 | — |
| 1846O | 66 | 485.00 | 5,250.00 | — |
| 1847 | 30 | 375.00 | 3,500.00 | — |
| 1847C | 23 | 1,150.00 | 7,000.00 | — |
| 1847D | 16 | 1,250.00 | 7,500.00 | — |
| 1847O | 124 | 400.00 | 3,500.00 | — |
| 1848 | 7 | 950.00 | 8,000.00 | — |
| 1848 CAL above Eagle | 1 | 14,000.00 | 35,000.00 | — |
| 1848C | 17 | 1,500.00 | 16,750.00 | — |
| 1848D | 14 | 1,325.00 | 11,500.00 | — |
| 1849 | 23 | 500.00 | 2,350.00 | — |
| 1849C | 10 | 1,400.00 | 24,000.00 | — |
| 1849D | 11 | 1,375.00 | 21,500.00 | — |
| 1850 | 253 | 225.00 | 1,150.00 | — |
| 1850C | 9 | 1,400.00 | 19,750.00 | — |
| 1850D | 12 | 1,200.00 | 19,750.00 | — |
| 1850O | 84 | 475.00 | 4,750.00 | — |
| 1851 | 1,373 | 185.00 | 325.00 | — |
| 1851C | 15 | 1,275.00 | 15,000.00 | — |
| 1851D | 11 | 1,300.00 | 14,500.00 | — |
| 1851O | 148 | 250.00 | 4,750.00 | — |
| 1852 | 1,160 | 185.00 | 325.00 | — |
| 1852C | 8 | 1,675.00 | 18,500.00 | — |
| 1852D | 4 | 2,400.00 | 25,000.00 | — |
| 1852O | 140 | 300.00 | 5,250.00 | — |
| 1853 | 1,405 | 185.00 | 375.00 | — |
| 1853D | 3 | 2,650.00 | 23,500.00 | — |
| 1854 | 596 | 185.00 | 375.00 | — |
| 1854C | 7 | 1,900.00 | 18,500.00 | — |
| 1854D | 2 | 5,000.00 | 25,000.00 | — |
| 1854O | 153 | 250.00 | 1,700.00 | — |
| 1854S (Rare) | 246 Pieces | 50,000.00 | — | — |
| 1855 | 235 | 185.00 | 425.00 | — |
| 1855C | 4 | 2,850.00 | 27,500.00 | — |
| 1855D | 1 | 7,500.00 | 39,000.00 | — |
| 1856 | 384 | 185.00 | 450.00 | 35,000.00 |
| 1856C | 10 | 2,150.00 | 17,000.00 | — |
| 1856D | 1 | 11,500.00 | 50,000.00 | — |
| 1856O | 21 | 750.00 | 7,500.00 | — |
| 1856S | 71 | 400.00 | 4,850.00 | — |
| 1857 | 214 | 185.00 | 400.00 | — |
| 1857D | 2 | 2,350.00 | 16,000.00 | — |
| 1857O | 34 | 375.00 | 4,750.00 | — |
| 1857S | 69 | 360.00 | 6,750.00 | — |
| 1858 | 47 | 260.00 | 1,500.00 | 15,000.00 |
| 1858C | 9 | 1,300.00 | 9,750.00 | — |
| 1859 | 39 | 260.00 | 500.00 | 15,000.00 |
| 1859D | 2 | 2,650.00 | 26,500.00 | — |
| 1859S | 15 | 1,200.00 | 7,750.00 | — |
| 1860 | 23 | 290.00 | 1,375.00 | 15,000.00 |
| 1860C | 7 | 1,950.00 | 22,500.00 | — |
| 1860S | 36 | 700.00 | 4,350.00 | — |
| 1861 | 1,248 | 185.00 | 375.00 | 15,000.00 |

|  | Mintage in Thousands | Ex. Fine | Unc. | Proof |
|---|---|---|---|---|
| 1861S | 24 | 1,000.00 | 6,750.00 | — |
| 1862 | 99 | 300.00 | 1,350.00 | 6,500.00 |
| 1862S | 8 | 2,400.00 | 18,500.00 | — |
| 1863 | 30 Pieces | — | — | 37,500.00 |
| 1863S | 11 | 1,500.00 | 17,500.00 | — |
| 1864 | 3 | 11,500.00 | 37,500.00 | 10,000.00 |
| 1865 | 2 | 9,250.00 | 37,500.00 | 13,000.00 |
| 1865S | 23 | 625.00 | 4,250.00 | — |
| 1866 | 3 | 3,750.00 | 18,500.00 | 10,000.00 |
| 1866S | 39 | 825.00 | 9,250.00 | — |
| 1867 | 3 | 850.00 | 5,000.00 | 10,000.00 |
| 1867S | 28 | 850.00 | 5,750.00 | — |
| 1868 | 4 | 425.00 | 2,350.00 | 10,500.00 |
| 1868S | 34 | 330.00 | 4,500.00 | — |
| 1869 | 4 | 475.00 | 3,000.00 | 7,250.00 |
| 1869S | 30 | 475.00 | 4,500.00 | — |
| 1870 | 5 | 450.00 | 3,800.00 | 8,000.00 |
| 1870S | 16 | 450.00 | 5,000.00 | — |
| 1871 | 5 | 360.00 | 2,600.00 | 7,250.00 |
| 1871S | 22 | 325.00 | 2,600.00 | — |
| 1872 | 3 | 850.00 | 4,750.00 | 7,250.00 |
| 1872S | 18 | 425.00 | 4,500.00 | — |
| 1873 | 178 | 185.00 | 325.00 | 6,250.00 |
| 1873S | 27 | 500.00 | 3,150.00 | — |
| 1874 | 4 | 475.00 | 2,600.00 | 8,000.00 |
| 1875 | 420 Pieces | 5,250.00 | 17,500.00 | 17,500.00 |
| 1875S | 12 | 325.00 | 4,750.00 | — |
| 1876 | 4 | 685.00 | 3,650.00 | 6,000.00 |
| 1876S | 5 | 550.00 | 4,000.00 | — |
| 1877 | 2 | 800.00 | 3,850.00 | 10,000.00 |
| 1877S | 35 | 185.00 | 700.00 | — |
| 1878 | 286 | 185.00 | 325.00 | 10,000.00 |
| 1878S | 178 | 185.00 | 385.00 | — |
| 1879 | 89 | 185.00 | 325.00 | 6,750.00 |
| 1879S | 44 | 300.00 | 1,700.00 | — |
| 1880 | 3 | 375.00 | 1,600.00 | 7,250.00 |
| 1881 | 1 | 3,150.00 | 8,250.00 | 5,250.00 |
| 1882 | 4 | 325.00 | 800.00 | 5,000.00 |
| 1883 | 2 | 425.00 | 2,200.00 | 5,150.00 |
| 1884 | 2 | 410.00 | 1,675.00 | 5,150.00 |
| 1885 | 1 | 1,725.00 | 4,500.00 | 5,650.00 |
| 1886 | 4 | 300.00 | 1,375.00 | 5,500.00 |
| 1887 | 6 | 250.00 | 850.00 | 4,750.00 |
| 1888 | 16 | 230.00 | 375.00 | 5,000.00 |
| 1889 | 18 | 210.00 | 375.00 | 6,250.00 |
| 1890 | 9 | 230.00 | 500.00 | 5,250.00 |
| 1891 | 11 | 200.00 | 450.00 | 5,350.00 |
| 1892 | 3 | 250.00 | 850.00 | 5,000.00 |
| 1893 | 30 | 190.00 | 350.00 | 4,850.00 |
| 1894 | 4 | 225.00 | 850.00 | 4,850.00 |
| 1895 | 6 | 210.00 | 450.00 | 4,750.00 |
| 1896 | 19 | 190.00 | 325.00 | 4,850.00 |
| 1897 | 30 | 190.00 | 325.00 | 4,750.00 |
| 1898 | 24 | 190.00 | 325.00 | 4,750.00 |
| 1899 | 27 | 190.00 | 375.00 | 4,750.00 |
| 1900 | 67 | 210.00 | 325.00 | 4,750.00 |
| 1901 | 91 | 185.00 | 325.00 | 4,750.00 |
| 1902 | 134 | 185.00 | 325.00 | 4,750.00 |

|  | Mintage in Thousands | Ex. Fine | Unc. | Proof |
|---|---|---|---|---|
| 1903 | 201 | 185.00 | 325.00 | 4,750.00 |
| 1904 | 161 | 185.00 | 325.00 | 4,750.00 |
| 1905 | 218 | 185.00 | 325.00 | 4,750.00 |
| 1906 | 176 | 185.00 | 325.00 | 4,750.00 |
| 1907 | 336 | 185.00 | 325.00 | 4,750.00 |

## INDIAN HEAD TYPE

|  | Mintage | Ex. Fine | Unc. | Proof |
|---|---|---|---|---|
| 1908 | 565 | 180.00 | 270.00 | 8,500.00 |
| 1909 | 442 | 180.00 | 285.00 | 14,500.00 |
| 1910 | 493 | 180.00 | 270.00 | 8,500.00 |
| 1911 | 704 | 180.00 | 285.00 | 8,500.00 |
| 1911D | 56 | 975.00 | 3,000.00 | — |
| 1912 | 616 | 180.00 | 285.00 | 8,500.00 |
| 1913 | 722 | 180.00 | 285.00 | 8,750.00 |
| 1914 | 240 | 200.00 | 400.00 | 8,500.00 |
| 1914D | 448 | 180.00 | 280.00 | — |
| 1915 | 606 | 180.00 | 270.00 | 8,500.00 |
| 1925D | 578 | 180.00 | 265.00 | — |
| 1926 | 446 | 180.00 | 265.00 | — |
| 1927 | 388 | 180.00 | 265.00 | — |
| 1928 | 416 | 180.00 | 265.00 | — |
| 1929 | 532 | 180.00 | 265.00 | — |

# 43.
# THREE-DOLLAR GOLD PIECES
# 1854–1889

|  | Mintage in Thousands | V. Fine | Unc. | Proof |
|---|---|---|---|---|
| 1854 | 139 | 525.00 | 1,750.00 | 40,000.00 |
| 1854D | 1 | 7,250.00 | 80,000.00 | — |
| 1854O | 24 | 775.00 | 16,000.00 | — |
| 1855 | 51 | 525.00 | 1,850.00 | — |
| 1855S | 7 | 950.00 | 25,000.00 | — |
| 1856 | 26 | 525.00 | 2,350.00 | 17,000.00 |
| 1856S | 35 | 575.00 | 9,000.00 | — |
| 1857 | 21 | 525.00 | 2,850.00 | 15,000.00 |
| 1857S | 14 | 700.00 | 14,000.00 | — |
| 1858 | 2 | 725.00 | 7,250.00 | 15,000.00 |
| 1859 | 16 | 525.00 | 2,350.00 | 11,000.00 |
| 1860 | 7 | 585.00 | 2,450.00 | 11,000.00 |
| 1860S | 7 | 725.00 | 13,500.00 | — |
| 1861 | 6 | 650.00 | 2,850.00 | 12,000.00 |
| 1862 | 6 | 650.00 | 2,850.00 | 11,500.00 |
| 1863 | 5 | 675.00 | 2,800.00 | 10,000.00 |
| 1864 | 3 | 685.00 | 2,550.00 | 11,000.00 |
| 1865 | 1 | 975.00 | 7,250.00 | 13,500.00 |
| 1866 | 4 | 700.00 | 2,750.00 | 13,000.00 |
| 1867 | 3 | 700.00 | 2,550.00 | 11,500.00 |
| 1868 | 5 | 650.00 | 2,475.00 | 11,500.00 |
| 1869 | 3 | 750.00 | 3,500.00 | 11,500.00 |
| 1870 | 4 | 585.00 | 3,500.00 | 11,000.00 |
| 1870S (Unique) | — | — | — | 1,000,000.00 |
| 1871 | 1 | 710.00 | 3,100.00 | 17,500.00 |
| 1872 | 2 | 675.00 | 2,650.00 | 12,000.00 |
| 1873 Closed 3 | — | 2,900.00 | 25,000.00 | 22,500.00 |
| 1873 Open 3 | 25 Pieces | — | — | 27,500.00 |
| 1874 | 42 | 525.00 | 1,750.00 | 13,000.00 |
| 1875 | 20 Pieces | — | — | 75,000.00 |
| 1876 | 45 Pieces | — | — | 24,000.00 |
| 1877 | 1 | 1,075.00 | 11,750.00 | 15,000.00 |

|  | Mintage in Thousands | V. Fine | Unc. | Proof |
|---|---|---|---|---|
| 1878 | 82 | 525.00 | 1,750.00 | 15,000.00 |
| 1879 | 3 | 625.00 | 2,250.00 | 11,000.00 |
| 1880 | 1 | 650.00 | 2,300.00 | 10,750.00 |
| 1881 | 1 | 1,200.00 | 4,750.00 | 9,250.00 |
| 1882 | 2 | 800.00 | 2,450.00 | 9,250.00 |
| 1883 | 1 | 700.00 | 2,500.00 | 9,250.00 |
| 1884 | 1 | 1,100.00 | 2,450.00 | 9,250.00 |
| 1885 | 1 | 1,100.00 | 3,000.00 | 9,250.00 |
| 1886 | 1 | 1,000.00 | 3,100.00 | 9,250.00 |
| 1887 | 6 | 600.00 | 1,800.00 | 9,250.00 |
| 1888 | 5 | 600.00 | 1,800.00 | 9,250.00 |
| 1889 | 2 | 600.00 | 1,800.00 | 9,250.00 |

# 44.
# STELLAS
# 1879–1880
## ($4 GOLD PIECES)

|  | Mintage in Thousands | Proof-65 |
|---|---|---|
| 1879 Flowing hair | 415 Pieces | 95,000.00 |
| 1879 Coiled hair (Very rare) | 10 Pieces | 275,000.00 |
| 1880 Flowing hair (Very rare) | 15 Pieces | 160,000.00 |
| 1880 Coiled hair (Very rare) | 10 Pieces | 375,000.00 |

# 45.
# HALF EAGLES
# 1795–1929

## ($5 GOLD PIECES)
## CAPPED BUST TYPE

**1795–1798**  **1795–1807**

|  | Mintage in Thousands | V. Fine | Unc. |
|---|---|---|---|
| 1795 Small Eagle, All Kinds | 9 | 8,000.00 | 37,500.00 |
| 1795 Large Eagle, All Kinds | 9 | 13,750.00 | 85,000.00 |
| 1796 over 95 | 6 | 10,500.00 | 70,000.00 |
| 1797 15 Stars, Small Eagle, All Kinds | 4 | 14,500.00 | 130,000.00 |
| 1797 16 Stars, Small Eagle, All Kinds | 4 | 13,000.00 | 120,000.00 |
| 1797 over 95, Large Eagle | (included above) | 13,250.00 | 150,000.00 |
| 1798 Small Eagle (Very rare) | — | 150,000.00 | — |
| 1798 Large Eagle, 13 star reverse, All Kinds | 25 | 2,350.00 | 16,000.00 |
| 1798 Large Eagle, 14 star reverse, All Kinds | 25 | 2,400.00 | 30,000.00 |
| 1799 | 7 | 2,350.00 | 16,500.00 |
| 1800 | 38 | 1,850.00 | 6,750.00 |
| 1802 over 1 | 53 | 1,850.00 | 7,000.00 |
| 1803 over 2 | 34 | 1,850.00 | 6,850.00 |
| 1804 | 30 | 1,900.00 | 7,250.00 |
| 1805 | 33 | 1,950.00 | 6,750.00 |
| 1806 | 64 | 1,900.00 | 6,250.00 |
| 1807 | 32 | 1,950.00 | 6,850.00 |

## LIBERTY CAP TYPE

1807–1812                1813–1834

|  | Mintage in Thousands | V. Fine | Unc. |
|---|---:|---:|---:|
| 1807 | 52 | 1,800.00 | 5,500.00 |
| 1808 over 7, All Kinds | 56 | 1,850.00 | 9,750.00 |
| 1808, All Kinds | 56 | 1,775.00 | 6,000.00 |
| 1809 over 8 | 34 | 1,800.00 | 6,250.00 |
| 1810 | 100 | 1,775.00 | 5,500.00 |
| 1811 | 100 | 1,775.00 | 5,500.00 |
| 1812 | 58 | 1,800.00 | 5,750.00 |
| 1813 | 95 | 2,100.00 | 6,750.00 |
| 1814 over 3 | 15 | 2,575.00 | 9,000.00 |
| 1815 (Rare) | 1 | 50,000.00 | 150,000.00 |
| 1818 | 49 | 2,375.00 | 8,250.00 |
| 1819 | 52 | 16,500.00 | 40,000.00 |
| 1820 | 264 | 2,550.00 | 10,000.00 |
| 1821 | 35 | 10,000.00 | 33,500.00 |
| 1822 (Very rare) | 18 | — | — |
| 1823 | 14 | 3,100.00 | 16,500.00 |
| 1824 | 17 | 9,250.00 | 28,500.00 |
| 1825 over 21, All Kinds | 29 | 7,250.00 | 28,500.00 |
| 1825 over 24 (Rare), All Kinds | 29 | — | 325,000.00 |
| 1826 | 18 | 7,000.00 | 23,500.00 |
| 1827 | 25 | 8,000.00 | 28,500.00 |
| 1828 over 27, All Kinds (Rare) | 28 | 12,000.00 | 110,000.00 |
| 1828, All Kinds | 28 | 6,750.00 | 47,500.00 |
| 1829 (Rare) | 57 | 45,000.00 | 120,000.00 |
| 1830 | 126 | 4,850.00 | 13,750.00 |
| 1831 | 141 | 5,100.00 | 17,000.00 |
| 1832 | 157 | 5,000.00 | 13,250.00 |
| 1833 | 194 | 4,900.00 | 11,000.00 |
| 1834 | 50 | 4,900.00 | 18,000.00 |

## CLASSIC HEAD TYPE

|  | Mintage in Thousands | Ex. Fine | Unc. |
|---|---|---|---|
| 1834 | 658 | 500.00 | 2,650.00 |
| 1835 | 372 | 500.00 | 3,250.00 |
| 1836 | 553 | 475.00 | 2,650.00 |
| 1837 | 207 | 525.00 | 3,500.00 |
| 1838 | 287 | 500.00 | 3,575.00 |
| 1838C | 17 | 3,850.00 | 35,000.00 |
| 1838D | 21 | 3,750.00 | 26,000.00 |

## CORONET TYPE

1839–1865              1865–1908

|  | Mintage in Thousands | V. Fine | Ex. Fine | Unc. |
|---|---|---|---|---|
| 1839 | 118 | 250.00 | 435.00 | 3,500.00 |
| 1839C | 17 | 950.00 | 2,450.00 | 26,000.00 |
| 1839D | 19 | 800.00 | 2,100.00 | 18,500.00 |
| 1840 | 137 | 225.00 | 350.00 | 4,100.00 |
| 1840C | 19 | 750.00 | 2,450.00 | 23,000.00 |
| 1840D | 23 | 750.00 | 1,650.00 | 18,500.00 |
| 1840O | 40 | 325.00 | 800.00 | 10,000.00 |
| 1841 | 16 | 350.00 | 850.00 | 5,600.00 |
| 1841C | 21 | 675.00 | 1,450.00 | 16,500.00 |
| 1841D | 29 | 800.00 | 1,250.00 | 16,000.00 |
| 1841O | 50 Pieces | — | — | — |
| 1842 | 28 | 325.00 | 1,150.00 | 12,500.00 |
| 1842C | 28 | 800.00 | 1,500.00 | 13,750.00 |
| 1842D | 160 | 725.00 | 1,250.00 | 14,000.00 |
| 1842O | 16 | 1,000.00 | 3,450.00 | 21,500.00 |
| 1843 | 611 | 210.00 | 240.00 | 1,700.00 |
| 1843C | 44 | 750.00 | 1,400.00 | 14,000.00 |
| 1843D | 98 | 625.00 | 1,100.00 | 11,500.00 |
| 1843O | 517 | 250.00 | 1,000.00 | 11,250.00 |
| 1844 | 340 | 210.00 | 225.00 | 1,850.00 |
| 1844C | 24 | 875.00 | 2,850.00 | 19,500.00 |
| 1844D | 89 | 650.00 | 1,050.00 | 12,000.00 |
| 1844O | 365 | 225.00 | 350.00 | 4,500.00 |
| 1845 | 417 | 210.00 | 225.00 | 1,875.00 |
| 1845D | 90 | 675.00 | 1,100.00 | 13,000.00 |
| 1845O | 41 | 385.00 | 675.00 | 11,500.00 |
| 1846 | 396 | 210.00 | 225.00 | 2,750.00 |
| 1846C | 13 | 950.00 | 2,850.00 | 23,500.00 |
| 1846D | 80 | 650.00 | 1,200.00 | 12,500.00 |
| 1846O | 58 | 350.00 | 925.00 | 12,750.00 |
| 1847 | 916 | 210.00 | 225.00 | 1,500.00 |
| 1847C | 84 | 650.00 | 1,250.00 | 14,000.00 |
| 1847D | 64 | 600.00 | 1,250.00 | 8,000.00 |
| 1847O | 12 | 1,800.00 | 6,750.00 | 24,000.00 |
| 1848 | 261 | 210.00 | 225.00 | 1,500.00 |

|  | Mintage in Thousands | V. Fine | Ex. Fine | Unc. | Proof |
|---|---|---|---|---|---|
| 1848C | 64 | 675.00 | 1,250.00 | 19,000.00 | — |
| 1848D | 47 | 600.00 | 1,375.00 | 14,500.00 | — |
| 1849 | 133 | 210.00 | 260.00 | 2,500.00 | — |
| 1849C | 65 | 550.00 | 1,250.00 | 14,000.00 | — |
| 1849D | 39 | 750.00 | 1,250.00 | 14,500.00 | — |
| 1850 | 64 | 260.00 | 575.00 | 3,500.00 | — |
| 1850C | 64 | 575.00 | 1,250.00 | 15,000.00 | — |
| 1850D | 44 | 625.00 | 1,500.00 | 22,000.00 | — |
| 1851 | 378 | 210.00 | 225.00 | 2,900.00 | — |
| 1851C | 49 | 600.00 | 1,000.00 | 16,000.00 | — |
| 1851D | 63 | 650.00 | 1,650.00 | 15,000.00 | — |
| 1851O | 41 | 550.00 | 1,250.00 | 11,750.00 | — |
| 1852 | 574 | 210.00 | 225.00 | 1,400.00 | — |
| 1852C | 73 | 550.00 | 1,100.00 | 8,000.00 | — |
| 1852D | 92 | 550.00 | 1,250.00 | 13,000.00 | — |
| 1853 | 306 | 210.00 | 225.00 | 1,650.00 | — |
| 1853C | 66 | 550.00 | 1,250.00 | 8,000.00 | — |
| 1853D | 90 | 525.00 | 950.00 | 7,250.00 | — |
| 1854 | 161 | 210.00 | 235.00 | 2,100.00 | — |
| 1854C | 39 | 525.00 | 1,500.00 | 17,000.00 | — |
| 1854D | 56 | 525.00 | 1,200.00 | 14,500.00 | — |
| 1854O | 46 | 285.00 | 500.00 | 7,500.00 | — |
| 1854S (Rare) | 268 Pieces | — | — | — | — |
| 1855 | 117 | 210.00 | 225.00 | 1,650.00 | — |
| 1855C | 40 | 775.00 | 1,700.00 | 16,500.00 | — |
| 1855D | 22 | 750.00 | 1,375.00 | 18,000.00 | — |
| 1855O | 11 | 650.00 | 2,100.00 | 23,500.00 | — |
| 1855S | 61 | 400.00 | 1,000.00 | 14,500.00 | — |
| 1856 | 198 | 210.00 | 235.00 | 2,150.00 | — |
| 1856C | 28 | 575.00 | 1,150.00 | 21,000.00 | — |
| 1856D | 20 | 575.00 | 1,250.00 | 13,500.00 | — |
| 1856O | 10 | 600.00 | 1,300.00 | 21,500.00 | — |
| 1856S | 105 | 300.00 | 600.00 | 6,500.00 | — |
| 1857 | 98 | 210.00 | 225.00 | 1,650.00 | — |
| 1857C | 31 | 575.00 | 1,250.00 | 12,000.00 | — |
| 1857D | 17 | 575.00 | 1,175.00 | 20,000.00 | — |
| 1857O | 13 | 575.00 | 1,375.00 | 21,500.00 | — |
| 1857S | 87 | 300.00 | 525.00 | 9,250.00 | — |
| 1858 | 15 | 250.00 | 600.00 | 3,750.00 | — |
| 1858C | 39 | 650.00 | 1,250.00 | 14,000.00 | — |
| 1858D | 15 | 650.00 | 1,400.00 | 16,500.00 | — |
| 1858S | 19 | 675.00 | 2,500.00 | 23,500.00 | — |
| 1859 | 17 | 325.00 | 575.00 | 17,250.00 | — |
| 1859C | 32 | 625.00 | 1,450.00 | 16,500.00 | — |
| 1859D | 10 | 725.00 | 1,700.00 | 14,000.00 | — |
| 1859S | 13 | 1,350.00 | 3,500.00 | 32,500.00 | — |
| 1860 | 20 | 285.00 | 575.00 | 4,000.00 | — |
| 1860C | 15 | 850.00 | 1,950.00 | 14,500.00 | — |
| 1860D | 15 | 800.00 | 2,000.00 | 18,500.00 | — |
| 1860S | 21 | 1,150.00 | 2,000.00 | 22,500.00 | — |
| 1861 | 688 | 210.00 | 225.00 | 1,350.00 | — |
| 1861C | 7 | 1,650.00 | 3,600.00 | 32,500.00 | — |
| 1861D | 2 | 4,350.00 | 7,250.00 | 47,500.00 | — |
| 1861S | 18 | 1,100.00 | 4,350.00 | 32,500.00 | — |
| 1862 | 4 | 650.00 | 1,500.00 | 19,000.00 | — |
| 1862S | 10 | 3,500.00 | 6,500.00 | 60,000.00 | — |
| 1863 | 2 | 1,175.00 | 3,500.00 | 22,500.00 | — |
| 1863S | 17 | 1,275.00 | 4,000.00 | 32,500.00 | — |

|  | Mintage in Thousands | V. Fine | Ex. Fine | Unc. | Proof |
|---|---|---|---|---|---|
| 1864 | 4 | 600.00 | 1,875.00 | 14,500.00 | — |
| 1864S | 4 | 4,750.00 | 11,750.00 | 32,500.00 | — |
| 1865 | 1 | 1,350.00 | 3,750.00 | 24,000.00 | — |
| 1865S | 28 | 1,350.00 | 2,600.00 | 16,500.00 | — |
| 1866S No Motto | 9 | 1,600.00 | 3,900.00 | 31,000.00 | — |
| 1866 Motto on Reverse | 7 | 750.00 | 1,450.00 | 17,500.00 | 27,500.00 |
| 1866S | 35 | 1,150.00 | 2,750.00 | 23,500.00 | — |
| 1867 | 7 | 500.00 | 1,600.00 | 8,500.00 | 21,000.00 |
| 1867S | 29 | 1,300.00 | 2,750.00 | 26,000.00 | — |
| 1868 | 6 | 650.00 | 1,000.00 | 9,750.00 | 27,500.00 |
| 1868S | 52 | 450.00 | 1,400.00 | 20,000.00 | — |
| 1869 | 2 | 875.00 | 2,100.00 | 21,000.00 | 27,500.00 |
| 1869S | 31 | 450.00 | 1,650.00 | 24,000.00 | — |
| 1870 | 4 | 700.00 | 1,775.00 | 17,000.00 | 27,500.00 |
| 1870CC | 7 | 4,500.00 | 12,500.00 | 100,000.00 | — |
| 1870S | 17 | 1,200.00 | 2,500.00 | 26,000.00 | — |
| 1871 | 3 | 800.00 | 1,675.00 | 17,500.00 | 27,500.00 |
| 1871CC | 21 | 1,100.00 | 3,000.00 | 40,000.00 | — |
| 1871S | 25 | 500.00 | 950.00 | 13,500.00 | — |
| 1872 | 2 | 800.00 | 1,850.00 | 16,750.00 | 16,500.00 |
| 1872CC | 17 | 1,100.00 | 4,000.00 | 41,000.00 | — |
| 1872S | 36 | 425.00 | 775.00 | 10,000.00 | — |
| 1873 | 112 | 210.00 | 240.00 | 775.00 | 20,000.00 |
| 1873CC | 7 | 1,750.00 | 9,250.00 | 37,000.00 | — |
| 1873S | 31 | 525.00 | 1,250.00 | 21,000.00 | — |
| 1874 | 4 | 575.00 | 1,500.00 | 17,000.00 | 16,500.00 |
| 1874CC | 21 | 725.00 | 1,450.00 | 22,500.00 | — |
| 1874S | 16 | 550.00 | 1,900.00 | 21,000.00 | — |
| 1875 | 220 Pieces | 45,000.00 | 55,000.00 | 170,000.00 | 70,000.00 |
| 1875CC | 12 | 1,300.00 | 4,250.00 | 32,500.00 | — |
| 1875S | 9 | 600.00 | 2,350.00 | 23,500.00 | — |
| 1876 | 1 | 1,000.00 | 2,250.00 | 11,500.00 | 15,000.00 |
| 1876CC | 7 | 1,050.00 | 4,250.00 | 22,500.00 | — |
| 1876S | 4 | 1,500.00 | 3,250.00 | 27,500.00 | — |
| 1877 | 1 | 800.00 | 2,500.00 | 11,500.00 | 20,000.00 |
| 1877CC | 9 | 950.00 | 2,750.00 | 22,500.00 | — |
| 1877S | 27 | 375.00 | 625.00 | 8,750.00 | — |
| 1878 | 132 | 175.00 | 190.00 | 375.00 | 20,000.00 |
| 1878CC | 9 | 2,750.00 | 6,750.00 | 36,000.00 | — |
| 1878S | 145 | 175.00 | 200.00 | 650.00 | — |
| 1879 | 302 | 175.00 | 190.00 | 350.00 | 15,000.00 |
| 1879CC | 17 | 475.00 | 1,075.00 | 18,500.00 | — |
| 1879S | 426 | 175.00 | 210.00 | 825.00 | — |
| 1880 | 3,166 | 175.00 | 190.00 | 250.00 | 12,500.00 |
| 1880CC | 51 | 385.00 | 700.00 | 9,250.00 | — |
| 1880S | 1,349 | 175.00 | 190.00 | 250.00 | — |
| 1881 | 5,709 | 175.00 | 190.00 | 250.00 | 12,500.00 |
| 1881CC | 14 | 465.00 | 1,350.00 | 10,500.00 | — |
| 1881S | 969 | 175.00 | 190.00 | 250.00 | — |
| 1882 | 2,515 | 175.00 | 190.00 | 250.00 | 12,500.00 |
| 1882CC | 83 | 365.00 | 500.00 | 5,000.00 | — |
| 1882S | 970 | 175.00 | 190.00 | 250.00 | — |
| 1883 | 233 | 175.00 | 190.00 | 350.00 | 12,500.00 |
| 1883CC | 13 | 425.00 | 950.00 | 17,500.00 | — |
| 1883S | 83 | 185.00 | 210.00 | 1,000.00 | — |
| 1884 | 191 | 175.00 | 190.00 | 675.00 | 12,500.00 |
| 1884CC | 16 | 500.00 | 900.00 | 17,500.00 | — |
| 1884S | 177 | 175.00 | 190.00 | 350.00 | — |

|   | Mintage in Thousands | V. Fine | Ex. Fine | Unc. | Proof |
|---|---|---|---|---|---|
| 1885 | 602 | 175.00 | 190.00 | 250.00 | 12,500.00 |
| 1885S | 1,212 | 175.00 | 190.00 | 250.00 | — |
| 1886 | 388 | 175.00 | 190.00 | 250.00 | 12,500.00 |
| 1886S | 3,268 | 175.00 | 190.00 | 250.00 | — |
| 1887 | 87 Pieces | — | — | — | 60,000.00 |
| 1887S | 1,912 | 175.00 | 190.00 | 250.00 | — |
| 1888 | 18 | 185.00 | 225.00 | 575.00 | 10,000.00 |
| 1888S | 294 | 185.00 | 200.00 | 1,150.00 | — |
| 1889 | 8 | 300.00 | 450.00 | 1,050.00 | 12,500.00 |
| 1890 | 4 | 400.00 | 650.00 | 2,150.00 | 12,500.00 |
| 1890CC | 54 | 310.00 | 375.00 | 1,100.00 | — |
| 1891 | 61 | 185.00 | 200.00 | 475.00 | 10,000.00 |
| 1891CC | 208 | 275.00 | 375.00 | 725.00 | — |
| 1892 | 754 | 175.00 | 190.00 | 250.00 | 12,500.00 |
| 1892CC | 83 | 300.00 | 400.00 | 1,400.00 | — |
| 1892O | 10 | 475.00 | 925.00 | 2,950.00 | — |
| 1892S | 298 | 175.00 | 190.00 | 750.00 | — |
| 1893 | 1,528 | 175.00 | 190.00 | 250.00 | 11,000.00 |
| 1893CC | 60 | 260.00 | 425.00 | 1,350.00 | — |
| 1893O | 110 | 230.00 | 325.00 | 850.00 | — |
| 1893S | 224 | 175.00 | 190.00 | 250.00 | — |
| 1894 | 958 | 175.00 | 190.00 | 250.00 | 11,000.00 |
| 1894O | 17 | 210.00 | 360.00 | 1,175.00 | — |
| 1894S | 56 | 250.00 | 375.00 | 2,750.00 | — |
| 1895 | 1,346 | 175.00 | 190.00 | 250.00 | 10,000.00 |
| 1895S | 112 | 215.00 | 285.00 | 2,900.00 | — |
| 1896 | 59 | 175.00 | 190.00 | 280.00 | 10,000.00 |
| 1896S | 155 | 215.00 | 250.00 | 1,300.00 | — |
| 1897 | 868 | 175.00 | 190.00 | 250.00 | 10,000.00 |
| 1897S | 354 | 185.00 | 200.00 | 925.00 | — |
| 1898 | 633 | 175.00 | 190.00 | 260.00 | 10,000.00 |
| 1898S | 1,397 | 175.00 | 190.00 | 250.00 | — |
| 1899 | 1,711 | 175.00 | 190.00 | 250.00 | 9,500.00 |
| 1899S | 1,545 | 175.00 | 190.00 | 260.00 | — |
| 1900 | 1,406 | 175.00 | 190.00 | 250.00 | 9,500.00 |
| 1900S | 329 | 175.00 | 190.00 | 350.00 | — |
| 1901 | 616 | 175.00 | 190.00 | 250.00 | 9,500.00 |
| 1901S | 3,648 | 175.00 | 190.00 | 250.00 | — |
| 1902 | 173 | 175.00 | 190.00 | 250.00 | 9,500.00 |
| 1902S | 939 | 175.00 | 190.00 | 250.00 | — |
| 1903 | 227 | 175.00 | 190.00 | 250.00 | 9,500.00 |
| 1903S | 1,855 | 175.00 | 190.00 | 250.00 | — |
| 1904 | 392 | 175.00 | 190.00 | 250.00 | 9,500.00 |
| 1904S | 97 | 175.00 | 200.00 | 950.00 | — |
| 1905 | 302 | 175.00 | 190.00 | 250.00 | 10,000.00 |
| 1905S | 881 | 175.00 | 190.00 | 525.00 | — |
| 1906 | 349 | 175.00 | 190.00 | 250.00 | 9,500.00 |
| 1906D | 320 | 175.00 | 190.00 | 250.00 | — |
| 1906S | 598 | 175.00 | 190.00 | 250.00 | — |
| 1907 | 626 | 175.00 | 190.00 | 250.00 | 9,500.00 |
| 1907D | 888 | 175.00 | 190.00 | 250.00 | — |
| 1908 | 422 | 175.00 | 190.00 | 250.00 | — |

# INDIAN HEAD TYPE

|  | Mintage in Thousands | Ex. Fine | Unc. | Proof |
|---|---:|---:|---:|---:|
| 1908 | 578 | 225.00 | 350.00 | 11,500.00 |
| 1908D | 148 | 225.00 | 350.00 | — |
| 1908S | 82 | 450.00 | 1,350.00 | — |
| 1909 | 627 | 225.00 | 350.00 | 11,500.00 |
| 1909D | 3,424 | 225.00 | 350.00 | — |
| 1909O | 34 | 1,050.00 | 7,000.00 | — |
| 1909S | 297 | 235.00 | 1,400.00 | — |
| 1910 | 604 | 225.00 | 350.00 | 11,500.00 |
| 1910D | 194 | 225.00 | 385.00 | — |
| 1910S | 770 | 240.00 | 1,050.00 | — |
| 1911 | 915 | 225.00 | 350.00 | 11,500.00 |
| 1911D | 73 | 450.00 | 3,750.00 | — |
| 1911S | 1,416 | 240.00 | 650.00 | — |
| 1912 | 790 | 225.00 | 350.00 | 12,000.00 |
| 1912S | 392 | 240.00 | 1,700.00 | — |
| 1913 | 916 | 225.00 | 350.00 | 13,000.00 |
| 1913S | 408 | 250.00 | 1,500.00 | — |
| 1914 | 247 | 225.00 | 385.00 | 11,500.00 |
| 1914D | 247 | 225.00 | 350.00 | — |
| 1914S | 263 | 235.00 | 1,350.00 | — |
| 1915 | 588 | 225.00 | 350.00 | 15,000.00 |
| 1915S | 164 | 350.00 | 2,250.00 | — |
| 1916S | 240 | 270.00 | 600.00 | — |
| 1929 | 662 | 4,300.00 | 6,500.00 | — |

# 46.
# EAGLES
# 1795-1933

## ($10 GOLD PIECES) BUST TYPE

      1795-1797           1797-1804

|  | Mintage in Thousands | V. Fine | Unc. |
|---|---|---|---|
| 1795 | 6 | 10,500.00 | 65,000.00 |
| 1796 | 4 | 11,250.00 | 72,500.00 |
| 1797 Small Eagle | 4 | 13,500.00 | 175,000.00 |
| 1797 Large Eagle | 11 | 3,750.00 | 21,000.00 |
| 1798 over 97, 9 Stars Left, 4 Right | 1 | 12,000.00 | 75,000.00 |
| 1798 over 97, 7 Stars Left, 6 Right | 1 | 25,000.00 | 180,000.00 |
| 1799 | 37 | 3,500.00 | 11,000.00 |
| 1800 | 6 | 3,750.00 | 18,000.00 |
| 1801 | 44 | 3,500.00 | 11,250.00 |
| 1803 | 15 | 3,500.00 | 14,500.00 |
| 1804 | 4 | 4,150.00 | 26,500.00 |

## CORONET TYPE

|  | Mintage in Thousands | Ex. Fine | Unc. |
|---|---:|---:|---:|
| 1838 | 7 | 3,000.00 | 25,000.00 |
| 1839 Type of 1838 | 38 | 2,000.00 | 22,500.00 |

### 1840–1865    1866–1907

| | | | |
|---|---:|---:|---:|
| 1839 Type of 1839 | — | 3,500.00 | 31,500.00 |
| 1840 | 47 | 650.00 | 13,000.00 |
| 1841 | 63 | 485.00 | 9,500.00 |
| 1841O | 3 | 4,750.00 | 32,500.00 |
| 1842 | 82 | 525.00 | 13,000.00 |
| 1842O | 27 | 525.00 | 18,000.00 |
| 1843 | 75 | 485.00 | 17,000.00 |
| 1843O | 175 | 475.00 | 11,500.00 |
| 1844 | 6 | 3,000.00 | 17,500.00 |
| 1844O | 119 | 425.00 | 13,500.00 |
| 1845 | 26 | 800.00 | 17,000.00 |
| 1845O | 48 | 725.00 | 13,500.00 |
| 1846 | 20 | 1,250.00 | 22,500.00 |
| 1846O | 82 | 1,000.00 | 16,000.00 |
| 1847 | 862 | 375.00 | 3,500.00 |
| 1847O | 572 | 375.00 | 4,750.00 |
| 1848 | 145 | 425.00 | 5,350.00 |
| 1848O | 36 | 1,300.00 | 18,000.00 |
| 1849 | 654 | 375.00 | 3,600.00 |
| 1849O | 24 | 2,000.00 | 24,000.00 |
| 1850 | 291 | 375.00 | 4,250.00 |
| 1850O | 58 | 750.00 | 16,500.00 |
| 1851 | 176 | 450.00 | 7,000.00 |
| 1851O | 263 | 425.00 | 6,500.00 |
| 1852 | 263 | 400.00 | 4,600.00 |

|  | Mintage in Thousands | Ex. Fine | Unc. | Proof |
|---|---|---|---|---|
| 1852O | 18 | 1,100.00 | 25,000.00 | — |
| 1853 | 201 | 400.00 | 3,850.00 | — |
| 1853O | 51 | 425.00 | 8,000.00 | — |
| 1854 | 54 | 450.00 | 6,000.00 | — |
| 1854O | 53 | 725.00 | 13,000.00 | — |
| 1854S | 124 | 375.00 | 12,000.00 | — |
| 1855 | 122 | 375.00 | 3,800.00 | — |
| 1855O | 18 | 1,350.00 | 20,000.00 | — |
| 1855S | 9 | 2,400.00 | 31,500.00 | — |
| 1856 | 60 | 375.00 | 3,800.00 | — |
| 1856O | 15 | 1,800.00 | 17,500.00 | — |
| 1856S | 68 | 485.00 | 9,750.00 | — |
| 1857 | 17 | 875.00 | 13,500.00 | — |
| 1857O | 6 | 1,850.00 | 20,000.00 | — |
| 1857S | 26 | 800.00 | 11,000.00 | — |
| 1858 | 3 | 6,850.00 | 35,000.00 | — |
| 1858O | 20 | 650.00 | 9,250.00 | — |
| 1858S | 12 | 3,350.00 | 31,000.00 | — |
| 1859 | 16 | 650.00 | 12,000.00 | — |
| 1859O | 2 | 7,850.00 | 50,000.00 | — |
| 1859S | 7 | 4,850.00 | 45,000.00 | — |
| 1860 | 15 | 650.00 | 8,500.00 | — |
| 1860O | 11 | 1,300.00 | 14,250.00 | — |
| 1860S | 5 | 6,750.00 | 45,000.00 | — |
| 1861 | 113 | 375.00 | 3,100.00 | — |
| 1861S | 16 | 3,100.00 | 36,000.00 | — |
| 1862 | 11 | 1,050.00 | 17,500.00 | — |
| 1862S | 13 | 3,600.00 | 38,000.00 | — |
| 1863 | 1 | 8,500.00 | 57,500.00 | — |
| 1863S | 10 | 3,300.00 | 26,500.00 | — |
| 1864 | 4 | 3,900.00 | 16,500.00 | — |
| 1864S | 3 | 14,000.00 | 55,000.00 | — |
| 1865 | 4 | 3,750.00 | 34,000.00 | — |
| 1865S | 17 | 9,850.00 | 47,500.00 | — |
| 1866S No Motto | 9 | 3,350.00 | 46,500.00 | — |
| 1866 With Motto | 4 | 1,750.00 | 16,500.00 | 32,500.00 |
| 1866S | 12 | 3,650.00 | 25,000.00 | — |
| 1867 | 3 | 2,600.00 | 28,500.00 | 32,500.00 |
| 1867S | 9 | 6,100.00 | 45,000.00 | — |
| 1868 | 11 | 750.00 | 13,750.00 | 32,500.00 |
| 1868S | 14 | 1,900.00 | 25,000.00 | — |
| 1869 | 2 | 2,850.00 | 35,000.00 | 32,500.00 |
| 1869S | 6 | 2,650.00 | 30,000.00 | — |
| 1870 | 4 | 1,300.00 | 17,500.00 | 32,500.00 |
| 1870CC | 6 | 24,500.00 | 77,500.00 | — |
| 1870S | 8 | 2,400.00 | 35,000.00 | — |
| 1871 | 2 | 2,700.00 | 18,500.00 | 45,000.00 |
| 1871CC | 7 | 5,000.00 | 47,500.00 | — |
| 1871S | 17 | 2,000.00 | 28,500.00 | — |
| 1872 | 2 | 3,500.00 | 26,000.00 | 35,000.00 |
| 1872CC | 6 | 8,250.00 | 60,000.00 | — |
| 1872S | 17 | 950.00 | 25,000.00 | — |
| 1873 | 1 | 10,500.00 | 46,500.00 | 26,500.00 |
| 1873CC | 5 | 9,750.00 | 46,500.00 | — |
| 1873S | 12 | 1,700.00 | 31,000.00 | — |
| 1874 | 53 | 300.00 | 2,350.00 | 35,000.00 |

|  | Mintage in Thousands | Ex. Fine | Unc. | Proof |
|---|---|---|---|---|
| 1874CC | 17 | 2,750.00 | 7,750.00 | — |
| 1874S | 10 | 2,850.00 | 6,000.00 | — |
| 1875 (Very rare) | 120 Pieces | 65,000.00 | — | 100,000.00 |
| 1875CC | 8 | 8,750.00 | 51,000.00 | — |
| 1876 | 1 | 7,000.00 | 55,000.00 | 22,500.00 |
| 1876CC | 5 | 7,250.00 | 48,000.00 | — |
| 1876S | 5 | 1,850.00 | 40,000.00 | — |
| 1877 | 1 | 5,250.00 | 42,500.00 | 22,500.00 |
| 1877CC | 3 | 4,650.00 | 37,500.00 | — |
| 1877S | 17 | 750.00 | 24,000.00 | — |
| 1878 | 74 | 260.00 | 1,000.00 | 22,500.00 |
| 1878CC | 3 | 8,500.00 | 42,500.00 | — |
| 1878S | 26 | 750.00 | 21,000.00 | — |
| 1879 | 385 | 260.00 | 650.00 | 22,500.00 |
| 1879CC | 2 | 13,000.00 | 45,000.00 | — |
| 1879O | 2 | 4,250.00 | 32,500.00 | — |
| 1879S | 224 | 260.00 | 1,075.00 | — |
| 1880 | 1,645 | 260.00 | 375.00 | 22,500.00 |
| 1880CC | 11 | 775.00 | 8,000.00 | — |
| 1880O | 9 | 675.00 | 8,000.00 | — |
| 1880S | 506 | 260.00 | 450.00 | — |
| 1881 | 3,877 | 260.00 | 350.00 | 21,000.00 |
| 1881CC | 24 | 600.00 | 6,250.00 | — |
| 1881O | 8 | 825.00 | 6,000.00 | — |
| 1881S | 970 | 260.00 | 350.00 | — |
| 1882 | 2,324 | 260.00 | 350.00 | 21,000.00 |
| 1882CC | 17 | 1,150.00 | 8,750.00 | — |
| 1882O | 11 | 600.00 | 5,750.00 | — |
| 1882S | 132 | 325.00 | 450.00 | — |
| 1883 | 209 | 260.00 | 350.00 | 21,000.00 |
| 1883CC | 12 | 700.00 | 7,500.00 | — |
| 1883O | 1 | 6,000.00 | 35,000.00 | — |
| 1883S | 38 | 260.00 | 900.00 | — |
| 1884 | 77 | 260.00 | 700.00 | 20,000.00 |
| 1884CC | 10 | 900.00 | 11,000.00 | — |
| 1884S | 124 | 260.00 | 550.00 | — |
| 1885 | 254 | 325.00 | 450.00 | 15,000.00 |
| 1885S | 228 | 325.00 | 400.00 | — |
| 1886 | 236 | 275.00 | 425.00 | 14,000.00 |
| 1886S | 826 | 260.00 | 385.00 | — |
| 1887 | 54 | 350.00 | 775.00 | 13,500.00 |
| 1887S | 817 | 260.00 | 400.00 | — |
| 1888 | 133 | 325.00 | 550.00 | 13,000.00 |
| 1888O | 21 | 260.00 | 525.00 | — |
| 1888S | 649 | 260.00 | 400.00 | — |
| 1889 | 4 | 475.00 | 2,400.00 | 18,000.00 |
| 1889S | 425 | 260.00 | 400.00 | — |
| 1890 | 58 | 260.00 | 675.00 | 17,000.00 |
| 1890CC | 18 | 425.00 | 1,750.00 | — |
| 1891 | 92 | 260.00 | 350.00 | 12,000.00 |
| 1891CC | 104 | 425.00 | 750.00 | — |
| 1892 | 798 | 260.00 | 350.00 | 15,000.00 |
| 1892CC | 40 | 450.00 | 3,000.00 | — |
| 1892O | 29 | 260.00 | 425.00 | — |
| 1892S | 116 | 260.00 | 450.00 | — |
| 1893 | 1,841 | 260.00 | 350.00 | 15,000.00 |

|  | Mintage in Thousands | Ex. Fine | Unc. | Proof |
|---|---|---|---|---|
| 1893CC | 14 | 675.00 | 6,250.00 | — |
| 1893O | 17 | 375.00 | 625.00 | — |
| 1893S | 141 | 260.00 | 425.00 | — |
| 1894 | 2,471 | 260.00 | 350.00 | 15,000.00 |
| 1894O | 108 | 325.00 | 900.00 | — |
| 1894S | 25 | 375.00 | 3,750.00 | — |
| 1895 | 568 | 260.00 | 350.00 | 10,000.00 |
| 1895O | 98 | 260.00 | 525.00 | — |
| 1895S | 49 | 325.00 | 2,350.00 | — |
| 1896 | 76 | 325.00 | 400.00 | 10,000.00 |
| 1896S | 124 | 310.00 | 3,000.00 | — |
| 1897 | 1,000 | 260.00 | 350.00 | 14,000.00 |
| 1897O | 43 | 260.00 | 675.00 | — |
| 1897S | 235 | 310.00 | 825.00 | — |
| 1898 | 812 | 350.00 | 350.00 | 11,000.00 |
| 1898S | 474 | 260.00 | 425.00 | — |
| 1899 | 1,262 | 260.00 | 350.00 | 9,500.00 |
| 1899O | 37 | 350.00 | 550.00 | — |
| 1899S | 841 | 260.00 | 425.00 | — |
| 1900 | 294 | 265.00 | 350.00 | 9,500.00 |
| 1900S | 81 | 300.00 | 875.00 | — |
| 1901 | 1,719 | 260.00 | 350.00 | 9,500.00 |
| 1901O | 72 | 325.00 | 400.00 | — |
| 1901S | 2,813 | 260.00 | 350.00 | — |
| 1902 | 83 | 325.00 | 400.00 | 9,500.00 |
| 1902S | 470 | 260.00 | 350.00 | — |
| 1903 | 126 | 325.00 | 400.00 | 9,500.00 |
| 1903O | 113 | 325.00 | 425.00 | — |
| 1903S | 538 | 260.00 | 385.00 | — |
| 1904 | 162 | 260.00 | 385.00 | 9,500.00 |
| 1904O | 109 | 325.00 | 385.00 | — |
| 1905 | 201 | 260.00 | 350.00 | 10,000.00 |
| 1905S | 369 | 260.00 | 1,100.00 | — |
| 1906 | 165 | 260.00 | 350.00 | 9,500.00 |
| 1906D | 981 | 260.00 | 350.00 | — |
| 1906O | 87 | 325.00 | 450.00 | — |
| 1906S | 457 | 325.00 | 525.00 | — |
| 1907, All Kinds | 1,204 | 260.00 | 350.00 | 9,500.00 |
| 1907D | 1,030 | 260.00 | 350.00 | — |
| 1907S | 211 | 325.00 | 550.00 | — |

## INDIAN HEAD TYPE

                No Motto           Motto

|  | Mintage in Thousands | Ex. Fine | Unc. | Proof |
|---|---|---|---|---|
| 1907 Wire Edge, Periods before and after Legends | 500 Pieces | 8,500.00 | 13,750.00 | — |
| 1907 Rolled Edge, Periods (Rare) | 42 Pieces | 21,500.00 | 29,500.00 | — |
| 1907 No Periods | 239 | 320.00 | 525.00 | — |
| 1908 No Motto | 34 | 325.00 | 800.00 | — |
| 1908D No Motto | 210 | 325.00 | 675.00 | — |
| 1908 With Motto | 341 | 310.00 | 475.00 | 15,000.00 |
| 1908D With Motto | 837 | 310.00 | 750.00 | — |
| 1908S | 60 | 385.00 | 1,675.00 | — |
| 1909 | 185 | 310.00 | 475.00 | 16,000.00 |
| 1909D | 122 | 310.00 | 575.00 | — |
| 1909S | 292 | 310.00 | 625.00 | — |
| 1910 | 319 | 325.00 | 475.00 | 15,000.00 |
| 1910D | 2,357 | 310.00 | 450.00 | — |
| 1910S | 811 | 310.00 | 675.00 | — |
| 1911 | 506 | 310.00 | 475.00 | 17,000.00 |
| 1911D | 30 | 750.00 | 3,850.00 | — |
| 1911S | 51 | 650.00 | 1,150.00 | — |
| 1912 | 405 | 310.00 | 475.00 | 17,000.00 |
| 1912S | 300 | 310.00 | 685.00 | — |
| 1913 | 442 | 310.00 | 500.00 | 15,000.00 |
| 1913S | 66 | 750.00 | 3,850.00 | — |
| 1914 | 151 | 310.00 | 550.00 | 17,000.00 |
| 1914D | 344 | 310.00 | 550.00 | — |
| 1914S | 208 | 310.00 | 700.00 | — |
| 1915 | 351 | 310.00 | 550.00 | 21,000.00 |
| 1915S | 59 | 750.00 | 3,250.00 | — |
| 1916S | 139 | 340.00 | 850.00 | — |
| 1920S (Rare) | 127 | 7,250.00 | 22,500.00 | — |
| 1926 | 1,014 | 310.00 | 425.00 | — |
| 1930S | 96 | 7,000.00 | 10,000.00 | — |
| 1932 | 4,463 | 310.00 | 425.00 | — |
| 1933 (Rare) | 313 | — | 65,000.00 | — |

## 47.
## DOUBLE EAGLES
## 1850–1932

### ($20 GOLD PIECES) CORONET TYPE

**1849–1865**      **1866–1907**

| | Mintage in Thousands | Ex. Fine | Unc. |
|---|---:|---:|---:|
| 1849 Unique—U.S. Mint Collection | — | — | — |
| 1850 | 1,170 | 650.00 | 4,250.00 |
| 1850O | 141 | 1,100.00 | 30,000.00 |
| 1851 | 2,087 | 625.00 | 3,000.00 |
| 1851O | 315 | 750.00 | 14,000.00 |
| 1852 | 2,053 | 610.00 | 3,250.00 |
| 1852O | 190 | 700.00 | 13,000.00 |
| 1853 | 1,261 | 610.00 | 5,000.00 |
| 1853O | 71 | 1,000.00 | 22,500.00 |
| 1854 | 758 | 600.00 | 5,500.00 |
| 1854O (Rare) | 3 | 55,000.00 | — |
| 1854S | 141 | 700.00 | 3,500.00 |
| 1855 | 365 | 650.00 | 8,500.00 |
| 1855O | 8 | 6,000.00 | 75,000.00 |
| 1855S | 880 | 600.00 | 8,250.00 |
| 1856 | 330 | 625.00 | 8,500.00 |
| 1856O (Rare) | 2 | 70,000.00 | — |
| 1856S | 1.19 | 600.00 | 3,850.00 |
| 1857 | 439 | 600.00 | 3,950.00 |
| 1857O | 30 | 1,600.00 | 25,000.00 |
| 1857S | 971 | 600.00 | 4,250.00 |
| 1858 | 212 | 850.00 | 4,750.00 |
| 1858O | 35 | 1,750.00 | 23,500.00 |
| 1858S | 847 | 610.00 | 8,000.00 |
| 1859 | 44 | 1,875.00 | 38,500.00 |
| 1859O | 9 | 6,500.00 | 38,500.00 |
| 1859S | 636 | 600.00 | 4,750.00 |
| 1860 | 578 | 600.00 | 3,950.00 |

|  | Mintage in Thousands | Ex. Fine | Unc. |
|---|---|---|---|
| 1860O | 7 | 5,650.00 | 50,000.00 |
| 1860S | 545 | 600.00 | 5,850.00 |
| 1861 | 2,976 | 600.00 | 2,400.00 |
| 1861O | 18 | 3,000.00 | 25,000.00 |
| 1861S | 768 | 600.00 | 8,750.00 |
| 1862 | 92 | 1,250.00 | 11,500.00 |
| 1862S | 854 | 625.00 | 13,750.00 |
| 1863 | 143 | 685.00 | 13,750.00 |
| 1863S | 967 | 600.00 | 6,750.00 |
| 1864 | 204 | 825.00 | 10,000.00 |
| 1864S | 794 | 675.00 | 8,000.00 |
| 1865 | 351 | 625.00 | 5,750.00 |
| 1865S | 1,043 | 600.00 | 4,250.00 |
| 1866S No Motto | — | 2,850.00 | 27,500.00 |
| 1866 With Motto | 699 | 700.00 | 4,750.00 |
| 1866S | 842 | 700.00 | 12,000.00 |
| 1867 | 251 | 625.00 | 1,850.00 |
| 1867S | 921 | 725.00 | 13,250.00 |
| 1868 | 99 | 925.00 | 8,250.00 |
| 1868S | 838 | 685.00 | 7,750.00 |
| 1869 | 175 | 750.00 | 5,250.00 |
| 1869S | 687 | 600.00 | 4,750.00 |
| 1870 | 155 | 775.00 | 8,000.00 |
| 1870CC (Very rare) | 4 | 65,000.00 | 140,000.00 |
| 1870S | 982 | 625.00 | 4,500.00 |
| 1871 | 80 | 800.00 | 3,500.00 |
| 1871CC | 17 | 4,750.00 | 38,500.00 |
| 1871S | 928 | 650.00 | 3,450.00 |
| 1872 | 252 | 625.00 | 2,650.00 |
| 1872CC | 30 | 1,375.00 | 24,000.00 |
| 1872S | 780 | 585.00 | 2,850.00 |
| 1873 | 1,710 | 585.00 | 775.00 |
| 1873CC | 22 | 1,600.00 | 24,000.00 |
| 1873S | 1,041 | 585.00 | 1,650.00 |
| 1874 | 367 | 625.00 | 1,000.00 |
| 1874CC | 115 | 775.00 | 7,750.00 |
| 1874S | 1,241 | 600.00 | 1,400.00 |
| 1875 | 296 | 600.00 | 775.00 |
| 1875CC | 111 | 775.00 | 2,400.00 |
| 1875S | 1,230 | 585.00 | 825.00 |
| 1876 | 584 | 585.00 | 775.00 |
| 1876CC | 138 | 775.00 | 3,500.00 |
| 1876S | 1,597 | 585.00 | 725.00 |
| 1877 | 398 | 475.00 | 625.00 |
| 1877CC | 43 | 950.00 | 15,000.00 |
| 1877S | 1,735 | 475.00 | 625.00 |
| 1878 | 544 | 475.00 | 625.00 |
| 1878CC | 13 | 1,450.00 | 18,750.00 |
| 1878S | 1,739 | 475.00 | 875.00 |
| 1879 | 208 | 525.00 | 1,000.00 |
| 1879CC | 11 | 1,550.00 | 27,500.00 |
| 1879O | 2 | 4,400.00 | 30,000.00 |
| 1879S | 1,224 | 475.00 | 1,250.00 |
| 1880 | 51 | 475.00 | 2,600.00 |
| 1880S | 836 | 490.00 | 1,050.00 |
| 1881 | 2 | 6,500.00 | 40,000.00 |
| 1881S | 727 | 475.00 | 1,050.00 |

|  | Mintage in Thousands | Ex. Fine | Unc. |
|---|---|---|---|
| 1882 | 1 | 13,500.00 | 55,000.00 |
| 1882CC | 39 | 775.00 | 6,350.00 |
| 1882S | 1,125 | 500.00 | 875.00 |
| 1883 (Rare) | 92 Pieces | — | — |
| 1883CC | 60 | 725.00 | 4,000.00 |
| 1883S | 1,189 | 500.00 | 650.00 |
| 1884 (Rare) | 71 Pieces | — | — |
| 1884CC | 81 | 775.00 | 2,600.00 |
| 1884S | 916 | 500.00 | 625.00 |
| 1885 | 1 | 7,450.00 | 31,500.00 |
| 1885CC | 9 | 1,650.00 | 10,500.00 |
| 1885S | 684 | 500.00 | 625.00 |
| 1886 | 1 | 10,500.00 | 36,000.00 |
| 1887 (Rare) | 121 Pieces | — | — |
| 1887S | 283 | 500.00 | 700.00 |
| 1888 | 226 | 500.00 | 650.00 |
| 1888S | 860 | 475.00 | 600.00 |
| 1889 | 44 | 525.00 | 700.00 |
| 1889CC | 31 | 875.00 | 3,500.00 |
| 1889S | 775 | 475.00 | 625.00 |
| 1890 | 76 | 525.00 | 625.00 |
| 1890CC | 91 | 700.00 | 2,400.00 |
| 1890S | 803 | 475.00 | 625.00 |
| 1891 | 1 | 4,500.00 | 25,000.00 |
| 1891CC | 5 | 2,375.00 | 13,500.00 |
| 1891S | 1,288 | 475.00 | 525.00 |
| 1892 | 5 | 1,375.00 | 5,000.00 |
| 1892CC | 27 | 800.00 | 3,250.00 |
| 1892S | 930 | 475.00 | 525.00 |
| 1893 | 344 | 475.00 | 525.00 |
| 1893CC | 18 | 800.00 | 2,150.00 |
| 1893S | 996 | 475.00 | 525.00 |
| 1894 | 1,369 | 475.00 | 525.00 |
| 1894S | 1,049 | 475.00 | 525.00 |
| 1895 | 1,115 | 475.00 | 525.00 |
| 1895S | 1,144 | 475.00 | 525.00 |
| 1896 | 793 | 475.00 | 525.00 |
| 1896S | 1,404 | 475.00 | 525.00 |
| 1897 | 1,383 | 475.00 | 525.00 |
| 1897S | 1,470 | 475.00 | 525.00 |
| 1898 | 170 | 500.00 | 550.00 |
| 1898S | 2,575 | 475.00 | 525.00 |
| 1899 | 1,669 | 475.00 | 525.00 |
| 1899S | 2,010 | 475.00 | 525.00 |
| 1900 | 1,875 | 475.00 | 525.00 |
| 1900S | 2,460 | 475.00 | 525.00 |
| 1901 | 112 | 475.00 | 525.00 |
| 1901S | 1,596 | 500.00 | 525.00 |
| 1902 | 31 | 475.00 | 825.00 |
| 1902S | 1,754 | 475.00 | 525.00 |
| 1903 | 287 | 475.00 | 525.00 |
| 1903S | 954 | 475.00 | 525.00 |
| 1904 | 6,257 | 475.00 | 525.00 |
| 1904S | 5,134 | 475.00 | 525.00 |
| 1905 | 59 | 525.00 | 1,000.00 |
| 1905S | 1,813 | 525.00 | 600.00 |

|  | Mintage in Thousands | Ex. Fine | Unc. |
|---|---|---|---|
| 1906 | 70 | 500.00 | 725.00 |
| 1906D | 620 | 475.00 | 525.00 |
| 1906S | 2,066 | 475.00 | 525.00 |
| 1907 | 1,452 | 475.00 | 525.00 |
| 1907D | 842 | 475.00 | 525.00 |
| 1907S | 2,166 | 475.00 | 525.00 |

## SAINT-GAUDENS TYPE

| | | | |
|---|---|---|---|
| 1907 High Relief Roman Numerals (MCMVII) Wire Rim, All Kinds | 11 | 4,500.00 | 7,750.00 |
| 1907 High Relief Flat Rim, All Kinds | 11 | 4,500.00 | 7,750.00 |

### 1907–1908                     1980–1932 Motto

| | | | |
|---|---|---|---|
| 1907 No Motto | 362 | 485.00 | 600.00 |
| 1908 | 4,272 | 485.00 | 525.00 |
| 1908D | 664 | 485.00 | 525.00 |
| 1908 With Motto | 156 | 500.00 | 575.00 |
| 1908D | 350 | 500.00 | 575.00 |
| 1908S | 22 | 1,000.00 | 3,850.00 |
| 1909 over 8, All Kinds | 161 | 625.00 | 1,200.00 |
| 1909, All Kinds | — | 600.00 | 725.00 |
| 1909D | 53 | 700.00 | 1,200.00 |
| 1909S | 2,775 | 500.00 | 575.00 |
| 1910 | 482 | 475.00 | 525.00 |
| 1910D | 429 | 475.00 | 525.00 |
| 1910S | 2,128 | 500.00 | 550.00 |
| 1911 | 197 | 500.00 | 600.00 |

|  | Mintage in Thousands | Ex. Fine | Unc. |
|---|---|---|---|
| 1911D | 847 | 475.00 | 525.00 |
| 1911S | 776 | 475.00 | 525.00 |
| 1912 | 150 | 525.00 | 625.00 |
| 1913 | 169 | 525.00 | 575.00 |
| 1913D | 394 | 475.00 | 550.00 |
| 1913S | 34 | 750.00 | 1,100.00 |
| 1914 | 95 | 550.00 | 650.00 |
| 1914D | 453 | 475.00 | 550.00 |
| 1914S | 1,498 | 475.00 | 525.00 |
| 1915 | 152 | 475.00 | 650.00 |
| 1915S | 568 | 475.00 | 525.00 |
| 1916S | 796 | 475.00 | 550.00 |
| 1920 | 228 | 475.00 | 525.00 |
| 1920S | 558 | 8,750.00 | 30,000.00 |
| 1921 | 530 | 15,000.00 | 40,000.00 |
| 1922 | 1,376 | 475.00 | 525.00 |
| 1922S | 2,658 | 700.00 | 875.00 |
| 1923 | 566 | 475.00 | 525.00 |
| 1923D | 1,702 | 475.00 | 525.00 |
| 1924 | 4,324 | 475.00 | 525.00 |
| 1924D | 3,050 | 975.00 | 1,875.00 |
| 1924S | 2,928 | 975.00 | 2,250.00 |
| 1925 | 2,832 | 475.00 | 525.00 |
| 1925D | 2,939 | 1,555.00 | 3,400.00 |
| 1925S | 3,777 | 1,325.00 | 5,850.00 |
| 1926 | 817 | 475.00 | 525.00 |
| 1926D | 481 | 2,650.00 | 8,500.00 |
| 1926S | 2,042 | 1,100.00 | 1,850.00 |
| 1927 | 2,947 | 475.00 | 525.00 |
| 1927D (Rare) | 180 | — | — |
| 1927S | 3,107 | 3,750.00 | 14,000.00 |
| 1928 | 8,816 | 475.00 | 525.00 |
| 1929 | 1,780.00 | 6,750.00 | 10,000.00 |
| 1930S | 74 | 8,250.00 | 25,000.00 |
| 1931 | 2,938 | 8,000.00 | 22,500.00 |
| 1931D | 107 | 7,750.00 | 18,000.00 |
| 1932 | 1,102 | 10,000.00 | 19,000.00 |

(Note: Nearly all Philadelphia Mint Double Eagle dates exist as Proof; all are very rare with values typically ranging from $15,000.00 to $30,000.00 for Choice examples.)

# 48.
# PRIVATE AND TERRITORIAL GOLD COINS

## GEORGIA

|  | V. Good | Ex. Fine |
|---|---|---|
| 1830 $2.50 TEMPLETON REID (Very rare) | — | 50,000.00 |
| 1830 $5.00 TEMPLETON REID (Very rare) | — | 125,000.00 |
| 1830 TEN DOLLARS (Very rare) | 110,000.00 | — |
| NO DATE TEN DOLLARS (Very rare) | 85,000.00 | — |

## NORTH CAROLINA

|  | Fine | Unc. |
|---|---|---|
| $1.00 AUGUST BECHTLER | 900.00 | 3,500.00 |
| $5.00 AUGUST BECHTLER | 4,000.00 | 14,500.00 |
| $1.00 CHRISTOPHER BECHTLER | 1,000.00 | 3,500.00 |
| $2.50 | 2,750.00 | 12,000.00 |
| $5.00 | 3,750.00 | 13,000.00 |

## CALIFORNIA
### NORRIS, GRIEF AND NORRIS

| | | |
|---|---|---|
| 1849 $5.00 | 2,750.00 | 20,000.00 |

## MOFFAT & CO.

|  | V. Fine | Ex. Fine |
|---|---|---|
| 1849 $10.00 | 3,500.00 | 7,500.00 |
| 1849 $5.00 | 1,500.00 | 3,250.00 |
| 1850 $5.00 | 1,500.00 | 3,250.00 |
| 1852 $10.00 | 3,250.00 | 5,750.00 |

## AUGUSTUS HUMBERT
## U.S. ASSAYER

|  | V. Fine | Ex. Fine |
|---|---|---|
| 1851 FIFTY DOLLARS 880 THOUS. "Target" Reverse | 8,500.00 | 12,500.00 |
| 1851 FIFTY DOLLARS 887 THOUS. "Target" Reverse | 8,500.00 | 12,500.00 |
| 1852 FIFTY DOLLARS 887 THOUS. "Target" Reverse | 9,000.00 | 12,500.00 |
| 1852 FIFTY DOLLARS 900 THOUS. "Target" Reverse | 9,500.00 | 13,500.00 |
| 1851 50 DC Several Varieties: AUGUSTUS HUMBERT UNITED STATES ASSAYER OF GOLD CALIFORNIA 1851 | 12,500.00 | 16,000.00 |
| 1852 TWENTY DOLLARS 1852 over 1 | 3,750.00 | 6,750.00 |
| 1853 TWENTY DOLLARS 884 THOUS. | 3,000.00 | 4,250.00 |
| 1853 TWENTY DOLLARS 900 THOUS. | 2,450.00 | 3,250.00 |

|  | Fine | Ex. Fine |
|---|---|---|
| 1852 TEN DOLLARS 1852 over 1 | 2,000.00 | 4,750.00 |
| 1852 TEN DOLLARS 884 THOUS. | 1,100.00 | 2,650.00 |
| 1853 TEN DOLLARS 884 THOUS. (Rare) | 4,000.00 | 11,500.00 |
| 1853 TEN DOLLARS 900 THOUS. | 2,250.00 | 4,750.00 |

## BALDWIN & COMPANY

|  | V. Fine | Unc. |
|---|---|---|
| 1850 TEN DOLLARS | 30,000.00 | — |
| 1851 TWENTY DOLLARS (Rare) | — | — |
| 1851 TEN DOLLARS | 9,000.00 | — |
| 1850 FIVE DOLLARS | 5,500.00 | 20,000.00 |

## SCHULTZ & COMPANY

| | | |
|---|---|---|
| 1851 FIVE DOLLARS | 35,000.00 | 55,000.00 |

## DUNBAR & COMPANY

| | | |
|---|---|---|
| 1851 FIVE DOLLARS (Rare) | 60,000.00 | — |

## WASS, MOLITOR & COMPANY

|  | Fine | Ex. Fine |
|---|---|---|
| 1855 FIFTY DOLLARS | 15,000.00 | 30,000.00 |
| 1855 TWENTY DOLLARS, Small Head | 7,500.00 | 18,000.00 |
| 1855 TWENTY DOLLARS, Large Head (Rare) | — | 60,000.00 |
| 1852 TEN DOLLARS, Small Head | 3,500.00 | 10,000.00 |
| 1852 TEN DOLLARS, Large Head | 2,000.00 | 5,000.00 |
| 1855 TEN DOLLARS | 7,500.00 | 16,500.00 |
| 1852 FIVE DOLLARS, Small Head | 2,000.00 | 7,500.00 |
| 1852 FIVE DOLLARS, Large Head | 2,000.00 | 7,500.00 |

## KELLOGG & COMPANY

| | | |
|---|---|---|
| 1855 FIFTY DOLLARS (Rare) | — | — |
| 1854 TWENTY DOLLARS | 1,500.00 | 3,750.00 |
| 1855 TWENTY DOLLARS | 1,500.00 | 3,750.00 |

Between 1852 and 1882, round and octagonal one-dollar, fifty-cent, and twenty-five-cent gold pieces were also issued in California. After an act of 1864 made private coinage illegal, their makers were anonymous; their initials, however, can be found on some coins.

There are many copies of these small coins, some made to be worn as charms. Genuine pieces all show their denomination—"1/2 Dol.," or "1/2 Dollar," or "half dollar," etc.

These coins are valued as follows:

|  | V. Fine | Unc. |
|---|---|---|
| .25 Round Indian or Liberty Heads | 75.00 | 150.00 |
| .25 Octagonal Indian or Liberty Heads | 85.00 | 225.00 |
| .50 Round Indian or Liberty Heads | 100.00 | 225.00 |
| .50 Octagonal Indian or Liberty Heads | 110.00 | 275.00 |
| 1.00 Round Indian Heads | 550.00 | 2,500.00 |
| 1.00 Octagonal Indian or Liberty Heads | 125.00 | 1,000.00 |
| 1.00 Round Liberty Heads | 500.00 | 2,000.00 |

(Washington Heads bring about 50% more.)

## OREGON

### OREGON EXCHANGE COMPANY

|  | Fine | Ex. Fine |
|---|---|---|
| 1849 TEN DOLLARS (Rare) | 25,000.00 | 55,000.00 |
| 1849 FIVE DOLLARS | 7,500.00 | 22,500.00 |

## UTAH

### MORMON GOLD

|  | Fine | V. Fine |
|---|---|---|
| 1849 TWENTY DOLLARS (Rare) | 30,000.00 | — |
| 1849 TEN DOLLARS (Rare) | 90,000.00 | — |

|  | Fine | Ex. Fine |
|---|---|---|
| 1849 FIVE DOLLARS................................. | 4,500.00 | 10,000.00 |

| 1849 TWO AND ONE-HALF DOLLARS ............. | 5,500.00 | 12,500.00 |
| 1850 FIVE DOLLARS............................... | 6,000.00 | 15,000.00 |

| 1860 FIVE DOLLARS............................... | 9,500.00 | 25,000.00 |

## COLORADO

### CLARK, GRUBER & COMPANY

| 1860 TWENTY DOLLARS (Rare).................... | 30,000.00 | 70,000.00 |
| 1860 TEN DOLLARS ............................... | 3,750.00 | 9,000.00 |
| 1861 TWENTY DOLLARS ......................... | 5,000.00 | 17,500.00 |

|  | Fine | Ex. Fine |
|---|---|---|
| 1861 TEN DOLLARS | 1,750.00 | 6,000.00 |
| 1861 FIVE DOLLARS | 1,500.00 | 5,750.00 |
| 1861 TWO AND ONE-HALF DOLLARS | 1,350.00 | 3,250.00 |

## CLARK & CO.

|  |  |  |
|---|---|---|
| 1860 FIVE DOLLARS | 1,350.00 | 3,250.00 |
| 1860 TWO AND ONE-HALF DOLLARS | 1,150.00 | 2,500.00 |

## JOHN PARSONS & COMPANY

|  |  |  |
|---|---|---|
| (1861) Undated 2 1/2 D (Rare) | — | 40,000.00 |
| (1861) Undated FIVE D (Rare) | — | 50,000.00 |

## J.J. CONWAY & COMPANY

|  |  |  |
|---|---|---|
| (1861) 2-1/2 DOLL'S (Rare) | — | 45,000.00 |
| (1861) FIVE DOLLARS (Rare) | — | 60,000.00 |
| 1861 TEN DOLLARS (Very rare) | — | — |

# 49.
# HARD TIMES TOKENS

These are tokens, usually satirically political in nature, which were privately struck and issued in the period 1832–1844. The tokens are copper or brass and are predominantly the same size as the large one-cent piece of the period. Descriptions of the major types follow. (Tradesman's or advertising tokens of the same approximate period encompass hundreds of varieties which are outside the scope of this listing. The value of the more common of the commercial varieties are: Good $10.00; Fine $15.00; Ex. Fine $40.00; Unc. $150.00.)

| Type | Good | Fine | Ex. Fine | Unc. |
|---|---|---|---|---|
| 1. Jackson Head Right/Legend in Wreath | 3,000.00 | 4,500.00 | 9,000.00 | — |
| 2. Jackson Bust Right/Legend | 65.00 | 135.00 | 500.00 | — |
| 3. Jackson Bust Facing/Eagle | 175.00 | 250.00 | 700.00 | — |
| 4. Van Buren Bust Facing/Chest | — | 2,500.00 | 4,000.00 | 10,000.00 |
| 5. Van Buren Bust Right/Eagle | — | 300.00 | 700.00 | 1,650.00 |
| 6. Van Buren Bust Left/Safe | — | 75.00 | 175.00 | 375.00 |
| 7. Seward Bust Left/Eagle | 65.00 | 175.00 | 300.00 | 750.00 |
| 8. Verplanck Bust Left/Eagle | 50.00 | 125.00 | 275.00 | 575.00 |
| 9. Ship Left/Victorious Whigs of New York | 125.00 | 300.00 | 725.00 | — |
| 10. Liberty Cap/Ship | 750.00 | 1,750.00 | 3,250.00 | — |
| 11. Cow Right/Ship | 50.00 | 100.00 | 375.00 | 1,000.00 |
| 12. Kneeling Woman/Legend | 50.00 | 85.00 | 140.00 | 600.00 |
| 13. Liberty Head Left/Legend "Mint Drop" | 15.00 | 30.00 | 75.00 | 275.00 |
| 14. Man Standing Left/Jackass | 10.00 | 15.00 | 65.00 | 225.00 |
| 15. Man in Chest/Jackass | 10.00 | 15.00 | 40.00 | 150.00 |
| 16. Pig Running Left/Bust Over Legend | 10.00 | 20.00 | 50.00 | 185.00 |
| 17. Turtle Right/Jackass | 10.00 | 15.00 | 40.00 | 150.00 |
| 18. Liberty Head Left/Legend "Not One Cent" | 10.00 | 15.00 | 40.00 | 150.00 |
| 19. Liberty Head Left/Legend "May Tenth" | 10.00 | 15.00 | 40.00 | 150.00 |
| 20. Phoenix/Legend | 10.00 | 15.00 | 40.00 | 175.00 |
| 21. Ship/Shipwreck | 10.00 | 15.00 | 40.00 | 150.00 |
| 22. Shipwreck/Man in Chest | 10.00 | 15.00 | 40.00 | 150.00 |
| 23. Ship/Legend | 10.00 | 15.00 | 40.00 | 150.00 |
| 24. Ship/Liberty Head | 25.00 | 65.00 | 150.00 | 375.00 |
| 25. Half-Cent | 25.00 | 50.00 | 150.00 | 450.00 |

# 50.
## CIVIL WAR TOKENS

These are copper or brass tokens, privately struck during the years 1860–1866, ostensibly to help alleviate the shortage of Federal cents caused by hoarding. Although they were approximately the size of an Indian Head cent, many were underweight. As they were sold to merchants by their manufacturers at a discount from face value, this underweight condition is to be expected—war profiteers existed then as now. Several hundred varieties of the patriotic kind exist, and prices are listed for the major types. Many thousands of varieties exist for the merchants' or advertising types, and they fall beyond our scope (values for common advertising Civil War tokens— Good $5.00; Fine $8.00; Ex. Fine $13.00; Unc. $35.00.)

|  | Good | Fine | Ex. Fine | Unc. |
|---|---|---|---|---|
| 1. Liberty Head Left | 7.00 | 10.00 | 15.00 | 40.00 |
| 2. Liberty Head Right | 8.00 | 11.00 | 17.00 | 45.00 |
| 3. Indian Head Left | 5.00 | 8.00 | 13.00 | 35.00 |
| 4. Washington Head Left | 25.00 | 40.00 | 65.00 | 150.00 |
| 5. Washington Head Right | 10.00 | 15.00 | 30.00 | 60.00 |
| 6. Lincoln Head Left | 15.00 | 25.00 | 40.00 | 100.00 |
| 7. Lincoln Head Right | 15.00 | 28.00 | 50.00 | 125.00 |
| 8. McClellan Head Left | 7.00 | 15.00 | 20.00 | 65.00 |
| 9. McClellan Head Right | 7.00 | 15.00 | 20.00 | 60.00 |
| 10. Franklin Head Left | 20.00 | 55.00 | 80.00 | 250.00 |
| 11. Franklin Head Right | 15.00 | 30.00 | 65.00 | 200.00 |
| 12. Flying Eagle Right | 35.00 | 65.00 | 125.00 | 500.00 |
| 13. Flying Eagle Left | 40.00 | 75.00 | 150.00 | 450.00 |
| 14. Upright Eagle | 25.00 | 55.00 | 80.00 | 250.00 |
| 15. Eagle on Shield | 8.00 | 10.00 | 15.00 | 35.00 |
| 16. Cannon | 11.00 | 15.00 | 20.00 | 60.00 |
| 17. Man on Horseback | 11.00 | 15.00 | 20.00 | 60.00 |
| 18. Flag | 5.00 | 8.00 | 13.00 | 35.00 |
| 19. Ship | 11.00 | 18.00 | 35.00 | 75.00 |
| 20. Walking Man | 11.00 | 18.00 | 35.00 | 75.00 |
| 21. Scroll | 30.00 | 75.00 | 175.00 | 700.00 |
| 22. Wreath | 5.00 | 8.00 | 13.00 | 35.00 |

# 51.
# COINS OF HAWAII

There was an issue of dimes, quarters, half-dollars and dollars struck by King Kalakaua in 1883; these were manufactured at the San Francisco Mint, although no mintmark appears on the pieces. There was also an issue of cents in 1847, bearing the bust of Kamehameha III and the legend "Apuni Hawaii, Hapa Haneri." (Beware of Spurious Specimens, which have an unnatural golden appearance.)

|  | Good | Fine | Ex. Fine | Unc. | Proof |
|---|---|---|---|---|---|
| 1847 Cent | 100.00 | 225.00 | 500.00 | 1,500.00 | — |
| 1883 Dime | 25.00 | 60.00 | 225.00 | 1,500.00 | 8,000.00 |
| 1883 Quarter | 25.00 | 45.00 | 85.00 | 250.00 | 9,000.00 |
| 1883 Half-Dollar | 35.00 | 75.00 | 250.00 | 1,650.00 | 11,000.00 |
| 1883 Dollar | 125.00 | 250.00 | 650.00 | 4,750.00 | 15,000.00 |

# 52.
# PHILIPPINE ISLANDS

From 1903 to 1945 the coinage of the Philippines was under the sovereignty of the United States of America. Types are uniform, as follows:

1/2¢, 1¢, 5¢—Man leaning on anvil, "Filipinas" below eagle on shield, "United States of America" around.

10¢, 20¢, 50¢, 1 Peso—Standing female, "Filipinas" below "United States of America" around eagle on shield.

Prices are for most common dates.

|  |  | Fine | Ex. Fine | Unc. |
|---|---|---|---|---|
| Half Centavo | 1903–08 | 0.50 | 2.00 | 15.00 |
| One Centavo | 1903–36 | 1.00 | 2.00 | 15.00 |
| One Centavo | 1937–44 | — | 0.25 | 2.00 |
| Five Centavos | 1903–28 | 1.00 | 3.00 | 20.00 |
| Five Centavos | 1930–45 | — | — | 2.00 |
| Ten Centavos | 1903–06 | 2.00 | 4.00 | 40.00 |
| Ten Centavos | 1907–45 | — | — | 2.00 |
| Twenty Centavos | 1903–06 | 3.00 | 6.00 | 45.00 |
| Twenty Centavos | 1907–29 | 2.00 | 4.00 | 25.00 |
| Fifty Centavos | 1903–06 | 5.00 | 15.00 | 100.00 |
| Fifty Centavos | 1907–21 | 3.00 | 6.00 | 25.00 |
| One Peso | 1903–06 | 10.00 | 20.00 | 120.00 |
| One Peso | 1907–12 | 4.00 | 10.00 | 65.00 |

## COMMEMORATIVES

|  | Fine | Ex. Fine | Unc. |
|---|---|---|---|
| 1936 50 Centavos, Facing Busts | 25.00 | 45.00 | 75.00 |
| 1936 Peso, Murphy & Quezon | 45.00 | 75.00 | 150.00 |
| 1936 Peso, Roosevelt & Quezon | 45.00 | 75.00 | 150.00 |

Note: After World War II, many hundreds of these commemoratives were dredged up from Manila Bay, where they had lain since their dumping at the time of the Japanese invasion. These pieces bear the scars of long immersion in saltwater—pits, pockmarks, corrosion, etc.—and are worth very little as collectors' pieces.